Mathematics in the early years

The Clemsons' clear and readable book takes the reader from debates about how children learn and what children know and can do when they start school, through to a discussion of how mathematics can be managed in school and classroom, and how it can be assessed and evaluated. Linking these two parts of the book is a section on the subject of mathematics itself, from which the non-specialist reader can gain a view of what mathematics is, what needs to be thought about in planning and offering a curriculum and the special dilemmas faced in teaching and offering mathematics as a subject. A bank of case studies offers an opportunity to see mathematics in action in a variety of classrooms, and a final chapter makes suggestions for stimulating in-service training.

David Clemson and **Wendy Clemson** are both experienced teachers and are the authors of a number of books for teachers, parents and children. David is Reader in Primary Education at Liverpool John Moore's University and Wendy is a freelance writer, working on a variety of writing projects related to the education of young children.

Teaching and learning in the first three years of school
Series Editor *Joy Palmer*

This innovatory and up-to-date series is concerned specifically with curriculum practice in the first three years of school. Each book includes guidance on:

- subject content
- planning and organisation
- assessment and record keeping
- in-service training

This practical advice is placed in the context of the National Curriculum and the latest theoretical work on how children learn at this age and what experiences they bring to their early years in the classroom.

Mathematics in the early years

David Clemson and Wendy Clemson

London and New York

First published 1994
by Routledge
11 New Fetter Lane, London EC4P 4EE

Simultaneously published in the USA and Canada
by Routledge
29 West 35th Street, New York, NY 10001

Reprinted in 1997

Typeset in Palatino by
Ponting–Green Publishing Services, Chesham, Bucks
Printed and bound in Great Britain by
Biddles Ltd., Guildford and King's Lynn

Printed on acid free paper

British Library Cataloguing in Publication Data
A catalogue record for this book is available from the British
Library

Library of Congress Cataloging in Publication Data
Clemson, David.
    Mathematics in the early years/David and
    Wendy Clemson.
        p.   cm. – (Teaching and learning in the first three
    years of school)
    Includes bibliographical references and index.
    1. Mathematics–Study and teaching (Primary).
    I. Clemson, Wendy.   II. Title.   III. Series.
    QA135.5C547   1994
    372.7′049–dc20   93–40268
                                                  CIP

ISBN 0–415–09628–6

Contents

Part VI In-service education

Illustrations

FIGURES

TABLES

Editor's preface

Each book in this series focuses on a specific curriculum area. The series relates relevant learning theory or a rationale for early years learning to the practical development and implementation of subject-based topics and classroom activities at the infant level (i.e. Reception, Y1, Y2). It seems that the majority of existing books on primary education and the primary curriculum focus on pupils aged 7–11 years. It is hoped that this series presents a refreshing and much needed change in that it specifically addresses the first three years in school.

Each volume is intended to be an up-to-date, judicious mix of theory and practical classroom application, offering a wealth of background information, ideas and advice to all concerned with planning, implementing, monitoring and evaluating teaching and learning in the first three years in school. Theoretical perspectives are presented in a lively and interesting way, drawing upon recent classroom research findings wherever possible. Case studies and activities from a range of classrooms and schools illuminate many of the substantial issues related to the subject area in question.

Readers will find a similar pattern of contents in all the books in the series. Each discusses the early learning environment, transition from home- to school-based learning, and addresses the key questions of what this means for the early years teacher and the curriculum. Such discussion inevitably incorporates ideas on the knowledge which young children may have of subjects and an overview of the subject matter itself which is under scrutiny. As the thrust of the series is towards young children learning subjects, albeit in a holistic way, no doubt readers will wish to consider what is an appropriate content or rationale for the subject in the early years. Having considered young children as learners, what they are bringing into school in terms of prior knowledge, the teacher's task and the subject matter itself, each book then turns its attention to appropriate methods of planning, organising, implementing and evaluating teaching and learning activities. Crucial matters such as assessment, evaluation and record-keeping are dealt with in their own right, and are also referred to and discussed in ongoing examples of good practice. Each book concludes with useful suggestions for further staffroom discussion/INSET activities and advice on resources.

As a whole, the series aims to be inspirational and forward-looking. As all readers know so well, the National Curriculum is not 'written in concrete'. Education is a dynamic process. While taking due account of the essential National Curriculum framework, authors go far beyond the level of description of rigid content guidelines to highlight *principles* for teaching and learning. Furthermore, they incorporate two key messages which surely underpin successful, reflective education, namely 'vision' and 'enthusiasm'. It is hoped that students and teachers will be inspired and assisted in their task of implementing successful and progressive plans which help young learners to make sense of their world and the key areas of knowledge within it.

Joy A. Palmer

Foreword

Our purpose in writing this book is to help teachers of infants to improve children's learning of mathematics. We recognise that this is not a simple task. We do, however, have such a regard for the commitment, professionalism, insight and downright common sense that so many teachers of young children demonstrate, that we believe if anyone can improve children's learning they can.

We have raised a number of the important issues for consideration when teachers are thinking about infants and mathematics. Inevitably, the points we have presented fit a number of general and overarching themes that permeate the book. While the reader can follow those strands of argument which arise for them personally when they use the book, it may also be useful to set down those that we see as important. They have to do with the following:

— the purposes of mathematics
— communication and mathematics
— mathematical knowledge
— change and mathematics

Thoughts about all of these themes are provoked by a reading of Chapter 8. If we look at some of the other places where the themes are addressed in the book the list goes as follows.

THE PURPOSES OF MATHEMATICS

— Mathematics education is a continuance and extension of what 'naturally' occurs in pre-school life (Chapter 2), and those everyday situations where we apply mathematical ideas provide powerful contexts to use for the settings for learning in school (Chapter 4).
— Mathematical 'literacy' is as important as linguistic literacy (Chapter 2).
— Mathematics comprises a debate about abstractions and is therefore important in human thinking (Chapter 3).
— Mathematics enables us to interpret and manipulate the data we meet

every day (Chapter 3), and this knowledge and skill should feature in the school curriculum (Chapter 4).
— A range of differing political ideologies affects the emphases in school mathematics curricula (Chapter 4).
— Mathematics makes a contribution to understanding in other curriculum areas (Chapter 7).

COMMUNICATION AND MATHEMATICS

— School mathematics involves parents (Chapter 2).
— Mathematics and language is a complex area of debate, involving, for example, talking about mathematics and the reading and writing of mathematics (Chapter 5).
— Coherent mathematics curricula demand co-ordination of effort in school (Chapter 6).
— There is an interchange of ideas between mathematics and other subjects (Chapter 7).
— Effective communication of children's mathematical progress to their families and to teaching colleagues is important (Chapter 9), as well as being invaluable in evaluation (Chapter 10).

MATHEMATICAL KNOWLEDGE

— Mathematical knowledge can be structured and we can set objectives about what children can learn (Chapter 1).
— The knowledge that children starting school, and their parents have of mathematics is important (Chapter 2).
— Mathematical knowledge comprises a number of key ideas (Chapter 3).
— There are a number of items which should form the minimum mathematical knowledge we think children should acquire in school (Chapter 4), and these can be described in terms of classroom treatment.
— There should be breadth and balance in school mathematics (Chapter 6).
— The mathematical knowledge or lack of it that teachers profess is important (Chapter 6).

CHANGE AND MATHEMATICS

— Views of how learning occurs can affect presentation of learning and therefore outcomes (Chapter 1).
— Views of children's early capacity for mathematics are changing (Chapter 2).
— Changes can be effected by involving parents in mathematics, and by

taking account of the image of mathematics projected in school (Chapter 2).
— Mathematical ideas are subject to change (Chapter 3).
— Assessing change in what children know (Chapter 9).
— Teachers are agents of change (Chapter 10).
— Teachers' knowledge and repertoire of skills in mathematics teaching can be augmented by INSET (Chapter 11).

We want this book to be enjoyable, whilst also being provocative and challenging. We also intend that it should be realistic. While its purpose is not to give 'tips' that can be used in the classroom tomorrow, we do hope that it triggers ideas about how to help children to become satisfyingly mathematical in their own eyes; and that it fuels teachers' ambitions to provide enjoyable, provocative and challenging mathematics for the children they teach.

Acknowledgements

Special thanks are due to teachers Jane Booth, Dorothy Nutley, Carol Sutcliffe and Mari Williams, and to the children, head teachers and staff of Gatley County Primary School, Hartford County Primary School, St. Matthew's Church of England School, Stretton, and Winnington Park County Primary School.

Our thanks also go to all the teachers on twenty-day mathematics courses at Liverpool John Moores University, and Chris Cheong and the Northern Advisory Teachers' Group.

We thank Sue Gifford of the Roehampton Institute for the children's work reproduced in Figures 4.3, 5.1 and 5.2. Figures 1.1 and 1.2 are adapted with permission of the publishers, from *Toward a Theory of Instruction* (1966) by Jerome S. Bruner, The Belknap Press of Harvard University Press; Figure 3.1 is adapted with permission of the publishers, from *Mathematics for the Million* (1936) by Lancelot Hogben, George Allen & Unwin, an imprint of HarperCollins Publishers Ltd., and Figure 4.1 has been adapted with permission of the publishers, from *An Introduction to the History of Education* (1982) by Richard Aldrich, Hodder & Stoughton. We acknowledge authorisation from the publishers indicated.

Finally and mostly, we would like to acknowledge the tolerance of our daughter, Frances. Without her help we most assuredly would not have been able to write this book.

Part I

A context for mathematics

GENERAL INTRODUCTION

Teachers carry out their teaching on the basis of a complex set of personal and professional values and beliefs. All the actions that we take as teachers are based on our theories. In some cases we adopt the theories of others – writers, colleagues or friends – but in all cases we adapt them to our own beliefs and preferences, those ways of operating which we feel good about, and those which we think efficacious.

It is one of the major planks of our educational thinking that equal opportunities for learning should be offered to all children. To offer all the children in our care these opportunities in mathematics we need to evaluate our beliefs about how children learn. We can then implement those theoretical perspectives which are appropriate in learning situations. We also need to take cognisance of the value of what children have already learned, and continue to learn at home. Account needs to be taken of the contribution parents can make to the mathematical education of their children, both before their schooldays and when they are of school age. It is important to examine prejudices we may harbour about children's potential. We may all have made assumptions about children, or justified our treatment of them, in terms of the homes and families they come from and according to whether they are girls or boys. These ideas need exploration to see if there is any foundation for them. Finally, as teachers we cannot escape our culpability in the provision of children's first impressions of school mathematics. If children quickly acquire the view that mathematics is 'sums' in books, or are denied access to the whole panoply of mathematics possibilities, it *is* the teacher's fault. These are the themes for this section and form the backcloth for what is said in the rest of the book.

In order to unpick all these issues we have organised Part I into two chapters. Chapter 1 explores how theoretical ideas about how children learn can have affected our personal theories of learning in mathematics. In Chapter 2 we look at the two most influential sets of people in young children's lives, namely their parents and their first teachers. Our contention is that when children are making a start on school mathematics, their parents have already affected their mathematics knowledge and experience. We also believe that parents can continue to make a contribution once their children start school. It is then that the chief responsibility for children's mathematical progress rests with the teachers. They can make or mar young mathematicians by their attitudes and expectations.

Chapter 1

How children learn

INTRODUCTION

In this chapter our main focus is on children's intellectual development in school, for it is with this that teachers have a particular concern. Even though it is difficult to measure and quantify intellectual growth and achievement, it is through assessment of these qualities that teachers and schools are commonly judged. We are focusing on that period of children's lives which extends from before they begin school to when they are 8 years old. During this short time there are monumental changes in what children know, understand and can do. To try to give the flavour of the learning children undertake, here are two snapshots of children at either end of our chronological time scale. We must stress that they are only examples and cannot do more than give a glimpse of this period of vital mathematical education. The first is part of a conversation between a researcher and Patrick (aged 4 years and one month):

MH:	How many is two and one more?
PATRICK:	Four.
MH:	Well, how many is two *lollipops* and one more?
PATRICK:	Three.
MH:	How many is two *elephants* and one more?
PATRICK:	Three.
MH:	How many is two *giraffes* and one more?
PATRICK:	Three.
MH:	So how many is *two* and one more?
PATRICK:	Six.

(Hughes 1986: 47)

The second is part of a session in which one of the authors was working with 8 year olds, using Logo. Katie had drawn a robot and decided she wanted to instruct the turtle to draw in a diagonal. In order to achieve this it was suggested that she drew a square on the screen. This she did, using 100 turtle steps for the length of the side, finishing with the turtle pointing vertically up the screen and in the bottom left hand corner.

KATIE: We'll turn it 45.
  DC: OK – left or right?
KATIE: Right.
  DC: What next?
KATIE: Forward . . . erm . . . well the square is 100 so forward 100.
(When the diagonal proved too short, Katie tried again.)
KATIE: Forward 150.
  DC: 150 more or where you started from?
KATIE: 50 more (when this proved too long, she had another go) . . . 40
         more . . . just a tiny bit more. We'll do 141. (Katie sat for a short
         while and then said) . . . If we make the square 200 then the
         diagonal will be 282.
  DC: Let's try it.
(This Katie did to good effect. At this point DC thought Katie would now
double the 200 square, but no . . .)
KATIE: If we make a 300 it will be 141 add 282 . . . 423.

(Clemson 1992: 6)

Here is evidence that Katie, who is thought by her teacher and DC to be a
typical 8 year old, can, without 'special' work, find the fundamental ideas
underpinning Pythagoras' theorem.

In our debate about children's learning we have to consider children like
Patrick and Katie and what we ask of them when doing mathematics. We
have to take account of children like Sharon who entered school at almost
5 years old and who was unable to count beyond three, not able to give the
word for 'yellow' and unable to give names to some things commonly
found on a breakfast table. While providing tasks which present progression for Sharon, we also probably find children like Stefan starting
school at the same time. Stefan already enjoyed making collections, could
build inventive and complex models from construction kits, sang counting
rhymes with accuracy and gusto and, through an interest in cars, already
knew about speed limits and common road signs. One of the important
backdrops to the provision of learning opportunities for Patrick and Katie
and Sharon and Stefan is a view of how these children learn.

There is no single comprehensive theory that explains how children
develop intellectually or how they learn. There are two main schools
of thought and each has something to offer the teacher in the infant
classroom. There are those who attempt to construct models of the
internal thought processes and associations these have with learning
(cognitive), and those whose starting point is the observation of behaviour (behaviourist).

We shall examine some facets of the work of a few influential individuals from each of the schools of thought, using as 'pegs' on which to
hang the argument the notions of children being 'ready, willing and able'

to learn what the teacher intends and the idea that learning conforms to a pattern which has a structure. We have therefore organised the main body of this chapter in relation to ideas about:

— the readiness of children to tackle new learning;
— the motivation of children in relation to mathematics and new learning;
— the ability of children to tackle new ideas;
— the structuring of learning in mathematics.

READINESS

The concept of 'readiness' is prevalent in primary schools and may be seen to pervade all that teachers of infants do in offering children learning opportunities in all areas of the curriculum. We may say things like 'I wonder if Bobby is ready for that book yet?' or 'I moved blue group on today because they were ready for tens and units'. The idea that children develop cognitively, rather as they do physically, is part of the belief system of many infant teachers. This comparison with physical development is important. The visibility and measurability of physical change has clear advantages for teachers for whom there is an imperative to do two things. The first is that they are required to justify their approach to teaching and learning. Secondly, they are asked to indicate the efficacy of the process through the assessment of change and progress. The desire to draw on substantive theories and observable and measurable change is absolutely understandable in our scientific culture. Indeed, it is that desire that probably led to the ready adoption of many of the cognitive ideas put forward by Jean Piaget.

Stages and ages

From the early nineteenth through to the second half of the twentieth century, there has developed in infant schools a philosophy of child-centredness based on the ideas of Rousseau, Froebel, Montessori and Dewey. It is therefore not surprising that the work of Piaget, with its focus on individual development in the child, should have profoundly affected the work of infant teachers. Indeed, between the First and Second World Wars the Consultative Committee to the Board of Education for England and Wales was much influenced by the work of Piaget as well as many notable progressive practitioners (Evans 1985).

Piaget's work, including his idea of 'stages' in development, has had a powerful impact on mathematics education. He suggests that children think differently from adults and that their thinking passes through five main stages which are equated to chronological age bands: sensori-motor period (birth to 2 years), pre-operational thought (2–4 years), intuitive thought (4–7 years), concrete operations (8–11 years), and formal operations (11–14 years). Of these, therefore, the suggestion is that the infant teacher is concerned with pre-operational thought and intuitive thought.

In coming to his views on the development of knowledge, Piaget worked with small numbers of children. He offered these children carefully constructed challenges and recorded their responses to the set tasks. These tasks and challenges were designed to 'test' the child's ability in particular aspects of perception and understanding. Mathematics figured prominently in the tasks that Piaget set.

Examples of children's thinking

An example of a challenge that Piaget offered to the small sample of children he worked with is to do with spatial concepts and perception (Piaget and Inhelder 1956). The conclusion drawn from this experiment was that children are unable to see things from any viewpoint except their own. This has, however, been vigorously challenged by a number of other researchers. For example, Donaldson (1978) reports studies made by Hughes in which, by setting the task in a modified way, it was shown that young children are able to see things from another person's point of view. Clearly the way a task is presented to a child can have a marked effect on the outcome. Another example serves to support this point.

In a series of experiments to do with the conservation of number[1] (Piaget 1952), the results obtained led Piaget to determine three stages of performance, and it was only at stage three, demonstrated largely by older children, that conservation of number was achieved. There has also been strong criticism of these particular experiments, including important comments about the language used and the way the task was presented to the child. For example:

> Children should not therefore be written off as 'non-conservers' if they fail on a Piagetian conservation task; they may well conserve in more favourable circumstances and may have a concept of number which is adequate for many basic number situations.
>
> (Dickson *et al*. 1984: 185)

Stages, ages and mathematics

Piaget's theory offered a template for children's acquisition of knowledge, and a 'scientific' explanation of children's understanding and capacity for tackling new concepts. Piagetian influence is still entrenched, leading to a ready acceptance of the possibility of developmental stages in respect of the acquisition of mathematical knowledge. Piaget's work also raises questions to regarding preparedness of children to tackle new ideas or novel formulations of existing information. We feel sure there are some teachers who, in talking about, for example, Patrick or Stefan (whom we talked of in the introduction to this chapter), would say they are 'ready' or not yet 'ready' to learn addition, on account of their ages.

There are so many critics of Piagetian theory today that the idea of 'readiness' based on his work, so warmly embraced in the 1960s, is now unacceptable. We cannot withhold opportunities from children on the basis that they are not yet ready to learn from them due to the stage of learning development that they might have reached. This is particularly so in relation to a child's age – one cannot state that 6 year old children have to wait until they are 7 or 8 in order to encounter particular ideas.

It is still the case that many mathematics schemes continue to evidence the influence of Piaget's stages. A recognition of that can help us to offset the limitations imposed on children's learning by the 'book, level or phase a year' approach, or the idea that children must 'do all of A before they are ready for B'. The teacher who remarked to us, 'I think Brian is really at Level four[2] in some parts of his mathematics but I must get him to do all the Levels two and three work first', seems to us to be adopting an age and stage approach which insists upon all work at a given level having, of necessity, to be undertaken before it is possible or even permissible for children to tackle work at the frontiers of their understanding. Whilst appreciating the reasons for this we would argue for support for children in doing what they are able to do rather than taking on a scheme wholesale along with principles of 'ages and stages' and all that this implies in relation to readiness.

The emphases in the theories of Bruner, another leading cognitive theorist, have much to do with 'stages' but little to do with 'ages'. In this respect they are different from those of Piaget. However, they may have just as important an effect on how we view children's learning.

Spirals in learning

Jerome Bruner's name is generally less well known in UK primary schools than that of Piaget, but his ideas are actually part and parcel of the everyday discussion of teaching and learning. Bruner also takes a developmental view of children, but he emphasises this in terms of ideas visited and re-visited. Following in the traditions of Dewey (e.g. 1938) he elaborates a model of learning based upon the concept of the spiral curriculum. By this is meant that children study a topic at one stage of their development and then return to it later in order to elaborate their understanding, and thereby develop a more sophisticated attitude. This view of curriculum design is one that has been central to much of primary philosophy in recent times, though it has not been adopted by the compilers of the National Curriculum.[3]

Modes of thinking

Bruner (1966) defines three modes of thinking; enactive, iconic, and symbolic. *Enactive* means learning through action, whereas *iconic* representation depends upon the use of images to detect patterns or pathways. *Symbolic* representation means the utilisation of symbols through which hypotheses can be explored and manipulated. These modes have clear connections with Piaget's stages of development although Bruner's modes are not so clearly age-related – we all make use of all of them to a greater or lesser degree in response to new learning, but there is the suggestion that young children incline towards the enactive mode.

By the representation of ideas Bruner means the outcomes of the processing of past experience. This entails children being able to 'stand away' from immediate stimuli in order to determine their response, and the development of a 'storage system' for information in order to make predictions and to extrapolate to new situations. Bruner sees memory as being the retrieval of relevant, useful and usable information coded from our past experience. This implies that if children are supported in organising their experience and guided in drawing out the kernel of ideas, they will be better able to respond to new situations and to develop refined and insightful perspectives. This process may be seen as one of growth, and Bruner makes extensive use of this term in offering 'benchmarks about the nature of intellectual growth' (1966: 5).

Modes of thinking and mathematics

It is possible to relate Bruner's modes of representation to our experience of children's learning of mathematics. We all understand the problems there would be in trying to learn from a manual: the skills of, for example, riding a bike, painting a picture, or swinging a conker. Indeed, even if someone is telling us what to do it is often difficult to translate what is said to us to the 'feel' of the conker swing. Reading and being told are not the same as doing. In mathematics we make use of this idea by letting children count on their fingers, laying out all the red crayons in order to count them, putting a hat on each of three teddies before attempting to say how many hats the teddies need, and so on. It is likely that the enactive mode is the pre-eminent mode for young children. Thus the imperative, for us in arranging learning situations for young children is to make them active and practical. Perhaps it is possible to have the children always doing some or all of the following during mathematics:

— moving around;
— using themselves (for example, their fingers) and their classmates; (for example), 'I can see my two eyes in the mirror, if you look in the mirror I can see four eyes';

— using the classroom environment; for example, 'Please go and touch something which you think is the same shape as this box', or 'Can you collect a set of red things from around the room?'

and to aid their 'representation of ideas' we should regard talk as essential and make everyday provision for the following:

— children to talk amongst themselves and set their own challenges as in this example recorded during children's first two days at school:

> John (4.11) and Ben (4.09) are sharing a pot of beads and a piece of string. Ben remarks, 'I'll do the same amount as you. All right?' and takes a turn at threading. Having threaded four beads Ben asks, 'Have I done the same amount?' John contemplates the string for a while then replies, 'Do two more.' Ben decides differently, however, and says 'I'll do three more,' adding, 'I'll pass you then.'
>
> (Bird 1991: 9)

— use talk as an integral part of mathematics, not only to support children in using their memories of what has gone before and refining their memories in the light of what they are doing today, but also in encouraging children to express their own thinking and their methods of working.

Children's 'picture maths' recording may be seen as fitting the iconic mode. When a child is presented with a picture of three butterflies and asked to draw a flower for each, iconic representation is in use. It is the case that there is now a widespread appreciation of the value of iconic representation in mathematics schemes and these are nowadays characterised by excellent illustrations and strong images including, sometimes, the use of cartoon characters to support the mathematical story line.

Symbolic representation includes letters, numerals and signs such as '=' or '+' in mathematics. Whatever the symbol, it is capable of theoretical, abstract manipulation. It is the case that expectations and pressures on teachers lead them to move to symbolic representation in mathematics as rapidly as possible. However, in view of the ways in which Bruner suggests that we all learn it is likely that too rapid a move to written symbolism is likely to be counter-productive for most children. This is not to say that children should not use symbols, for they will already, on entering school, be using symbolism when they speak. Rather we need to allow children to make use of all modes of representation, depending on which they themselves find appropriate. We will return to the question of the importance and meaning of language and symbols in relation to mathematics in Chapter 5.

Following Piaget and Bruner, studies that have replicated and challenged their work call into question ideas we may have about children needing to be 'ready' for a particular piece of learning. What children can learn has less to do with their 'stage or age' than with how the learning is presented and whether they are able to build on what they have already experienced. Children are not on a staircase or a moving pavement to mathematical understanding. They do not move 'up' in steps or 'along' in linear fashion. Their intellects do not need cosseting, or protecting from what is seen as 'too difficult' (Brown 1987). They will never be more 'ready'. They are ready now. However, we also have to address another issue which is thought to be important in class, and that is the motivation to learn what we teach.

WILLINGNESS

We take pleasure in doing those things which we like, and much less in those we dislike. Having to do things which we dislike is arduous, seems to take ages, is more like an ordeal, has to be got through. While it is not necessarily the case that we attain more in those things we like, we are often keen to keep trying things we like again and again to improve our personal performance. In distinguishing between attainment and 'keenness to improve a personal best' we are drawing attention to motivating forces which might be seen to be, on the one hand external or extrinsic and on the other personal or intrinsic. It is important therefore to consider why we take on new learning.

Why learn mathematics?

There is no obvious reason why children should wish to learn mathematics as it is taught. We rely on what we see as the 'natural' curiosity in young children allied with the social pressures that they experience, as the spur for mathematics learning to be seen as necessary and valid. However, the enthusiasm in children for what is seen as being mathematics in school seems to deteriorate rapidly. When we asked some 6 year olds to draw themselves doing mathematics, Tracy said, 'Do you mean proper mathematics like we do in our scheme books or shapes and patterns and things?' Roy drew a picture of himself as a tiny figure in the corner of the page, enveloped in an enormous open book covered with 'sums'. Veronica said, 'Mathematics at school is boring, all we ever do is "sheets".' If children feel this way; that mathematics is boring, limited and about sums and that is all, it is small wonder that they begin to see mathematics as something not very pleasant or meaningful.

Ausubel (1968) suggests that there are three factors involved in being motivated to undertake a task. They are:

— interest in the task;
— the effect the task has on our image of ourselves;
— whether the task accords us links with other people.

If we spell out these factors we can note their applicability to work in mathematics. Children or adults may be intrinsically interested in the task and see it as important. We teachers would like the nature of all mathematics tasks to be sufficient to motivate children, but Ausubel points to the contemporaneous effects of status and approval. Mathematics is accorded high status by both parents and teachers, and some children will attempt to 'learn' in order to acquire self-esteem and clearly approved success. However, peer approval may suggest that being good at mathematics is akin to being teacher's favourite, and therefore most undesirable. This discussion confirms that we have to be circumspect about the likely motivation of young children, for there may be lots of determining factors, which in turn may be contradictory. However, children can lay bare our convictions in discomforting, stereotypical ways which may indicate that we have rather limited views of what is motivating, and what school learning is really about.

When we watch small children playing 'school' there are some explicit and observable features of classroom life that constantly feature. They include some of the following:

— pupils are all given the same structured 'linear' task to do individually;
— ticks and crosses are put on the work;
— there are extremely severe punishments for anything 'wrong'.

Though this image of school life is partial and fragmentary it does map fairly closely the picture of mathematics sessions painted by adults who say they hated mathematics at school.[4] While it might be argued that what goes on in classrooms is not at all like this, or perhaps not like this nowadays, there is an element of truth in the caricature. Many teachers do use structured linear tasks and readily observable explicit aspects of performance in their classrooms. Children do experience the pressure of the right answer from some parents and teachers, and some children do feel punished for not getting their 'sums' correct. The 'play school' scenario presents and highlights 'right and wrong' and penalties for what is 'wrong'. These may be viewed by some as similar to the negative aspects of a behaviourist approach. However, behaviourism does have a positive use for teachers of infants in some circumstances. Set among a wide repertoire of strategies and techniques, individualised, highly-structured tasks which are closely monitored and on which children have frequent 'feedback' can be used to good effect.

Behaviourism and mathematics

Skinner (e.g. 1954) found in many series of experiments using animals that learning could be accomplished through structuring of the given tasks into series of small steps and rewarding each appropriate response immediately at every step. This work is known as 'stimulus-response' and led to the idea of programmed learning in the early 1960s. For a behaviourist the important areas of interest when applied to school learning are the sequence of small and carefully structured tasks given to children and the outcomes in terms of children's performance on the tasks. What happens within the child between the presentation of the task and the performance is not under consideration.

The important features of the programmed learning approach, as it was developed for use with humans, include:

— instant feedback;
— immediate reinforcement (reward);
— structured tasks (originally linear, but later versions allowed branching);
— individualised learning;
— self-pacing;
— mastery of each step in the learning sequence.

In practice, programmed learning machines were constructed in order to provide reliable tools for the provision of information and questions. The learner could then use pencil or keyboard to respond. Moving to the next 'frame' gave the answer, and so on.

Programmed learning machines had a very brief life in UK schools but some of the characteristics of programmed learning are evident in certain software currently available for computers in classrooms. Indeed, in the early days of software production a number of commercial packages were produced using programmed learning techniques. These have generally been relegated by teachers as 'drill', and more generic and open-ended software has become much more prevalent. This move, as was the case with the earlier programmed learning materials, is an attempt to offset one of the criticisms of such learning; namely that it is narrow in the material that can be programmed. But there may also be quality and control issues involved. Many software packages now offer visually exciting effects including animation, and more options and control of information to the user. As teachers choosing software for children to use, we need to assess when to provide externally programmed learning opportunities, and when to give opportunities where the learner is more self-determining. It would be foolish to turn away completely from instructional programs as they may, in some areas, offer an efficient and satisfying approach to a specific learning need.

Individualised tasks and quick feedback can be useful to teachers of infant mathematics. They do, however, have disadvantages which may concern motivation beyond the immediate task. In order to sustain children's work in mathematics (though not necessarily their enthusiasm), teachers resort to a few well-rehearsed ploys which involve testing, ticks, and turn-around. As mathematics appears to offer a rapid feedback on results, tests and the rehearsal of 'sums' which can be checked and accorded ticks are within the mathematics repertoire of every teacher. Turn-around of worksheets and scheme books is also seen, by some, as a measure of achievement. A page of ticks, or a finished workbook can boost a child's confidence in the short term and it is good to have an affirmation in answer to the question 'How am I doing?' This kind of work can also give a teacher external and demonstrable 'evidence' for learning. While all teachers know it is not the ultimate 'proof' of learning (for it does not tell us whether the child understands what is set down on the page or can use what they have learned in other settings) it can be seen as an important 'index' of learning in the opinion of parents, other adults, and even the children themselves. We recall these remarks made by children in schools we have worked in:

> 'We haven't done any work today' (when the child had not recorded work in a book).
> 'When are we going to start work?' (at the end of a mathematical discussion).

and Atkinson reports similar comments from children in a school she worked in:

> Maths was defined as 'doing the card' and when I tried to develop ideas or deal with difficulties, I got the reaction, 'But I've done that card'. My carefully thought out 'do and talk' maths activities . . . were not regarded as 'real' maths!
>
> (1992: 45)

It is clear that we do need to beware of giving children the impression that mathematics involves repetition or routinisation. Even from the few examples given above, we may conclude that a predominance of behaviourally based techniques in class may lead children to expect school mathematics to be inactive and cognitively limited. These ideas have powerful implications for what we envisage as a structure in learning (see p.16) and how we plan and organise what children actually do in mathematics.

ABILITY

In our view most teachers believe that some people have more 'natural ability' than others. By that they mean inherited ability. However, teachers' real focus is not in people's past but in their futures; that is, in helping them to realise their potential and not simply to demonstrate 'starting ability'. Having said this it is the common currency of staffroom talk and planning files to describe some children as 'high fliers', 'able', 'top group' and some as 'specials', 'slow learners', 'less able'.

We do not really know everything about children's ability. We all have our own idiosyncratic ways of telling how able children are. Added to these, we can test some aspects of children's performance and make predictions based on these test results. Our impressions are just that, and they are sometimes wrong. All experienced teachers can remember with shame that, though they may have 'done their best', it was not 'the best' that could have been done to help some children realise their potential. Just as we cannot entirely trust our impressions, we cannot trust test results either. No test tells more than part of the story and all have some weaknesses. The thrust of evidence about ability, from impressions that 'Toby's work is good for that of a 6 year old' to external test performances such as 'Sally scored more than any of the other year two children', is tied in to ideas we have about links between demonstrable ability and age.

Children's mathematical abilities

There is evidence that we constantly underestimate children's mathematical abilities. Bruner suggests the possibility of children meeting and grappling with complex ideas when young, and this, in our experience, is often earlier than many teachers expect. Bruner offers a number of examples of the ways in which young children gain initial insights into complex mathematical ideas. One such example, on the development of ideas concerning quadratic equations, makes use of Dienes apparatus (Dienes 1960, 1966). The work was done with four able 8 year old children using flats, longs and unit cubes. The act of faith required of the children was that the length of the sides of a flat were not known and that they could be called 'x'. As Bruner states:

> A certain humor helps establish in the pupils a proper contempt for measuring in this context, and the snob appeal of simply calling an unknown by the name 'x' is very great.'
>
> (1966: 60)

The children were asked to make a bigger square than the original flat using the materials available. This produced a construction like that in Figure 1.1.

Having produced a bigger square the children were then asked to produce a bigger square again, as in Figure 1.2.

These squares were described as:

— a single flat – 'an x-square';
— larger square – 'an x-square, two x-strips and a one square';
— next largest square – 'an x-square, four x-strips and four ones'.

These were then translated into symbols.

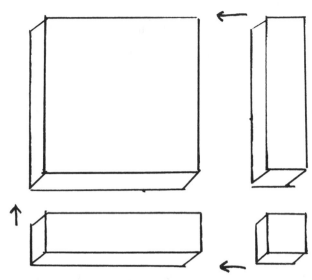

Figure 1.1 Making a bigger square
Source: Bruner 1966

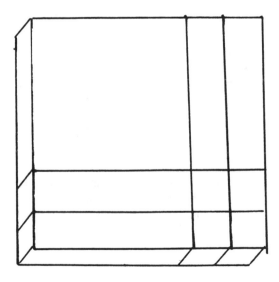

Figure 1.2 Making an even bigger square
Source: Bruner 1966

The first square was depicted as $x\square$ and the strips as 1x or simply x. The unit cubes were 'one by one' or simply 1. This led to a set of statements:

$x\square + 2x + 1$
$x\square + 4x + 4,$

and so on. But Bruner went further and the children constructed a set of relationships which were represented as (looking back at Figures 1.1 and 1.2 will help make clear what is happening):

$x\square + 2x + 1$ is x +1 by x + 1
$x\square + 4x + 4$ is x + 2 by x+ 2

which we could write as

$(x + 1)^2 = x^2 + x + 1$ and
$(x + 2)^2 = x^2 + 4x + 4$

This is impressive mathematics work.

Another example which amply demonstrates young children's abilities is reported by Hughes (1986). He let some 4 and 5 year olds use a simple version of Logo. Using mathematical commands they were able to control the turtle, steering it round obstacles. They were able to instruct the turtle to draw shapes on large pieces of paper. Finally they proved able to work on shape drawing on screen. In evaluating the potential of Logo with young children Hughes says:

> There is a problem reconciling the mathematics of Logo – with its emphasis on distance, space and angle – with the mathematics currently used in many schools. The Craigmillar[5] children, for example, were using concepts of angle considerably more advanced than those they encountered in their classroom.
>
> (1986: 165–6)

Bird, who worked with small groups of young children, says:

> The power of the children can be really astonishing, so much so that I often find that when teachers consider (the) case-studies they are all too readily prepared to remark that such-and-such a child must have been special in some way since 'normal' 4 and 5 year olds would not be able to do such things.
>
> (1991: 114)

STRUCTURE IN LEARNING

Mathematics is a subject in which there is an emphasis on the building of new knowledge on previous knowledge. Whatever our experience or training in the teaching of mathematics and whatever our current predilections, we would all agree that we put some order into our mathematics teaching, that we commonly teach some things before others and that we set objectives for children's learning. In doing so we may be drawing on theories akin to those of Gagné (1970).

Objectives for learning

An important corollary of the behavioural approach is the need to specify objectives. This means that in the construction of objectives it is necessary to keep in mind the way in which you will be able to assess the outcomes in relation to your chosen objective (Rowntree 1982). Gagné posits the importance of objectives in his work and he might be seen to bridge elements of cognitive and behavioural approaches.

Gagné devised a theory in which children learn by starting with simple capabilities and moving on and 'up' to more complex ones. It is assumed that they must master simpler capabilities in order to tackle more complex ones. Thus learning can be modelled as a hierarchy. The hierarchy can be constructed from the top down. For example, if we wished to teach children how to interpret a calendar, we would need to establish what all the steps were in learning to do this, place them in order and present them so. The steps might include, for example knowing the pattern of days of the week, being able to read the names for days of the week, knowing the pattern for months of the year, being able to read the words for these, knowing the numbers 1 to 31, and so on. Each of these would require further breaking down into specific capabilities which children need to learn. Gagné does acknowledge that learning hierarchies may provide not an immutable but an 'on the average' pathway to understanding.

Cognitive theorists also set store by structure in learning. Bruner, for example, though concerned with growth, is not expressing the same concerns as those who are associated with 'child-centred education'. He sees the fundamental importance of providing structured opportunities and challenging content to children and is not biased toward a process approach. He believes that there are ideas with which all children should grapple. In bringing forward his own ideas Bruner was not just a theoretician.

> Jerome Bruner stands out as having given committed attention to education in general and to curriculum in particular. His handling of problems in psychological development in the context of education is speculative and flexible because he is committed to the adventure of action as well as of theory.
>
> (Stenhouse 1975: 28)

While we may choose to structure children's learning objectives in detail and acknowledge 'growth' in the learner through a 'diet' of structured opportunities, if we wish to shift our focus to what has happened to the learner as a result of structured learning, then Richard Skemp's ideas are illuminating.

Kinds of understanding

Skemp (1971, 1989), focusing on cognition in learning, suggests that we construct schemata to link what we know already with our new learning. He also distinguishes between two kinds of understanding: 'instrumental' (acquired through 'habit' learning) and 'relational' (acquired through 'intelligent' learning). Those methods which we learned to get correct answers to sums fit the instrumental label, for we did understand in the sense of knowing how to set the numbers down and what to do to get the answer. We did not understand (and some of us still do not) why it was that the strategies we used got the answer required. By contrast, relational understanding is what we all associate with 'real' understanding and 'knowing'. The importance of this distinction for Skemp's ideas about the teaching of maths is that both kinds of understanding are deemed important.

For example, in teaching children numerals to add to their counts we may show them how we write ten – '10'. When subsequently recording the outcome of a count the children may write '10'. This is instrumental learning. An understanding of why we write ten in that way comes when they are learning place value, which may be much later in their infant career. Their understanding of why ten is written '10' would then be relational. We may choose to teach children to read a digital clock with confidence before they have an understanding of how long an hour or a minute feels. We may be happy for children to address and put a stamp on an envelope in their first year in school, and later to understand that the order of the address is to assist in sorting mail and the cost of the stamp is related to the postal service we require and the 'weight' of the letter. The challenge for the teacher is to use instrumental mathematics and relational mathematics, but each where it is appropriate according to the lesson content and the needs of the children. Skemp does contend that it is 'relational schemata' that provide promise if we are looking at children's education beyond what is short term.

Structure in mathematics

Gagné's ideas have importance for the planning of teaching, and for devising assessments, but they may have less potency in the daily classroom milieu. The watchword for the teacher is, be prepared! If you have worked out a rigorous series of steps for teaching, you will be able to evaluate how successful you were in achieving coverage. The dynamic of the classroom may allow children to assure you that they know some of the steps already, or can skip some of the steps, and permit them to follow a path to learning which is meaningful for them even if it does not fit the teaching plans.

Bruner's work indicates to us the need to offer children appropriate challenges using suitable materials and the pertinent language, and to do so in the context of the growth of experience. However, given current systems and structures it is certainly problematic for teachers to offer this to their classes. We should, perhaps, be more concerned with the 'how' of offering new learning opportunities than the accepted demand of the chosen content. This too can be problematic, for the National Curriculum Council working party for mathematics constructed a school curriculum which has as its basis the idea that children need to be taught some concepts before others; that mastery of the first concepts (Level one) are a precursor for an understanding of those that come next (Level two), and so on. Skemp's work reminds us that we need to take account of what it means for children to 'understand ' what they have done in mathematics, and that we can strive for different kinds of understanding according to our goals.

REVIEW

Both cognitive and behaviourist theorists have offered much to fuel our thinking about giving children opportunities in mathematics. However, it seems that many of the shortcomings in children's experience of mathematics in school may be due to an over-zealous adoption and adherence to aspects of developmental and behaviourist ideas.

The evidence seems to suggest that the following are some of the implications for teachers of young children:

— We can be eclectic in our adoption of a theoretical perspective, according to the specific learning task at issue.
— Our focus should be on the extension of children's horizons *regardless of age*, not the limitation of opportunities on the basis of crude judgements of children as intellectually part-formed (and not yet ready). It is time to shake off the widely held assumption that there is content that is too hard, or inappropriate, for young children.
— There is no theoretical justification for processing children at different rates through the *same* material. Rather, depending on the interests and desires of the child, a wide range of mathematical ideas should be available to children, and in a variety of classroom created contexts. Though many mathematics schemes do offer variety, they tend to do this in relation to developmental ideas which have their roots in a concept of appropriateness for the age of the child, and thus each

kind of activity is limited by the belief of the authors about developmental stages.

— Mathematics must involve activity, thinking and talk as a part of what children are used to doing in class, as these are crucial in early learning.

— We can influence young children's keenness to learn mathematics by making the tasks they do of interest to them (making them have what Atkinson (1992: 39) calls 'human sense'), by showing them we really think mathematics is important and fun and that it is therefore good to be a person who likes mathematics.

— We must guard against underestimating children's capabilities.

— Objectives for learning must be flexible enough to allow the teaching to fit the direction learning takes, and not the other way about.

NOTES

1 Conserving number means recognising that the number assigned to a collection of objects is the same no matter how the collection is arranged.

2 The Level referred to by this teacher is that defined within the Statutory Orders for Mathematics in the National Curriculum (England and Wales).

3 The National Curriculum in England and Wales offers quite a different model of the curriculum, in that it is layered with levels being prerequisite for subsequent levels.

4 See Chapter 2, Home and School, for more evidence of adults' attitudes to mathematics and, e.g. Richards (1982).

5 Craigmillar Primary School in Edinburgh.

Chapter 2

Home and school

INTRODUCTION

Starting school is, for many children, the very first step they take towards an independent life. Because it is so momentous it can be argued that the adults involved need to do their best to ensure the success of the venture in children's eyes. In this chapter we focus on some issues teachers may think about while trying to arrange that children starting school get a good impression of what school mathematics is all about. Children already know a good deal about mathematics before their first lesson. Much of their experience will have happened within sight of mum or dad. There are also aspects of being a child and being in a family that may affect children's approach to mathematics.

First, teachers have a complex task in getting to know about the children who are just starting school. They are required to collect facts and begin records that trace children through their school careers. They form impressions about what individual children are like and make judgements of an everyday kind about the children's families and homes. They also make decisions about children's first learning experiences at school; likely starting points, likely progression, and short-term objectives including the learning of the 'rules and regulations' of the school. Though we may not write them down, if asked to articulate objectives we may say things like 'help Tim to "settle" better when mum leaves him', or 'show Reena how to keep her belongings tidy'. Additionally the objectives include skills; for example, 'give Ali practice in holding and using scissors correctly' and 'show Daniel how to hold a pencil'. Added to this are objectives related to concept mastery; 'red group work on counting, ordering and sorting to five'.

The differences between home and school are legion. Some writers talk about 'bridging the gap' because the 'learning experiences, the discipline, the communication requirements, the physical and social environments of these worlds are very different' (Tizard and Hughes 1984: 263). We have different expectations of children in school when compared with home.

These expectations apply to a whole range of things and underlie the behaviour and thinking we let children know is appropriate in school. In school, we ask children to work on situations, objects and ideas which have little to do with choosing to 'do what you like'. Donaldson (1978) argues that children entering school have prodigious skills when dealing with 'real-life' situations in which they have objectives and can see those of other people. However, they do not reflect on what they have done away from specific situations. They also do not notice how they use their skills in dealing with these situations, nor can they muster these skills as and when they wish. According to Donaldson this is exactly what we expect in school.

> Education . . . requires . . . (the child) . . . to call the powers of his mind into service *at will* and use them to tackle problems which do not arise out of the old familiar matrix but which are 'posed' – presented in abrupt isolation and presented, to begin with at least, by some other person whose purposes are obscure.
>
> (Donaldson 1978: 121–2)

This view is supported by Tizard and Hughes: 'It is the school's role to introduce children to a way of thinking and knowing the world which is independent of their own experiences' (1984: 263).

Entry to school marks a point of change for children but in no sense do they 'begin again'. Prior learning is important and should be seen as useful and usable. In maximising children's learning opportunities in school, we need to take account of what children have already learned about mathematics and in mathematics. Parents and teachers both have a part to play in setting children on the road to 'mathematical literacy'. It is to the contribution of parents that we turn first.

PARENTS' CONTRIBUTION

Attitudes to mathematics

The Cockcroft Report (1982: 62) states that 'Parents can exercise, even if unknowingly, a considerable influence on their children's attitudes to mathematics'. It seems that their own schooling has much to do with how people in adulthood view mathematics (Cockcroft 1982: 62). Richards (1982: 59) reports that if people are asked 'to sum up their view of mathematics at school many people would describe it in terms of one, if not all of the three "d's" – dull, difficult and disliked.' We have argued thus:

> It is the case that most of us have been turned off mathematics at school and society reinforces being 'hopeless at maths' as a good thing! How often are we struck by the knowledge of literature that guests on the

radio and TV have and how often do those same guests willingly admit to being no good at maths? Being mathematically 'illiterate' is actually as limiting as being unable to read.

(Clemson and Clemson 1990: 73–4)

Despite a welter of negative feelings about mathematics The Mathematical Association suggests that this is an area in which 'parents are often extremely anxious for their children to show success' (1987b: 1). It reports: 'a recent survey in a national newspaper claimed that only 20 per cent of the sample admitted liking mathematics while 82 per cent believed it to be the single most important subject taught in school!' (1987: 2). Thus some children just starting school may already have feelings like the following:

— mum and/or dad don't like mathematics
— mathematics is hard
— mathematics is important
— mum and/or dad want me to be good at mathematics (despite thinking they are no good at it themselves)

It is worth adding here that many teachers in primary schools, whether they are parents or not, seem to share the attitudes held by other adults. For example, Walden and Walkerdine (1982) supply us with evidence of a lack of confidence in their own mathematics among primary school teachers. Thus the reception class teacher in school has to try to minimise the effects of the negative feelings children may have about mathematics. Account needs to be taken of the fact that teachers' attitudes may support and perpetuate these feelings.

Pre-school mathematics experiences

All children have access to mathematics before they attend school. The kinds of experience that are provided may not be regarded as mathematical by people in general. Whilst all adults can identify cooking and meeting a train on time as involving mathematics, in other everyday experiences the mathematics is sometimes not so obvious. It is important for teachers to have a store of examples of pre-school mathematical experiences. They can be used to reassure those parents who feel under-confident about helping the pre-school children in the family and they can also be used to illustrate what we mean by mathematics when we talk to parents. Some examples of the 'mathematical' events that may regularly have been part of children's lives before they came to school include:

— To do with number – sorting the shopping, matching the socks, arranging food on a plate, laying the table;

— To do with measures – going on the beach, having a bath, watching mum or dad do some baking, being measured for shoes;
— To do with spatial concepts – packing a bag, putting things away in drawers or cupboards, hoovering or sweeping;
— To do with putting things in order – making 'collections' (perhaps newspapers for recycling or clothes or toys for a jumble sale), setting out shoes, making journeys (for example, walk, bus, walk, then arrive at auntie's house).

Children may also have had experiences that we adults distinguish as play:

— To do with number – using coloured pens and paints in making patterns, threading beads, singing rhymes and songs;
— To do with measures – playing in the paddling pool and sand pit;
— To do with spatial concepts – doing jigsaws, playing on climbing frames, riding a tricycle, kicking a ball, building models with construction toys or junk, making a play camp;
— To do with putting things in order – play house or shop, sorting out toys.

It is clear that many of these experiences and countless others are available to very many children. In fact they may feature more frequently in the experience of children who have never been further than the local park, than those whose babyhood holidays have been spent in Lanzarote and whose grandparents buy them 'mathematics workbooks' in the supermarket.

Parents helping their children's school mathematics

Along with their negative attitudes to mathematics as a subject some parents may also feel that school mathematics these days is anathema. If we can persuade parents that they can help their own children, and that mathematics in school is not unpleasant, this will not only help the children we teach, but may also serve to change adults' attitudes to mathematics. It was pointed out in the Plowden Report (CACE: 1967) that parental interest has a big effect on achievement and that the level of interest depends on how much parents know about school. Clearly informing parents can result in mathematical gains for their children.

We believe teachers can support parents in continuing to help their children's mathematics in two ways. The first of these is by letting parents know that ordinary everyday life presents plenty of mathematical opportunity. We suspect that because adults' memories of their own early schooling can be hazy, they focus on the fairly constant characteristics of schooling as a whole. They therefore associate learning with sitting still, books and writing. Parents need convincing that mathematics at home is not 'homework' that has to be 'set' and 'marked' by the teacher. A walk round the block, visiting the park or local shops, playing a game of dominoes and doing household chores can yield more mathematics than any page of 'sums'. McPherson and Payne argue:

> Some parents may wish to have it explained to them that many everyday experiences and discussions provide the solid foundations on which a teacher can build the children's mathematical futures; experiences such as playing with water, cooking, playing board games, laying the table and having discussions, for example, about what is happening in the world, the shapes around them, the time it takes to get somewhere, tomorrow's visit by the doctor or granny's visit next Tuesday.
>
> (1987: 87)

The second way that teachers can support parents is to give them a chance to find out what school mathematics is like now. Workshops, exhibitions and parent/child projects are all ways of showing parents what mathematics is about and give them opportunities to 'have a go'. The Mathematical Association suggests these ways of presenting mathematics to parents:

> Static – displays of work, displays of resources, talks, stalls selling books and games.
> Dynamic – pupils at work, resources to be tried out, workshops, mathematical games and entertainments.
>
> (1987: 7)

There have been interventionist projects to promote mathematics at home in much the same way that researchers and teachers have enlisted parents' help with reading. These projects point up the benefits of parents helping their children. See, for example, Merttens and Vass (1990) which describes the IMPACT (Maths with Parents and Children and Teachers) project. Run in several hundred schools, it involves children taking home weekly mathematics tasks that can be shared with their parents. The Mathematical Association (1987: 44–7) describes the Stutton Project.[1] At this school there was a home reading partnership already established and the teachers decided to try extending it to mathematics. To start the venture, a booklet about metric measurement was produced in school. Meetings were held first for parents, and then parents and children. At the second meeting the activities in the booklet were set up so that children and adults could try them. Families were invited to borrow school equipment and do the activities at home over a six week period. During this time on one morning a week the activities were carried through in school and parents were invited along. A teacher involved wrote that the school 'engaged in a meaningful way with . . . parents, in pursuit of the kind of powerful partnership which . . . could improve mathematical education'

(Mathematical Association 1987: 46). It is to the teachers' contributions to children's mathematics as they start school that we turn next.

TEACHERS' RESPONSIBILITIES

Providing equal opportunities

There is now a large body of research which indicates that children who are perceived as 'advantaged' are higher achievers in education. If we group children according to social class, ethnicity or gender, the trend in results reveals that on the whole, working-class children, children from ethnic minority groups and girls do less well at school in terms of achievement. It contravenes common sense to assume that intellectual potential is lacking in all these children. However, the expectations that the parents of these children have, the level of expectation that the children have for themselves and the expectations that their *teachers* have may substantially affect how well the children do in school. In other words this outcome is only inevitable if it is what we expect. Children arrive at school having, for various reasons, had markedly unequal opportunities and experience. We cannot afford to ignore what has gone before or goes on out of school. However, we cannot glibly assume that some children have less potential than others because their parents have particular jobs or are unemployed, because they are members of an ethnic minority group, or because they are girls.

Class and culture

The notion that children of families from different social classes have different ways of using language and different experiences has led to the idea that some children, merely by virtue of the social class their family belongs to, are, on entry to school, in some way deprived. Despite the lack of substance in this idea, it has affected some teachers in two ways. First, because language is the vehicle for learning, teachers may be tempted to begin to make assumptions about the learning powers of working-class children and underestimate them. Secondly, teachers may also take the view that their own effect on the children's likely levels of achievement may be limited.

> Beliefs in cultural deprivation ... encourage teachers to hold low expectations of these pupils and to underestimate the importance of changing teaching styles and curriculum provision [and] stereotyping certain social classes or cultural groups as 'the problem' in education ... [means] ... the role of the school in enhancing children's learning opportunities is thereby underestimated or even ignored.
>
> (Docking 1990: 19, 20)

Bernstein (1971) devised a theory to describe the ways language was used in working-class and middle-class families. One of the points he made was that in a middle-class home children are 'oriented towards universalistic' meanings which are not tied to a given context. In working-class homes the children are 'oriented towards particularistic' meanings which are context bound. This point is of importance to teachers because Bernstein goes on to argue that what goes on in schools involves universalistic meanings; that is those to which the middle-class children are already attuned. He is at pains to say that working-class children do not have speech and meaning systems that are 'linguistically or culturally deprived'. He would agree that we do have to begin where the children are and provide contexts of learning that connect with children's experience, their family and community, otherwise 'the child is not at home in the educational world'. '*If the culture of the teacher is to become part of the consciousness of the child, then the culture of the child must first be in the consciousness of the teacher*' (Bernstein 1971: 199).

This suggests that it is mandatory for teachers to take every opportunity to get to know as much as they can about children and their lives outside school. We are not suggesting that teachers endeavour to map out or tap into all the likely experiences of children before even meeting them. We do, however, think it helps to do a bit of 'best guessing' and act on that, so that there are some areas in which the teacher can immediately enter the world of the children. For example, we are reminded of the student teacher who decided that she would try to talk to some 5 year olds about their interests, but her recordings of her conversations make it clear that she had never watched and did not know the names of any of the television programmes for that age group. This presented barriers (if only temporary ones) to the possible sharing between teacher and children. Desforges and Cockburn have recorded teachers' remarks which support the importance of getting to know about children. For example:

> Children know so much that is useful to maths teaching. You have to try to keep in touch with their world. I try to watch children's TV and read their comics. It's not only important to the relationship – it's vital when they start choosing topics for graphs!
>
> (1987: 30)

We regret to report that we know of a head teacher who does not know who Miss Honey and Miss Trunchbull are. There are also teachers who have worked in schools for years and have never walked around outside the school perimeter fence, never looked at the kinds of houses the children live in, nor where they play and have never visited the local shop. If that is the case teachers may just as well arrive each morning from another planet, only to achieve vertical take-off from the playground at the end of the day!

The point we are making is that it is part of the professional interest of every teacher of young children to make discoveries about the lives of children. Only then can the milieu of the school, the kinds of things done and said, link with children's home life, and their whole life before they started school.

> We should start knowing that the social experience the child already possesses is valid and significant, and that this social experience should be reflected back to him as being valid and significant. It can be reflected back to him only if it is a part of the texture of the learning experience we create.
>
> (Bernstein 1971: 200)

There is evidence then that social class alone is not an indicator of children's capabilities. Tizard and Hughes' research with nursery children supports the view that 'working-class children are as competent at conceptual and logical thinking as middle-class children'. (1984: 159). We therefore cannot afford to make assumptions about class, culture and mathematics skills in children. Some children from ethnic minority groups are also from families that many would deem working class and so the points we have made about class are applicable to them. There are, however additional points to make.

Culture and ethnicity

While social class is linked to underachievement, prejudice and discrimination have led to *added* underachievement (exceeding that of whites) for children of ethnic minority groups.[2] And the prejudice occurs in schools as well as outside them. What is required is a change of 'attitudes amongst the White Majority, and . . . a pattern of education that enables *all* pupils to give of their best' (The Swann Report 1985 para 2.9, p. 769).

Docking (1990: 19) tells us that though some people hold 'stereotypic beliefs about deficits in children's home background' when the children come from 'minority families', research among Afro-Caribbean and Asian families demonstrates that these beliefs are not borne out. Tizard *et al.* (1988) carried out a longitudinal study of British children of Afro-Caribbean origin and white British children of UK origin from the ages of 4 to 7. They report that though many of the children in their sample might be seen as 'deprived . . . in the most important ways the children were by no means deprived . . . most of the children were given a great deal of love, support and encouragement by their families.'(Tizard *et al.* 1988: 84). They also found that over 'the three year infant period as a whole, black parents were more positive about helping their children at home than were white parents' (1988: 83). This confounds commonly held prejudice.

Despite this parental support and the fact that there were no appreciable differences in mathematics skills between the groups of children before school, it was white boys who made the most progress in mathematics in their infant years.

Beyond the glaring prejudices held about families of minority ethnic groups, there is considerable misunderstanding and confusion about multicultural education. Of course some children from ethnic minority groups do experience different cultural traditions at home from at school and teachers acknowledge this. Similarly, if the school we work in has a working-class or 'mixed' catchment area including working-class and middle-class families, we may recognise that of course 'multi-cultural issues' are of importance. However, if we work in a school where all or nearly all the children seem to come from white middle-class families there is a temptation to view home and school as entirely homogeneous. At a superficial level this view could be forgiven. After all, teachers are purveyors of middle-class culture, and would call them-selves middle class. They then make assumptions about the values and culture being inculcated at home. Evidence of mismatch occurs when teachers follow their own predilections, falsely secure in the confidence that all parents are like themselves. Consider issues like whether children should be sent out onto the playground in the rain, or whether a certain film is suitable for 5 year olds, or what are appropriate procedures when a child is rude and insubordinate, or which big businesses should sponsor the school newsletter. These may seem minor issues but they can convey messages to children about values and standards that are important. We ourselves can recall 'mistakes' we have made as teachers and that we know have been made by other teachers, when multicultural dimensions are forgotten.

In contrast, Alexander did find that some schools introduce

innovative practices in multicultural education, recognizing that this is quite a separate thing from ethnic minority provision, and that although they have no need for the latter, the former is relevant and important whatever the ethnic composition of their own catchment area.

(1992: 15)

There is a clear imperative for teachers to reflect on what is meant by the 'culture of the home' and whether they themselves accord inappropriate treatment to children on the basis of assumptions about their home or ethnic group. Being from a family of any particular class, culture or ethnic group does not, of itself, tell us anything about children's potential for learning. Prejudices that are commonly held in these areas can only interfere with our responsibility to offer children equal mathematical opportunities in school. Another concern in the area of equal opportunities in mathematics is the provision of the same chances for girls as boys.

Gender

Mathematics is a contentious area of the curriculum when gender issues are under discussion. Those infant teachers who are constantly alert to their own treatment of girls and boys may consider that this discussion has little to offer them in the context of their mathematics sessions. However, there is a body of research which has produced findings that set out differences between girls and boys in both their performance in and attitudes towards mathematics. Most theorists and practitioners would agree that the groundwork for later achievement happens before school and in the early years of schooling. We therefore suggest that such findings and their implications might offer pointers to ways in which infant teachers can give genuinely equal opportunities and similar access to mathematics learning to all children. Let us touch on what happens to girls and boys before school. Our everyday experience tells us that boys are treated differently to girls from birth. Despite a wealth of literature on this subject, emphasising that stereotypes are damaging to the opportunities for both girls and boys, there are still many people who argue vociferously for maintaining these stereotypes. As we have said elsewhere:

> A common argument raised in favour of giving the sexes different opportunities, is that girls and boys are *not* the same, and that they force the difference by announcing their preferences. Differences there undoubtedly are, but they may not be as great as we suppose, for there are subtle pressures on children, from birth, to conform to a gender-linked image. Most adults conspire in this.
>
> (Clemson and Clemson 1990: 109)

It may be argued that there are different ranges of behaviours commonly tolerated from girls and boys.[3] It may be that activities such as climbing trees and kicking a ball around, seen as boys' pursuits, go with the opportunities to explore shape and space. Perhaps these pursuits offer more than dance, which is taken up by more girls than boys. Many boys are expected to be more active and to take more initiative, which, it could be argued, may give them a headstart in 'setting to it' when given a practical task or investigation. Cockcroft (1982) supports this notion.

There may need to be a shift, in schools, in what is generally viewed as appropriate for girls and boys to do. An HMI survey of 1973, reported in Joffe and Foxman (1984: 49), revealed that in primary schools 'boys engage more than girls in using tools, construction, three-dimensional modelling and measurement.' They suggest that 'it may be that the stereotyping of activities as masculine or feminine is reinforced in schools as well as in society in general' (1984: 49–50). Our own experience seems to indicate that though children's attitudes and behaviour have many influences on them before school and that schools may perpetuate patterns already established, this is by no means an irretrievable situation. We found we were able to deliberately set up equal and even 'special' access for boys and girls. For example, the girls who avoided using resources like Lego 'with active encouragement and a stimulus like "make a hamster cage, a proscenium arch, a garden centre or a dragon" made models as enthusiastically and successfully as boys' (Clemson and Clemson 1990: 110). Some teachers may, despite their feelings to the contrary, be as culpable as any other adults in not recognising the extent to which stereotyping exists or limits children's opportunities. For example, many of the teachers in Alexander's study (1992: 16) said 'We treat everybody equally here'. During the study, however, the researchers found that what happened in schools did not support this assertion.

Much of the research work on children's school mathematics has been directed at children much older than 7, the implication being that there is little difference between boys and girls with regard to maths when they are young. However, Shuard (1986: 23) says, 'I shall suggest that by the third year of the junior school, boys are already ahead at those aspects of mathematics which are fruitful for future mathematical development and insight.'

There is some evidence that girls do better at computation but boys excel in all other aspects of maths. It seems that:

> As pupils grow older . . . problem solving and the understanding of mathematical concepts become more important, so that they are absolutely central to progress. Somehow, by the age of 10, more boys than girls have got themselves into a position where they are able to cope with these aspects of mathematics.
>
> (Shuard 1986: 34)

The implications of this research might lead us to offer girls chances to work harder at mathematics. However, this effort may produce outcomes that are not as we would wish, for, as Shuard (1986: 34) suggests, 'girls may put more effort into excelling at computational skills rather than at understanding the concepts and principles of mathematics.' With curriculum changes and the introduction of calculators and computers into classrooms, there has been a broader brief for what constitutes mathematics in schools. Children are beginning to be encouraged to use calculators to do computations that are not of an everyday kind, and girls' ability in computation may therefore may be less useful in these circumstances. Increased attempts to use practical, investigational and problem solving approaches seem to favour those areas of mathematics in which girls do less well and thus there may be a perpetuation or even an increase in the differences in the performance of girls and boys. In contrast to Shuard's suggestions, the Assessment of Performance Unit (DES 1988: 26) presents what they see as encouraging results that indicate that 'tests assessing problem solving strategies rather than mathematical content reveal that at age 11 boys' and girls' measured performance is almost the same.' However, with success rates of only 11 per cent (boys) and 12 per cent (girls) on an example item, it seems that rather than comment on the match in percentages, it may be more important to look at why all children appear to do so badly.

With regard to attitudes to mathematics Cockcroft reports:

> boys more often attribute their successes in mathematics to ability and their failures to lack of effort or bad luck, girls more often attribute their success to hard work or good luck and their failures to lack of ability. If this is the case, it underlines the need to do all that is possible to encourage girls to develop confidence in their mathematical powers.
>
> (1982: 64)

Indeed, this view is supported by the APU (DES 1988: 27–8) who, in commenting on the higher performance of boys in measuring tasks at age 11, say, 'it seems reasonable that some aspects of attitude, perhaps confidence, may be operating – positively in the case of boys and negatively in the case of girls.'

It is also important to mention here that it is possible that written materials, scheme books and the like can affect children's attitudes to mathematics and its importance to them, and their attitudes to themselves as people. For example, the Inner London Education Authority's Learning Resources Branch suggests:

> In mathematics materials sex stereotyping . . . can imply that men and women have different needs for mathematics . . . often the uses women have for mathematics are restricted by sex stereotyping – they are shown, for instance, using mathematics only to help them while cooking and shopping, whereas men are shown using mathematics in a wide range of pursuits. The implication is that girls will have only a limited use for mathematics in adult lfe, whereas for boys it is more important.
>
> (1985: 12)

Northam (1982) looked at a variety of mathematics books and concluded that children were presented as fitting sex stereotypes and 'physically and psychologically incapable of self-initiated action'. She goes on to say that 'the concept of the pupil in infant books is at odds with the definition of the pupil-mathematician' as portrayed in the teacher's notes. In one book she examined, the children are invited to make sets of boys and girls.

> In order to distinguish clearly between the two sets, differences are emphasised. Dress, demeanour and physical behaviour must be sharply contrasted so that the notion of 'set' is clarified. Thus we find no mopheaded, trousered boy/girl figures in the sets. All the girls are in dresses and have elaborate hairstyles; four out of five of them are

standing staring into space. The boys' hair is cropped short and out of seven boys, five are on the move.

(Northam 1982)

This is supported by the ILEA's Learning Resources Branch (1985: 11): sex stereotyping occurs . . . in some [mathematics materials] . . . where girls often occupy passive, domestic or service roles, such as dressing dolls, making tea, and helping the boys by passing them bricks for their models.'

It may be an important part of an evaluation of the appropriateness of materials in mathematics for teachers to review those books, worksheets, work cards, charts and display materials that they use regularly. Part of the review might include the following issues:

— Where children are depicted are there as many girls as boys?
— What are the images of girls like?
— What are the images of boys like?
— Do the girls look as though they are as active as the boys?
— Do the girls and the boys appear to be enjoying what they do?

Special needs

There are national directives in England and Wales relating to educational provisions for children having 'special needs'. In mathematics these state that 'all pupils, including those with s.e.n. (special educational needs), are entitled to participate in the National Curriculum and to derive the benefits of a broad and balanced mathematics education' (NCC 1989: 32). Thus the teacher of infants has the same general aims for all the children in the class. We have always been puzzled by the experts' choice of the words 'special needs', for 'every child has needs and for each individual these are special' (Clemson and Clemson 1990: 117). The children to whom the label 'special needs' is applied seem to us to have *additional* needs. Chazan *et al.* (1980) report on their research among pre-school children, in which, in order to identify such children, the following areas were identified as possible sources of difficulty: vision, hearing, locomotion, muscular control and co-ordination, mental ability, speech and language development, emotional, social and behavioural adjustment and general health. Perhaps inevitably a 'medical model' is often employed when looking at children before they enter school. Some of these categorisations may, however, be of little help to teachers. As Chazan and Laing point out:

we are now thinking much more in terms of what the child can actually do or not do. A clear and comprehensive profile of the child's assets and problem areas can provide a useful starting point for a developmental and educational programme, whether at home or at school.

(1982: 100)

The role of the teacher of infants is not only to devise individual work programmes for children who have been identified as demonstrating difficulties before they begin school, but also to be vigilant for difficulties that other adults, who know each child, may not have spotted. A teacher's expertise in continuous assessment of children's progress is crucial in the identification of children for whom the 'usual' classroom provision of learning opportunities is not enough. Following the recommendations of the Warnock Report (1978) which included the imperative to view parents as having an essential role in children's education, Her Majesty's Inspectorate (DES 1990: 2) reported that schemes similar to the Portage projects have been adopted in many parts of England and Wales: 'The Portage system originated in the United States. It involves professionals and parents working together, usually in the home, to assess the skills of the children concerned, then devising, implementing and evaluating precisely targeted teaching programmes.'

This model of teaching and learning has proved successful for many children. However, while enlisting parental help and participation is undoubtedly efficacious in raising children's attainment in mathematics, we remain unconvinced that the Portage type of teaching programme can lead to real mathematical understanding.

Recognising children's pre-school capabilities

It is generally acknowledged that children already have a prodigious store of knowledge and skills by school age. Donaldson argues that by 'the time they come to school, all normal children can show skill as thinkers and language users to a degree which must compel our respect' (1978: 121). However, evidence from nursery schools suggests that teachers do not take cognisance of the 'skills and interests' children show at home (Tizard and Hughes 1984). We would suggest that this applies to areas that we would see as mathematical and indeed McPherson and Payne agree with us:

> Often the existing and well developed capabilites of young children remain untapped or unrecognised. Even where their understanding is not ignored it is considerably underestimated. This aspect of mismatch and the consequent lack of continuity for the child could make it more difficult for him to learn mathematics.
>
> (1987: 76)

The idea that first teachers may sometimes pay little regard to children's 'past' and 'other' (that is other than classroom) experience has relevance for all teachers. Given the developmental theories (see Chapter 1) on which much infant teaching seems to be based it seems surprising that the notion seems to have taken hold that children's past has little to do with what is appropriate as present learning. Our own anecdotal evidence suggests that perhaps in efforts to control learning and ensure logical progression, teachers often start a learning episode from a point which they have chosen, not one related to the optimum place for the learner in the light of 'past' and 'other' experience. We heard a child complain recently, 'we just had to sit there for about half an hour while Mrs Bee told us all about fractions. She said this is a half. We knew that already.'

After studies on children of nursery age Hughes concludes:

> It now seems that most pre-school children can carry out simple additions and subtractions, often using appropriate counting strategies which may involve the assistance of their fingers. Most pre-school children can invent their own systems of written number notation, usually based on the fundamental principle of one-to-one correspondence, and can recognise and interpret these inventions up to a week after they have made them. Most pre-school children can use magnetic numerals to identify tins according to the number of objects inside, and will subsequently learn to use the magnetic symbols '+' and '–' in representing changes to the contents of the tins. Some pre-school children can even control the movements of a computer-driven Turtle robot by sending it simple mathematical commands . . . within their limits (children) appear to be competent users of number.
>
> (1986: 167–8)

The limits Hughes talks of are that the abilities of children relate to small numbers; the abilities are not evenly apparent in all children and as a rule children from middle-class areas are more competent; and to demonstrate their abilities children need 'problems that arise naturally in a context which the children find interesting, and where the rationale for working out an answer, using a symbol or writing something down is clearly spelt out.' (Hughes 1986: 168).

If we accept that children entering school already have years of mathematics experiences behind them it is then necessary to amass the kinds of experiences these might be in order to harness them for children's future learning. We can also begin with the children's own interests. As Hughes points out:

> An important first step for teachers of young children is to find out as much as they can about their children's mathematical background. Do they like numbers and counting? Do they ever play mathematical games at home – such as dice games or card games? Do they ever play with a calculator or a computer? Are there particular activities they like to do at home, such as cooking or shopping, which involve mathematical skills and where they appear to be knowledgeable?
>
> (1986: 176)

It is important, for example, that teachers recognise that children have ways of tackling mathematics when they start school. We need to be sensitive to their mathematics and their invented symbols before imposing school mathematics. 'Children's early written representations of number . . . are often ingenious and of considerable personal significance . . . and should be the basis of any early work on written symbolism' (Hughes 1986: 177).

Making mathematics inviting

It is difficult to imagine what school is like for those who are just starting. Our own infant experience is long ago, but it may be important for us to take a child's eye view of school mathematics when they begin, if only so that we can understand and help to extend it. For example, are young children quickly persuaded that school mathematics is to be seen as work? Does this work turn out to be work on paper, work you always need a pencil for, sitting down work, on your own work, work you get ticks for, work about numbers? As we know, mathematics is much more than this and it is necessary to make it more than this to every child.

What constitutes school mathematics for children is partly set by how mathematics is portrayed in the school as a whole. It is hard to speculate about the effects on children of all the decisions made about mathematics. In trying here to look at this from a young child's point of view we shall set out some general questions related to the information the children may be getting through all their senses on entry to school.

— Are resources colourful and tempting?
— Are resources where children can reach them?
— Are children allowed to touch resources even when they are not doing mathematics?
— Is there mathematics work on display?
— Are the displays at children's eye level?
— Does display work invite children to 'have a go'?
— How is mathematics discussed between adults and within earshot of the children?
— How does the teacher talk to the children about mathematics?
— Do the children hear the teacher using mathematics (doing dinner numbers for example)?
— How tempting is the range of sensations in the resources on offer (sand, water, soft toys, bendable materials, hard bricks, books with glossy pages, books offering things to touch, count and feel the shape of)?
— How are tastes and smells associated with mathematics? (Do children connect the making and tasting of cakes with mathematics? Or the smell of books, and is that the smell of old or new ones?)

REVIEW

In the light of all that we have discussed, the task of planning the children's first experiences of school mathematics may seem pretty intimidating. We need to know so much about the children. The overwhelming imperative must be to engage children with school mathematics in a way that continues to make sense for them, and in a way that enables mastery of important basic concepts; then outcomes like the following can be avoided. Choat (1980: 47–9) reports on the example of 5 year old Jane who after a short period of schooling had completed pages of additions correctly, including some that were displayed vertically. On enquiry Choat found that Jane had actually laid out bricks and had placed them all together and counted again to find the sum. Choat says:

> A 'back to basics' advocate visiting Jane's class, looking at her book, would be highly delighted with this 5 year old's achievements. The school would be following the correct approach and teaching children some 'mathematics'. But this is far from the truth. . . . It appeared that in her early number development Jane had not acquired: negative relations; mapping by one-to-one correspondence; the symbols to define more than, fewer than and the same as; seriation; ordinal sequence; combining by pictograms; combining by sets; bilateral symmetry; patterns by translational symmetry; patterns for numbers to 5; mapping to 2, 3, 4 and 5; patterns for numbers from 6 to 9; mapping to 6, 7, 8 and 9; using the number line to combine sets; and ordered pairs. Activities related to zero were disregarded also.
>
> (1980: 49)

We may argue with Choat about whether Jane should master *all* of these things before meeting 'sums', but there is little doubt that some important gaps have been left in what Jane should have learned. She had spent perhaps a single term in school. She had got her sums right and knew that was what the teacher (and probably her parents) wanted. Jane was apparently experiencing little difficulty with her mathematics when Choat met her. However, despite the signs of 'learning' having taken place, Jane was not receiving teaching appropriate to really enable her to *understand what she was doing*. Apart from the importance of making school mathematics meaningful to children, this chapter highlights three other important areas for consideration and debate. These are as follows:

— We can no longer regard children's early life as insignificant in terms of its contribution to school learning in mathematics. Pre-school experience in mathematics is legitimate and apposite. It needs tapping.
— Girls and boys are truly equal in the eyes of the teacher and they should therefore be proffered equal opportunities in mathematics. We should note that equal opportunity does not mean different but comparable. In

other words we cannot allow the boys to do investigation 'A' and the girls exercise 'B' instead. It means that boys and girls should be offered *the same* range of experiences during their infant years. Inequality of opportunity needs zapping.

— There needs to be reflection on the image of mathematics given to small children. It should not be seen as a dull, repetitive and passive subject in school. A teacher who asks the children regularly to all 'sit down, be quiet and get on with your maths' or says 'as you have been noisy you can miss PE and do extra maths' is doing a disservice to children, to learning and to the spirit of mathematics. Mathematics features significantly in our everyday lives. It alerts us to pattern, it helps us understand the world, and take control of our lives. The positive power of mathematics needs projecting.

NOTES

1 Stutton Church of England Primary School, Ipswich.
2 There are variations in achievement between children from different ethnic groups. For example, 'West Indian children, on average, are underachieving at school. Asian children, by contrast, show on average, a pattern of achievement which resembles that of White children' (though amongst Asians there are sub-groups that underachieve) (The Swann Report 1985).
3 See, for example, Belotti (1975) and Arcana (1983) for discussions about the rearing of girls and boys (though not based on UK material we would contend they have powerful messages for what we observe is happening in the UK and elsewhere).

Part II

The subject mathematics

GENERAL INTRODUCTION

Much of young children's experience of mathematics involves an active exploration of pattern – a central idea within all mathematical enquiry. Hardy states that 'A mathematician, like a painter or a poet, is a maker of patterns. If his patterns are more permanent than theirs, it is because they are made with *ideas*' (1992: 84). Whether through practical work with number bonds, plane shapes, sequences or three dimensional objects, children are looking for and finding patterns which can be used to develop general statements and theories. This process involves inductive reasoning (see Chapter 3, note 2).

Thus the hallmarks of mathematics which has meaning for small children involves two vital characteristics. First, the children are enabled to use what Bruner (see Chapter 1) called the enactive mode. They are 'up and doing', handling real fruit for counting, building with toy carriages to make a train, following a pathway they have drawn on the playground, and so on. Secondly, they are encouraged to use the particular mathematical experiences they have, to add to these in settings which sometimes they themselves and sometimes their teacher has devised, and thereby to accrue a wealth of personal mathematical ideas from which their own mathematical thinking and reasoning can further develop.

The reasons why we consider mathematics to be such an important part of any curriculum include the following:

— mathematics enables us to detect and replicate and marvel in pattern;
— mathematics employs our thinking power in challenging ways, involving both inductive and deductive reasoning (see Chapter 3, note 2);
— mathematical thinking can allow us to be creative.

Added to this we can look at the application of mathematical learning in 'real life', for example in the development of bar codes, the construction of buildings, and the calculation of interest on investments in building societies or banks. Mathematics allows us to formulate models as well as check designs and measure physical processes and phenomena. Mathematics is a logical activity and lies at the heart of technological and scientific developments. Mathematics also offers a means to explore natural phenomena such as the growth of plants and the characteristics of the atom.

With all of these attributes it is clear that mathematics must hold a central place in human activity and thinking and that it is the right of children to be given access to mathematics as a tool, as an intellectual process and as a means by which to manage their daily lives. It is the case, however, that we seem to be failing to educate most people into a creative and enjoyable engagement with mathematical processes and ideas. This is in part due to the ways in which we present and represent mathematics to children. In order to air some of the areas of debate about the subject mathematics, we have taken three facets and devoted a chapter to each. Chapter 3 is for teachers themselves, and not the children they teach. It is about some of the major themes in mathematical endeavour over many centuries. Chapter 4 looks at the ways in which mathematics has been defined and located within the primary school curriculum. In Chapter 5 the focus is the communication of mathematical knowledge.

Chapter 3

What mathematics is

INTRODUCTION

When working as classroom teachers, we regarded some subjects as straightforward and some as problematic; we knew a good bit about some things and felt our subject knowledge, whether or not it was part of the curriculum we were teaching, made us more confident and assured as teachers. In fact the more we knew besides what we actually taught, the more sense we could make of it and (hopefully) the more sense we could help the children to make of it. There were, of course, some subjects in which we knew less. To some degree this did not matter. We still felt we knew more than we were required to teach. However, we always felt less able to articulate why we were doing what we did in these areas. We never offered advice or explanations to colleagues in these subjects, and we would not have relished the idea of having to present our ideas to parents or governors. Our own experience thus seems to demonstrate that the more insight into a subject we have the better. This supposition alone justifies the content of this chapter; namely a presentation of the origins of some of the mathematical ideas we use today. There is, however, an even more powerful argument for writing something about the 'nature of mathematics'. It is that mathematics differs from all the other subjects that young children learn.

The difference that is important in the current discussion is that young children and their teachers can reach and work in mathematics near the frontiers of what is known. We cannot imagine taking, say, top infants through all that is known about the manners of the Victorians, or the physical geography of the nearest piece of coastline, or the chemistry of bread making even if we wanted to. It is, however, possible for top infants to 'play' with, say, patterns of numbers in ways that advanced mathematicians do; that is if we want them to. But we cannot let them do that, nor can we join in, if our subject knowledge is poor. Despite the closeness of the frontiers of mathematics we cannot review the whole of mathematics in one chapter of a book. What we can try to do is make a broad sweep and explain where some important mathematical ideas are derived from and why mathematics may have developed in the way it has.

In this chapter we take four overarching themes which have exercised and continue to occupy the minds of mathematicians. We will use these to illustrate both the history of mathematical ideas and their continuing evidence in today's classrooms. We see this chapter as suitable for teachers themselves, rather than to be 'handed on' to the children they teach, for we feel that some understanding of where ideas have come from helps to enhance the confidence necessary to the competent communication of ideas in class. The themes we take are counting and ordering, reasoning and proof, the importance of zero and the impact of science and technology.

COUNTING AND ORDERING

It is likely that mathematics has its origins in the applications necessary for the construction of circles and the counting of possessions. Ancient peoples constructed pyramids and stone circles, and developed the use of the tally stick. Arithmetic is thought to have its roots in the need to tally belongings; a process which involves the idea of one to one correspondence. The latter is a common activity in primary classrooms. Early counting systems made use of the simple tally stick on which one notch equated to one real object. The idea of grouping a set of notches developed and thereby the foundations of multiplication were constructed. We still use tallying systems, usually having 'five' as the grouping. Tallying does not require either stick or pencil and paper, for in using their fingers to count on children are using probably the oldest tallying approach of all. Finger counting has a long history and systems of counting using the fingers, and in some cases other body parts, were developed in many parts of the world.[1]

In tallying we are using *cardinal* numbers. Numbers are also used to indicate the order of events or objects, that is as *ordinal* descriptors. This dual use of numbers is ancient in origin but is still important nowadays. We help children to grasp the difference between, for example, 'two' and 'second' and to do so where the symbol '2' might be used in both cardinal and ordinal settings.

Associated with counting was the need to develop methods of recording. Symbols beyond the 'notch' were invented, including some which precede the zero to nine of our current system. Best known to us in schools are Roman numerals. These numerals are still used in particular contexts, including clock faces, sundials, television and film copyright dates, and, in their lower case form, as numbers for paragraphs in some documents.

From the early developments from the need to know 'how many?' there grew an increasingly more ordered and organised assembly of mathematical ideas. This order was laid down many thousands of years ago and we continue to base much of our argument and procedural approaches in mathematics on those early evangelists of reasoning and logic. Developments that are central to the work we do in schools are the arrival of the symbol zero, the consequent development of place value and the manipulation of numbers within a place value system. For these we look back in history at the work of Hindu mathematicians. However, before they were at work, there were important developments in other mathematical directions during classical Greek times.

REASONING AND PROOF

Whilst Palaeolithic and Neolithic peoples clearly had a grasp of a number of rudimentary mathematical ideas and processes it is from the Greek civilisation of the period of about 600 to 300 BC that we glean many outstanding contributions to mathematics. These were made by people such as Pythagoras, Euclid, Eratosthenes and Archimedes, whose names are still famous. As Kline states, 'from the point of view of the twentieth century, mathematics and, it may well be added, modern civilization began with the Greeks of the classical period' (1972: 42).

The early Greek mathematicians based their work on that of the Babylonians and the Egyptians (Kline 1972, Hollingdale 1991). But they advanced the study of mathematics in two significant ways. They developed a deductive approach.[2] Allied to this they established mathematics as an abstract subject, thereby moving it from a dependence, say, on the numbers of objects to a subject in which there was the possibility of models and ideals. These two developments underpin school mathematics. The Greek mathematicians also strove to explain mathematics through the use of *geometry*.[3] Many of us will be familiar with the notion of *theorems* in which logically argued proofs are used to establish things like the shortest distance between two points and the sum of the angles of a triangle.

The triangle

The triangle became one of the most fundamentally important shapes in mathematics even though it is essentially an abstract concept and does not exist commonly in the natural world. The ancient Egyptians used a plumb bob and shadow stick to measure the length of the shadow cast by the sun – at the summer solstice the shadow cast at noon is the shortest of the whole year. But in order to carry out this work there had to be an appreciation of imaginary lines which created a triangle. This sort of problem led to the use of right-angled triangles in the measurement of heights, distances and building. A way of determining the height of a

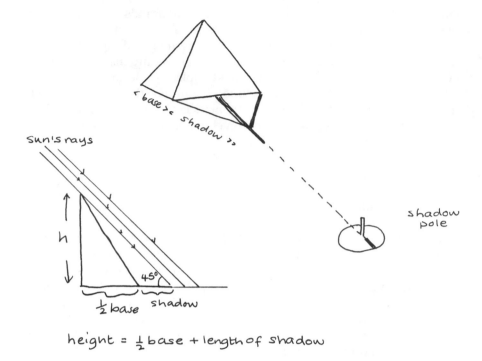

height = ½ base + length of shadow

Figure 3.1 A way of measuring the height of the Great Pyramid
Source: Adapted from Hogben 1936

pyramid which would be difficult to determine by other means is shown in
Figure 3.1. When the shadow cast by the stick touches the edge of the circle
which has a radius the same length as the stick, the height of the pyramid
can be determined by measuring its shadow and adding half the length of
the pyramid's base.

Some right-angled triangles became very important in building work.
According to some historians the Egyptians made use of the three-four-
five right-angled triangle to determine square corners. We can imagine
that a rope was tied with knots at equal distances. If it was then fixed so
that the hypotenuse of the triangle was five knots and the other two sides
were three knots and four knots respectively a right-angle is produced.
This relates to the well-known theorem of Pythagoras which is commonly
stated as the square on the hypotenuse of a right-angled triangle being
equal to the sum of the squares on the other two sides. This is more clearly
shown in a diagram (see Figure 3.2). Though this figure does not in itself
provide a proof of the theorem as required by the Greeks, it does help to
understand what the proposition is.

Once the right-angled triangle had been discovered and the whole

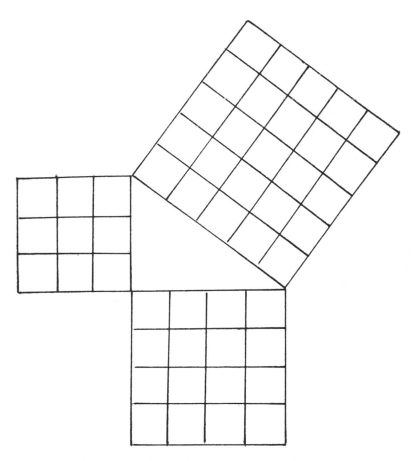

Figure 3.2 A right-angled triangle with the squares drawn in on the sides

business of the exploration of the characteristics and features of triangles had been embarked upon (and that of other shapes such as the circle) the foundations had been laid for development of a wide range of applications. These include building and surveying, navigation, accurate time-keeping, and the study of motion. In teaching young children about the triangle and the other two dimensional shapes, it is important, therefore, to appreciate that it is not the shape itself that is the subject of study but rather how that concept of a shape has application to our study of the built environment, the natural world and the mysteries of the universe. If children come to believe that a triangle is merely a shape which has three corners and is commonly drawn with its base horizontal then we have failed to grip the power and possibility of the exploration and use of such a shape.

We were working with a group of infants recently, where the children were sorting some '2-D' shapes. Morris was asked to find a set of triangles.

TEACHER: Can you lay them out so that we can see? Everyone have a look at those and see if you agree with Morris.

RICKIE: That one isn't a triangle (picking up a very acute angled triangle) because it's got one edge that's straight.

TEACHER: (picking up a 'fatter' right-angled triangle) What about that one then?

RICKIE: I'm not sure about that one.

TEACHER: Why are you not sure?

RICKIE: (turning the triangle round) When it's like this it's a triangle . . . that's a triangle . . . that's a triangle . . . but that isn't. (He rejects the right-angled triangle when it is placed with one side vertical.)

Rickie has yet to grasp something about the usefulness and ubiquitousness of the idea of a triangle, not only for the sake of his geometry but also for his understanding of its usefulness to him in getting to know about the world around him.

One way of making children excited about the importance of shapes is to embrace opportunities offered by some aspects of mathematics and art. From early times to the present people have been drawn to patterns of shapes that are symmetrical. Regular two-dimensional and three-dimensional shapes offer opportunities for the exploration of ideas like symmetry, reflection and rotation. There are pre-school toys which require a recognition of the fact that some three-dimensional shapes will go through holes that others will not, and that some of the shapes can be rotated and will still, in a number of positions, fit the hole. Children get the chance to experiment with ideas to do with symmetry and sequence when decorating books or making borders around displays. These ideas need to be locked into a study of shape and space as well as algebra.

ZERO AND PLACE VALUE

It was Hindu mathematicians who really laid the foundations of current arithmetic and algebra, for it was they who developed the place value system that we use. Until the arrival of a rigorous and consistent method for symbolising quantities with the use of only a few symbols, the progress of mathematics had been held back by the need for cumbersome recording in which there were many discrete symbols. For example, doing computation using Egyptian hieroglyphics is a lengthy business (see Figure 3.3).

In order to secure the system that we now accept the Hindu mathematicians had to invent 'zero'. But even as late as the fifteenth century it was asked, 'How . . . could a symbol which means 'nothing', when placed after another numeral, enhance its value tenfold?' (Hollingdale 1991: 96). We still face the problem of explaining this when teaching children place

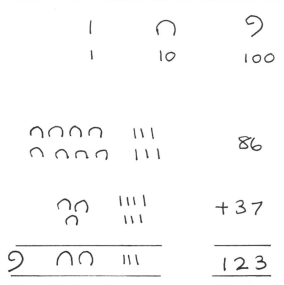

Figure 3.3 Example computation using Egyptian hieroglyphics

value. Hindu mathematicians also 'invented' negative numbers which they developed in relation to debts. The appearance of place value, the symbol zero and the availability of negative numbers allowed the development of the number line which we regularly put to good use in primary classrooms.

The use of zero allowed a very small number of symbols to represent all numbers to be written and manipulated. The corollary of this is the possibility of developing mathematical ideas limited only by the vision of human beings. The system which we use is elegant and simple and offers infinite variation with relatively few symbols to remember. However, this apparent simplicity conceals the fact that in writing, for example, 7 + 3 = 10 we offer children a condensed version of what is actually a very complex and full set of ideas and principles. Young children need to come to understand computation through a variety of experiences. For example, they need to be permitted to use real objects in number work. They need to tackle and master the ideas which we term 'one to one correspondence'. They also need to grasp the fundamental and profound meaning of zero. We have to help children understand the principles of place value so that they can manipulate symbols in what are, to them, novel ways. Of course all these kinds of experience can be offered in any order, according to each child's own patterns of learning. It is through amassing a wealth of experiences and then through the encouragement to use inductive reasoning in order to make links between these that children build their mathematical concepts. Hughes (1986: 121) reports on earlier work done by Ginsburg in the USA. He gives an illustration of the problems that can

Figure 3.4 A problem in setting down a computation

arise if a child has not understood the processes before being asked to respond to a computation set out as a standard algorithm (see Figure 3.4).

Whilst Ginsburg indicates that the child who produced this had substantial problems with numbers it does serve to indicate what can happen if the location of digits in space is not understood.

Having mastered the concepts and rules which govern our place value system children are fully equipped to handle much of the mathematics of number. Children are often particularly drawn to 'big numbers'. Many of us can remember talking of billions and trillions when we were little and trying to write or say the 'world's biggest number'. Faced with a graphics calculator, Amy, aged 7, filled the screen with digits and then gave the calculator the hardest sum she could contrive – again filling the screen with number-addition, sign-number and so on. Her shock, and then delight, at the fact that the calculator came up with the answer 'instantly' was enchanting. We all remember those moments when children start grappling with the idea of infinity – they challenge each other, and grown-ups, to produce the biggest number they can and are confounded when an adult can always top their largest number by one. Such incidents place quite young children only one step away from 'forever'. To understand the meaning of '10' is a major step. To understand and be able to write '1 000 000' and name it 'one million' is a smaller step and it is then only a very small conceptual step indeed to be able to portray a million as 10^6.

Number bonds, patterns and early algebraic ideas

Islamic mathematicians made major contributions to the development of mathematics in Europe. They not only undertook original work but kept Greek science alive (Fauvel and Gray 1987). Through the breadth of their mathematics they brought together arithmetic, algebra and geometry, offering the possibility of unified views based upon pattern. It is no accident that when children begin school algebra we start by looking at and making patterns. Of all the great Islamic mathematicians the one most commonly known today, rather for his poetry than his mathematics, is Omar Khayyám (circa 1050–1123). He was astronomer[4] to the Caliph at Merv. His mathematical work was much concerned with geometry in which he made extensive use of algebra. He is reported as writing that:

Whoever thinks algebra is a trick in obtaining unknowns has thought it in vain. No attention should be paid to the fact that algebra and geometry are different in appearance. Algebra are geometric facts which are proved.

(Hollingdale 1991: 101)

If we separate arithmetic, algebra and geometry, the proper relationships and connections between these subjects may not be clear to children. Teachers in primary schools in England and Wales will be particularly aware of this problem in relation to the National Curriculum. It is essential that we do not ignore the connections between number and shape and space, for even the way we describe some number patterns and sequences makes use of spatial concepts.

For example, a sequence of triangles can be made with counters, starting with one counter (see Figure 3.5).

Figure 3.5 Triangular numbers set out in counters

The numbers of counters are 1, 3, 6, 10, 15 and so on. These are known as the *triangular numbers*. The relationship between successive triangular numbers is easily discernible. As the sequence develops each number increases by the number of counters needed to enlarge the triangle by one row. So:

$1 + 2 = 3$
$3 + 3 = 6$
$6 + 4 = 10$
$10 + 5 = 15$

and so on.

Triangular numbers are related to another set of numbers – the *square numbers*. Square numbers are made by adding together consecutive triangular numbers.

$1 + 3 = 4$
$3 + 6 = 9$
$6 + 10 = 16$

and so on.

This relationship can be shown using counters, if we rearrange them into right-angled triangles (see Figure 3.6). This underlines the point that was made in Chapter 1 about the importance of enactive modes of

Triangular numbers 60

and   10 ●

added together make

the square number 16

Figure 3.6 Counters arranged as right-angled triangles

learning. We believe that in order truly to understand the use of the shape names 'triangle' and 'square' in describing numbers it is essential that we all make use of real objects. It is possible to figure the triangle and square numbers using pencil and paper and some rules, and this is commonly the way children are required to work, but it may actually be better for children to work with counters and the perception of shapes in order to really comprehend what is happening in many number sequences. It is, therefore important that young children set out, print, model and stick coloured shapes in patterns as a basis for the understanding of the generalisations that algebra allows us to make. If we let children learn the beginnings of algebra in this way they should be better equipped to tackle questions of the 3 + □ = 5 type.

Islamic ideas helped lay the foundations of some vital ideas in both number and algebra, in particular about the ways that numbers can and cannot be manipulated. In coming to understand that $3 + 2 = 2 + 3$, and that $4 \times 5 = 5 \times 4$, children are establishing their understanding of the *commutative* law. An operation is commutative if it does not matter in which order the numbers are worked on. They can then understand statements such as

$a + b = b + a$

This is crucial to their number and algebra work as is an understanding of the *associative* law. An operation involving three numbers is associative if it does not matter where the brackets are placed. For example:

$2 + (3 + 4) = (2 + 3) + 4$

can be set out as

$(2 + 3) + 4 = 2 + (3 + 4)$

We have learned the convention that operations enclosed by brackets are always carried out first, but wherever we put the brackets there is actually no difference in the solution to this 'sum'. However, this is not always the case. For example:

$2 \times (3 + 4)$ is not the same as $(2 \times 3) + 4$

There remains one other law that we need to understand, the *distributive* law. This is where we can do an operation on a combination of numbers and the result will be the same as if we had performed the operation on each in turn. This example shows that 'multiplication is distributive over addition':

$2 \times (3 + 4) = (2 \times 3) + (2 \times 4)$

Which, using symbols, would be written as:

$a (b + c) = ab + ac$

These three laws, together with the rules for addition and multiplication (subtraction and division being merely the inverse of these) are all the 'rules' that we need to carry out all basic number operations. Just five rules, that is all! The associative law should be within the ambit of every infant child.

MATHEMATICS, SCIENCE AND TECHNOLOGY

It is this theme that may be seen as currently contentious in schools. The development of new technologies is set to impinge on what mathematics is, or may become, for teachers and children. First, however, we will give examples of how scientific and technological developments in history have had an impact on mathematics. Kline (1972: 115) states that 'From the years 500 to 1400 there was no mathematician of note in the whole Christian world'. It needed the Renaissance for there to be a re-emergence of many of the ideas of the Greeks and for the works of the Islamic mathematicians to be incorporated into new thinking. European mathematics, such as it was, had been concerned with a study of the scriptures and the development of astrology. The concern was with the spiritual not the temporal. However, with the development of a number of apparently unconnected inventions, the prevailing doctrine came in for serious questioning. Gunpowder provided the possibility of controlled explosions. This invention – harnessed to the development of robust and fairly reliable artillery – led to a study of ways of making targeting more accurate. At the same time exploration, driven by commerce and trade, led to a need for accurate timekeeping. Navigation relied also on an understanding of the position of the sun, stars and planets. Mathematics and science once again became important and worthy areas of study. Inevitably there were clashes between the old order and the new thinkers and the fate of Galileo in the hands of the Inquisition was typical of this clash. In this combative atmosphere a number of great mathematicians and scientists emerged. They included Descartes, Fermat and Pascal and then, probably the greatest of them all, Newton.

Early in the Renaissance period there was a 'back to nature' approach which was concerned with our need to recognise that knowledge was to be found in the natural world rather than through dogma (Kline: 1972). Descartes, however, moved the debate to the idea that human beings could take command over nature through reason. He saw humans as the only creatures having souls, and combining 'both matter and intellect' (Thomas 1983); hence Descartes' assertion 'I think therefore I am'. These ideas, that it is possible to be rational, to reason and to gain mastery of the workings of the natural world from the heavens to the smallest particle of the Earth, contribute to a formal recognition of what we know as 'scientific method'. The age of *certainty* was born. And it is the belief of many that mathematics offers the most certainty of all – it is the subject of 'right answers'. For the last 300 years and more, scientists, and mathematicians, have been engaged in the pursuit of universal theories and general equations.

Along with the growth of an industrial society in the UK in the nineteenth century came an economy based upon the exploitation of raw materials, the use of sophisticated machinery, and the application of science and technology. The move from an agricultural society to the industrial needed two major planks for support: the idea that rational human behaviour achieved 'progress' and that all technological problems could be solved. This certainty, and the confidence with which it must be associated, allowed the Victorians to exploit natural resources, to develop schooling in order to fit different segments of the population for particular kinds of employment, and to adopt self adulatory attitudes to what was done in the name of 'progress'. It was also, however, a time when some started to question quite fundamental assumptions. The work of Darwin, for example, was widely debated. Less public notice was given to the growth of that field of mathematics which we know as *statistics*. This burgeoning of facts and figures has important effects on views of educational achievement and the content of the mathematics curriculum in school today.

Statistics

Whilst probabilities had been calculated for many centuries these were mainly in the fields of natural growth; that is people and plants, and in gambling. In the nineteenth century statistics started to be used to measure economic growth and intellectual achievements. Current views of children and their achievements are governed by statistical methods which have their roots in physical phenomena, and the probability of winning a race, a fight or a game or of drawing the winning card from the pack.

As teachers of infants, it is important that we help children come to understand the ideas embedded within the field of probability and chance.

We have heard teachers say that children do not think about statistical ideas much. We cannot agree, for we believe everyone (including young children) makes judgements and predictions about things like 'likelihood', 'average' and 'fairness' in everyday life. Children tell us who is shortest or tallest and who is 'normal-sized' in their class. They know how many times in a week they are likely to be able to have hot dogs for school dinner, and how many books will be out of the class library. They try to predict whether it will be wet play, and whether a game or a swop is fair. Whilst this is not rigorous it does show where we can begin to enlarge their understanding of the data that we are presented with every day.

Standard measures

The development of increasingly sophisticated measuring devices has gone hand in hand with the development of 'high technology'. The Romans, who offered little to the advancement of mathematical ideas, did refine many applied systems including the development of a regulated measuring system. For example, their measurement of length was organised and logically progressive in a way which we recognise today:

1 digitus	1.85 cm
4 digiti = 1 palmus	7.4 cm
4 palmi = 1 pes	29.6 cm
5 pes = 1 passus	1.48 m
125 passus = 1 stadium	185 m
8 stadia = 1 milliar	1480 m

Hands and feet featured prominently as starting points for their measuring system. We still use a 'hand' in the measurement of horses, and cannot entirely relinquish the use of the foot! It is still the case that the distance from nose to fingertips is used for measuring material on many a market stall (this gives a rough approximation of a yard). And not only the human body was used as a portable measure – barleycorns were used to 'standardise' the inch. But as soon as trade moved out of the parish some more accurate and universal standardisation was necessary. The creation of standard yards and metres with appropriate sub-divisions was the logical step and replicas of these measures were then manufactured and made widely available. There is much mathematics, history and economics to be generated from a consideration of the school ruler! The advent of electricity and then the use of electronics has led to even more accuracy in measurement of length, and mass and time.

When we ask young children to measure using spans and paces, to use water drops or sundials in work on time, and to compare volumes and masses in non-standard ways, we are taking them through methods we think people have used in the past. We can do so, not only to remind them of the history of measures, but so that they can be convinced of the need for standardisation of measurement. The advent of screw gauges, clinometers, measuring cylinders, fine balances and different sorts of rulers in the infant classroom reflects the concern that we all have with accurate measurement. Children can come to appreciate that measuring, no matter with what sophisticated means, is still liable to approximation – degrees of accuracy are a necessary part of our vocabulary when we measure.

Calculators and computers

In the last decade the power of calculators and computers has been put into the hands of children and their teachers. Aids to computation have, of course been with us for thousands of years. Hogben (1936: 45) suggests that the first step beyond the simple tally stick was the use of pebbles or shells which had a series of grooves in a flat surface. From there was made the step to beads on upright sticks and then in the closed frame of the abacus that we recognise today.

> It follows the megalithic culture routes around the world. The Mexicans and Peruvians were using the abacus when the Spaniards got to America. The Chinese and the Egyptians already possessed the abacus several millennia before the Christian era. The Romans took it from the Etruscans.

> (Hogben 1936: 45)

It is still to be found in infant classrooms today. As an aid to transactions and trade the abacus has been the single most important tool cheaply available to all of us. It has now been superseded, in many parts of the world, by the cheap, solar powered electronic calculator. The calculator allows us to handle other than the natural numbers.[5]

The use of calculators and computers in our classrooms should have a profound effect upon the way we view what is appropriate as school mathematics. Calculators and computers allow us to investigate problems which would have been beyond our reach because of the sheer slog of equivalent pencil and paper methods. Some people express a concern that the use of calculators somehow stops children from acquiring necessary mental methods. Experience indicates that where children are given full and open access to calculators they actually develop robust mental methods and good estimation skills.[6] Papert states:

> Faced with the heritage of school, math education can take two approaches. The traditional approach accepts school math as a given entity and struggles to find ways to teach it. Some educators use computers for this purpose. Thus, paradoxically, the most common use

of the computer in education has become force-feeding indigestible material left over from the pre-computer epoch.

(1980: 5)

Whilst Papert is expressing views about educators in the USA there is no doubt in our minds that the real possibilities for school mathematics in the UK which calculators and computers offer has yet to be realised.

REVIEW

The emphasis, in this chapter, has been to give teachers insight into how some aspects of mathematics have developed historically. To show just how relevant predominant themes in the history of mathematics are in classrooms now, here are some typical examples of the kinds of things being said by teachers in infant classrooms:

'Count how many'
'Which is third?'
'Show me how you got that'
'Where can you see right angles in the room?'
'How do we write one hundred and six'?
'If four add five make nine, what do five add four make?'
'What is twenty times ten?'
'Tosh and Sumi are playing that game. What are Sumi's chances of winning?'
'How will you measure across the hall?'

We have shown how all of these comments and questions have their origins in the mathematical themes worked on in a variety of cultures across the world over many centuries.

There is currently a growth of uncertainty in mathematics. Where mathematicians and scientists were so certain of there being universal truths, we now seem to be in a period in which the certainty of mathematics is being called into question (e.g. Stewart 1990). The principles behind scientific views of the universe are being questioned. Though we are not expected to get children to grapple with these issues we do have to prepare them to understand the debate and to realise that mathematics is not fixed and immutable but that it has breadth, beauty and significance. The advent of the computer has meant that the speed at which operations can be carried out is now so much faster than was available to the great mathematicians of the past. Infant teachers will be able to take advantage of the number and graphics software becoming available for children to use. We can harness new technologies in getting children to expand their vision of what is possible in mathematics. And to calculators and computers we can begin to add interactive video and CD roms.

NOTES

1   For example, the Venerable Bede writing in the eighth century gave details of such a system (Flegg 1984).

2   *Deductive* reasoning means to start from an agreed general point and develop, step by step, a series of propositions which lead to an accepted particular conclusion. This contrasts with *inductive* reasoning where we start from the particular and develop general statements. Polya (1957: 117) suggests that mathematics in the making is inductive whilst in rigorous presentation it is deductive.

3   This, literally, means earth measuring.

4   For many hundreds of years in India, China, Arabia and then Europe mathematics was associated with astronomy. Mathematics has many of its roots in studies and explanations of planetary motion and the location of the Earth in the heavens.

5   The natural numbers are the counting numbers. But these are not all the numbers known and used by us. Fractions, decimals, the use of pi and the square root of 2 are examples of these other numbers. For more on numbers see, for example, Buxton (1984).

6   See, for example, The Calculator-Aware Number Curriculum video developed through the Primary Initiatives in Primary Education (PRIME) project, published by Simon & Schuster for the National Curriculum Council (1991).

Chapter 4

The mathematics curriculum

INTRODUCTION

For teachers in classrooms it may seem that reflection on the content of a mathematics curriculum is beyond their brief. They may feel they are there to apportion, to manage and to sustain a curriculum but not to go beyond that. The problem, however, is that the school curriculum in mathematics, as in other subjects, is not 'neutral'. Carried through it are a set of values, principles about what is important, what is 'proper', what is 'right'. The issues raised in this chapter are intended to show that when we present children with a curriculum, its content and what it is like in action are based on principles which have to do with views of society. Though there may be a common set of mathematical areas that usually appear in mathematics curricula – for example, computational skills and measures – it is the principles adopted by curriculum designers that affect how curricula turn out. The ways we describe and define the curriculum can also affect its outcomes. We can look at the 'ends', the goals, what the children must achieve, or we can focus on the 'means', what happens in the educative process, the 'flow', the experience of learning. We can limit curriculum discussion to what may be statutorily required, or we can include more than that.

Aside from raising the theoretical stances taken in the study of curricula we felt it important to make our discussion relevant to teachers such as those in England and Wales, who are bound by a National Curriculum that is content driven. The history of curricula can certainly remind us of strengths and weaknesses and alert us to shortcomings in school mathematics now. However, we are acutely aware that if we abandon content models in favour of those espousing process as their parameters, we are in danger of rendering this part of the book hopelessly impractical for teachers in their work at present. We could, for example, make a powerful case for aesthetic experiences as being one of the main strands in the education of young children, and that studies involving anything the children wanted to do in this area should form the basis of teachers' thinking; and further, that young children would acquire mathematical concepts by doing so. However, it would take another book to develop that idea, and for some teachers it would go unread, for it would be too far from the classroom situation they face. Indeed, if we look very closely at what is currently being presented as process-linked mathematical experience for young children, it is actually not eschewing content.[1] We do not wish teachers to feel discouraged from employing process considerations as the central ideas in formulating their school and classroom plans. We are saying that there needs to be a consideration of content, whatever stance one takes ideologically.

With some ideas about issues in curriculum discussion at their finger-tips, we feel teachers can be more considered in their curriculum presentation, however they choose this to be. To explore the major themes of our discussion we shall focus in turn on the following:

- Ideologies
- Curriculum study
- Historical roots
- The contents of a mathematics curriculum for young children.

In order to illustrate how these dimensions impinge on any set of formal curriculum statements we also offer a critique of a current curriculum, the National Curriculum for England and Wales.

IDEOLOGIES

We have argued in the first section of this book that teachers, when tackling school mathematics, need to take account of their views of children and children as learners, the nature of mathematics and their own role and function. These are just as essential for compilers of mathematics curricula to consider. There are a number of different ideological stand-points where quite different views are taken, resulting in a set of distinct curriculum models. In order to critically examine these we shall adopt the analytical framework proposed by Ernest (1991). He suggests that there are three main ideological groups: utilitarians, purists and public educators.[2] He does sub-divide these categories, but for our purposes we can select from his detailed analysis a few points which illustrate the important differences in perspective of these groups in relation to the three key considerations above.

A utilitarian view

The child is seen as an 'empty vessel', self-centred and potentially naughty, and therefore in need of control and discipline. Children need to be made to work hard to acquire the techniques and skills of mathematics.

Assessment of the child's achievement is by external testing; cheating should be avoided. The child's ability is seen as inherited and generally fixed. Mathematics is seen as having universal truths and rules. The selection of mathematics content is linked to 'usefulness'. In acquiring mathematical knowledge children are prepared for useful roles in society where mathematics serves technological development. Society is seen as being hierarchical, and education meritocratic – those that succeed in education merit important jobs in society. The mathematics curriculum is often viewed, in common with other subjects, as containing a core which can be acquired by most children but which has elements which are only achievable by a relatively few, able, children. Schools should therefore be selective or there should be setting or banding by ability. The role of the teacher is to secure knowledge of the basics for the great majority of the children whilst ensuring that those with ability can proceed at a suitable rate and at the appropriate level.

A purist view

There are two traditions involved: humanist, and progressive. Both are liberal traditions but there are differences between them – they are similar in that they are both concerned with purity, 'the purity of subject matter or with pure creativity and personal development' (Ernest 1991: 137). The humanists see children as being civilised by learning about the valued elements of our culture. Children are seen as inheriting a 'cast of mind' which affects their ability to progress in relation to mathematics. Children need to be inducted into a curriculum which is constructed as a selection from our culture. The selection represents traditional values, topics of prevailing truth and worth, and a body of pure knowledge. The curriculum is laid out in relation to knowledge structures and mathematics is seen as being neutral – the child and teacher respond to mathematics. Teachers are seen as having a responsibility to explain and motivate the children and to pass on the culture and structure of the subject to them. We can see the influence of this ideology in the way in which particular individuals are 'educated'. Interestingly, though, such an educated person is seen nowadays (albeit superficially perhaps) as one who is familiar with the forms, structure and content of English literature, history and music rather than mathematics. Aspects of the old humanist tradition can still be detected in aspects of the National Curriculum (England and Wales) in the way in which certain texts are given particular status.

Progressive educators are concerned with process rather than product and place primacy on the child as a unique individual. This is a person-centred ideology which is characterised by an emphasis on human values such as warmth, empathy and non-threatening relationships. The child is seen as essentially 'innocent' and, given a supportive environment, able to flourish and grow. Whilst there is a recognition that children's abilities differ, all are seen as worthy and capable of achieving their own potential. A progressive, child-centred curriculum sees content, including mathematics, as personal and emphasises mathematics as a creative activity through which children can realise themselves. In developing mathematical ideas the child should explore and play, with activity being central. Teachers need to provide a stimulating and varied environment and support the child in personal explorations. Failure should be prevented and teacher-led assessments, which include the child's perspectives, is the approach to be adopted.

Much has been claimed, and asserted, about progressive education. Indeed, in recent times it has been vilified as being the cause of all the important failings of our education system. However, there is no real evidence that genuinely progressive approaches have really been fully implemented in schools. Rather it would seem that only some of the facets have taken hold; for example, most teachers of young children are concerned to provide a rich environment. In mathematics education there is even less evidence of 'progressivism' than in other subjects, certainly as applied to teaching method. The use of practical apparatus is, in many schools, the only sign that such ideas have impinged on mathematics at all. Mathematics is commonly taught in a hierarchical way, often using given schemes or syllabuses. It has been suggested that mathematics is a subject in which many teachers of young children are unsure or lack confidence in their own abilities and insights. Because this is so, mathematics will be taught separately and teachers are more likely to follow external prescriptions, that is to 'do as they are told' (Blenkin and Kelly 1987). Whatever the explanation, and this one does seem reasonable, it is our observation that the links that are forged between many other areas of the curriculum commonly exclude mathematics.

A public educator view

The concern here is with democracy and democratic processes. The public educator focuses on society in terms of justice, citizenship and social awareness. The child is seen as being fundamentally affected by the environment, social, physical and political. The aim of education must be to make the child question, able to make and take decisions, and to understand the processes and possibilities of negotiation. The ability of the child is not fixed but rather a product of the prevailing culture and cultural view. In order to assess a child's achievements and progress a variety of modes should be employed and use made of issues which are socially relevant and 'real'. This view of resources underpins the approach teachers should take and use should be made of questioning, discussion and contrasting views. A number of simulations and role-playing exercises that have appeared in recent years reflects this sort of approach and current concern. For example, environmental issues are often introduced in school nowadays. These contain elements of mathematics in the service of socially aware discussion with young children. Public educators view mathematics as being about social constructivism, by which is meant 'tentative, growing by human creation and decision-making, and connected with other realms of knowledge, culture and social life' (Ernest 1991: 207). Mathematics should not be externally imposed but rather appropriated by children and their teachers.

Ideology and curriculum presentation

We can clearly see the influence of utilitarian ideology in the way the National Curriculum of England and Wales has been conceived, in terms of both its structure and assessment arrangements. If we are implementing a curriculum devised by agencies employed by central government, head teachers or local authorities we need to take account of underlying views held by curriculum compilers. This insight gives us the power to offer the curriculum as intended, or to try to offset its worst shortcomings. If we devise the curriculum we teach, we can probably identify with one of the broad ideological groups named above. We can then reflect on how our perceptions about children, mathematics and ourselves as teachers are carried through that curriculum. As teachers we are responsible for the curriculum, whatever its form. Either we are the compilers or, if the curriculum is written by others in authority, we share culpability with all other adults in giving over that responsibility to others. We can fuel discussion about what should be in school curricula by examining the ways they are described.

CURRICULUM STUDY

There has recently been a growing appreciation that what is written down as the curriculum in a school may not be the curriculum as experienced by the child. If we follow the suggestions of Pollard and Tann (1987) about the use of the word curriculum, the former is the 'official' curriculum and the latter 'the curriculum as experienced'. They list two other ways in which the term curriculum can be used. If we apply them to mathematics, they are the hidden mathematics curriculum and the observed mathematics curriculum. The official curriculum, sometimes called 'formal', is 'an explicitly stated programme of learning intended for children' (Pollard and Tann 1987: 77). Curriculum as experienced is that which 'educates' (1987: 78). It is what the child actually gains and takes away from the classroom. The hidden curriculum is regarded as what children learn as a result of encountering the official curriculum but which was not explicitly part of that curriculum. The observed curriculum, that is, what is seen to occur, may be different from the official curriculum and can be gleaned through self-evaluation and research. It might be that opportunities to discuss this area will grow with the advent of appraisal in which teachers negotiate an observation of their teaching. There have been many attempts at organised observation, for example Galton *et al.* (1980). Through studies of the curriculum, both in practice and theory, models have been constructed. If we look at the ways the curriculum has been talked about above, it can be seen that models have to address the content of the curriculum and the processes of carrying it through.

One model is of particular interest to us as teachers of mathematics. It is the 'objectives model'. It was promoted out of a concern for the fact that the outcomes of previous curricula were so difficult to evaluate. The 'father' of the objectives approach, in modern times, is seen by many as Ralph Tyler. Whilst Tyler was not the first nor only theorist in this area he was extremely influential. Lawton (1981: 115)) refers to Tyler's book *Basic Principles of Curriculum and Instruction* written in 1949, as 'one of the foundation books in curriculum theory'. According to Davies (1976) Tyler looked at the ways objectives were written and concluded that to be clear they had to set out two things. These were: '1. *Behaviour* "the kind of behaviour to be developed in the student", and 2. *Content* "the content or area of life in which the behaviour is to operate"' (Davies 1976: 114). Tyler argued that in the act of teaching, the crucial items to address had to do with educational purpose, experiences to reach purpose, the ways of arranging these experiences and ways of knowing when the purpose has come about. These can be listed as:

1 aims and objectives;
2 content;
3 organisation;
4 evaluation.

(Lawton 1981: 115)

The use of behavioural objectives caused great dissent among a number of educationalists here and in the USA. Stenhouse (1975) offered a vigorous attack on the use of such devices. Rowntree provides a critique of objectives approaches:

> They are too difficult to formulate. . . . They put too much stress on trivial and easily measured behaviours. It is too dangerous to focus on behaviour anyway. Not all desirable results can be specified in advance. It is undemocratic to pre-specify. Objectives are too difficult for the teacher to work with.

(1982: 54)

However, he goes on to say that those who criticise objectives have not located difficulties in objectives themselves, but in the way they are set out and used. To Rowntree, objectives give us 'the most powerful approach to curriculum development that has yet become available to us' (1982: 58).

In contrast to objectives models where the minutiae of outcomes of learning are pre-set, Stenhouse, for example, sees the nub of education, namely 'induction into knowledge' (1975: 81) as '*successful to the extent that it makes the behavioural outcomes of the students unpredictable*' (1975: 82). He therefore proposes that a process model is appropriate for education, while training and instruction are compatible with objectives models. Using a process model, knowledge and understanding are at a premium, criterion-referenced assessment is appropriate, or at any rate examinations and tests that can be taken while children aspire to other goals, and the teacher is seen as 'a critic, not a marker' (Stenhouse 1975: 95). Objectives models, according to Stenhouse, are suitable for 'curricular areas which emphasize information and skills' (1975: 97). Norm-referenced assessments carried out through formal examinations are appropriate, and teachers are pre-eminently instructors. Whilst some areas of the early years curriculum have been seen as readily amenable to 'process' models, mathematics has not received this attention. Mathematics is seen as being very suitable for an objectives approach. As we shall see, the idea that mathematics is a subject for instruction rather than part of an education has its roots in the kind of mathematics curriculum offered nearly a century ago.

THE ROOTS OF THE PRESENT CURRICULUM

The Revised Code of 1862 might be seen as the first National Curriculum in Britain in that it contained statements about attainment labelled as standards, there being six of these for each subject. Linked to these standards came the legislation which has been known ever since as 'payment by results'.[3] The standards for arithmetic (the other subjects being reading and writing) were as shown in Table 4.1.

Clearly, this group of statements is intended to produce a particular set of arithmetical skills which can be characterised as applied, commercial and narrow. What was needed at the time was a work-force which could take on the new requirements of business and commerce; that is, ledgers and bills of account. This control and determination of the curriculum by particular sectors of society is a feature of much curriculum development and has been important in the development of the National Curriculum in England and Wales. By 1905 the curriculum for younger children was broader and labelled in familiar subject terms. The subjects were English, religious instruction, history, geography, nature study, physical training, art and craft (boys), needlework (girls), and music; but mathematics was still seen as being only arithmetic. However, well before the 1950s there

Table 4.1 Standards for arithmetic as set out in the Revised Code of 1862

Standard 1	Standard 2	Standard 3
Form on blackboard or slate, from dictation, figures up to 20; name at sight figures up to 20; add and subtract figures up to 10, orally, and from examples on blackboard.	A sum in simple addition and subtraction, and the multiplication table.	A sum in any simple rule as far as short division (inclusive).

Standard 4	Standard 5	Standard 6
A sum in compund rules (money).	A sum in compound rules (common weights and measures).	A sum in practice or bills of parcels.

Source: Adapted from Aldrich 1982: 81–2

was a recognition that besides arithmetic, geometry and algebra were necessary components in school mathematics.

Over the first half of the twentieth century we have witnessed the emergence of groups with quite different expectations of what the curriculum should be about. A gross simplification of this division would be the 'traditional' versus 'progressive' arguments. In fact, as we have already indicated, as far as mathematics is concerned, there has been little to observe in respect of 'progressive' as it applies to process. However, it is possible to see some influences of a progressive kind on mathematics content – what has been termed 'new maths'. This includes the idea that children should actually understand what they learn, rather than learn by rote in the hope that real understanding will come later. According to Choat, 'Acquiring mathematics through understanding was accompanied by mathematics which the majority of teachers had not encountered previously'. These included 'Sets, symmetry, multi-base, probability, graphs' (1980: 19–20).

Decimalisation brought more adjustments to the contents of school mathematics curricula. Prior to decimalisation of money in the early 1970s much of the mathematics experienced by children was to do with the manipulation of pounds, shillings, pence, halfpennies, and farthings. There was also a considerable amount of work done in relation to measures: tons, hundredweights, stones, pounds and ounces, and gallons, quarts and pints. In order to manipulate computations of money, weight and volume, children were generally taught each system separately rather than adopting an approach which was based upon the use of different number bases – no doubt due to the mixed bases to be found in many of the areas. Decimalisation brought the prospect, for some, of a disappearance of much of value in the mathematics curriculum. For others it seemed a golden opportunity to develop new mathematics based upon the progressive ideas which characterised much of the educational discourse in the 1960s. Associated with this there developed an emphasis on exploration and understanding, problem solving (not of the water in a bath sort of problem) and problem posing – simplistically, times tables were out, the investigation of number bonds was in! However, as with all changes, much was more to do with rhetoric than reality. Her Majesty's Inspectorate, for example, in *Mathematics 5–11* (DES 1979) engages in a contextual description of good practice that seems to embody a 'progressive' approach and then proceeds to a detailed discussion of the curriculum in terms of aims, objectives and close prescription – product rather than process orientated. However, what HMI did retain was the emphasis on a broad and balanced mathematics curriculum.

We can assess the extent of change in the mathematics curriculum over the century by comparing what was in the 1905 version with that in England and Wales today. We now have broadly the same subject array. However, mathematics is much more than the arithmetic of nearly a century ago and is also more than the arithmetic, algebra and geometry that it later became. We can make this clear by looking in detail at the National Curriculum as an example of what has evolved from the turn of the century. First, however, let us examine what we would see as the essential content of school mathematics for young children.

CURRICULUM CONTENT: A MODEL

We think it important, when talking about curriculum, to set down what we feel constitutes a list of topics young children should learn in mathematics. We believe that there is a body of knowledge which is important for 'mathematical literacy'. We have tried to produce a succinct group of content items, for we know that time for mathematics in school is limited and that many teachers feel there is too much to do; that there is 'curriculum overload'. The intention is that it should be possible for teachers to have a 'picture' of the whole mathematics curriculum. We know it is helpful to have a grasp of all that is important to work at in mathematics. This 'group of content items' does not carry with it an order for delivery or an order of complexity. It is therefore not hierarchical or cumulative and not tied in to children's ages. It is possible to start working on any one item. There are, however, some things which, in our opinion, best come after others, and we will make this clear as we discuss them in detail.

Number, and shape and space are the two parts of mathematics which subsume all mathematical ideas. There are parts of number which overlap with parts of shape and space, and this 'area of overlap' we call algebra.

For example, number patterns and shape patterns are linked and can be viewed algebraically. It is to ideas under the three headings (number, shape and space, and algebra) that children need to be introduced in their mathematics. Note that we talk of 'ideas', not rules or facts. This is quite intentional, for we wish the youngest of children to feel a 'glimmer of doubt' about the immutability of mathematics! From these three sets of ideas all applications of mathematical ideas come. What we have called applications develop from more fundamental concepts, and include all those things which people do that require mathematics of some sort. Thus the pattern of a honeycomb, weighing fruit at the supermarket, performing a dance routine or interpreting a digital clock are applications of mathematics. Though applications are derived from more fundamental ideas *this does not determine their order of presentation to young children*. We can begin with an idea and then apply it, or introduce children to applications and thereby give them experience of a fundamental idea in action.

The links between ideas in number, algebra and shape and space along with the applications of these ideas can be set out in a diagram (Figure 4.1). If we list what we would wish to comprise the content of each of these areas of mathematics for young children, they can be set out as shown in Table 4.2. Ideas and applications may be linked in a variety of ways, which teachers and children can determine. This content model therefore offers the antithesis of a 'fixed' prescription. Though we think children should learn the concepts within all of the items included, they can work on them in any order, at any age and establish links in a range of ways, through a mix of experiences and opportunities. An examination of each of the content items in turn will enable us to explain our thinking further.

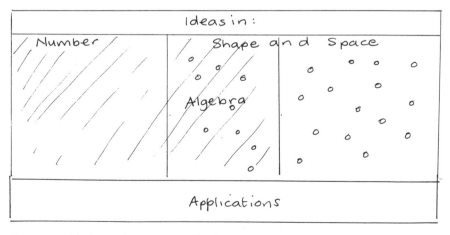

Figure 4.1 Mathematics coverage for the first three years of schooling

Table 4.2 Mathematics content for the first three years of schooling

Ideas in number	Ideas in algebra	Ideas in shape and space
Number line	Patterns	Two-dimensional and three-dimensional shapes
Computation	Sets	
	'Unknown' numbers	Angle and position
		Symmetry
Applications		
Measures – length, area and perimeter, time, 'mass', volume	Movement and direction	
Money	Shapes	Pattern
Fairness and likelihood		

Ideas in number

There are two main sets of ideas here. The first has to do with the number line. The second has to do with computation and the commutative law.

The number line

Using the idea of a number line we can convey to children the idea of cardinal number; that is counting 1,2,3, and so on. These are called natural numbers. To know about ordering numbers we must teach first, second, third; that is ordinal number. 'Real' numbers include all those we can imagine along the number line; for example, fractions and decimals. Children do need to know what it means to be 6½ years old, and the relationship between the little divisions and the centimetres on a ruler. This points up applications of number ideas. Children should also learn the importance of zero, both in expressing place value and in use when we create a scale like that for temperature. If we enter zero and negative numbers on a number line these, together with the positive numbers (the natural numbers), are called integers. Negative numbers are part of everyday experience, in weather forecasts and freezer temperatures, and can be introduced before fractions and decimals, as they may be easier for children to grasp (Haylock and Cockburn 1989).

Computation

In learning to do addition, subtraction, multiplication and division children should be encouraged to use their own methods and to do work in rough if they want to. The skill to do arithmetic 'in your head' is even more important now that children have access to calculators and computers. 'Mental methods' enable us quickly to see whether the electronically produced answers we are getting are what we expect. They help our powers of estimation. Right from the beginning of their schooling children can think mathematically. We have found that children are keen to do mental arithmetic at all those times when they are waiting for something to happen – try it in the dinner queue, while the videotape is winding back, and in those last few minutes before play time. Through repeated quick fire number puzzles, children can come to realise that addition and multiplication operations give the same outcome whichever way we do them. Thus 2 x 3 gives the same answer as 3 x 2. This is an example of the commutative law.

Algebra

We have placed algebraic ideas under three headings: patterns, sets and 'unknown' numbers.

Patterns

Pattern making and search for pattern in the natural world is something children delight in and can be presented again and again in different guises. Algebra is all about establishing and recognising general state-ments about numbers and shapes and we can begin, not with quadratic equations (though these will be part of children's mathematical experience before they reach secondary school) but with the applications of algebraic ideas in patterns.

Sets

Making collections, putting similar things together and 'sorting out' are activities that are part of our everyday lives from when we are very young. For example, when we get what we need for a job, tidy up or clear away we can use logical thinking to determine what we do. Logic is also important in dealing with the overwhelming amount of information we get through our senses all the time. We group and classify things in our environment.

Thus placing objects in sets means we are looking for patterns of similarities and differences. Work with 'sets' is about inclusion and exclusion, and demands complex logic when we begin to allow sets to overlap or break into sub-sets. This kind of work can support children's mathematics because it employs inductive and deductive thinking. Both are important to mathematics, as we have shown in Chapter 3.

'Unknown' numbers

This is to give children a sense that you can 'detect' a 'missing' or 'unknown' number by setting down the information you have and determining the answer, or set of possible answers, from that information. We find the use of the ideas embodied in 'function machines' very fruitful here. A function machine is a 'black box' which consistently operates on any number (or shape, or word) that is fed into it, for example, the 'add 2' robot in Figure 4.2.

Figure 4.2 A function machine: an add two robot

Machines such as this can be used at all levels of mathematical exploration. For example, Gifford (1990: 66–8) reports on her use of function machines in helping 6 and 7 year old children to begin, themselves, to 'use plus and minus signs to represent the actual operations of adding and subtracting'. The children used blocks to work out what was happening in their machines and then 'began to write statements like, 'three more' or 'put two', which they subsequently reduced to just '3m' and 'p2', thus using letters as symbols for the operations'. Examples of what the children wrote appear in Figure 4.3. Function machines also serve to engage children in a discussion of evidence for the certainty of an answer. For example, if asked to determine the operation being carried out in the 'machine' in Figure 4.4 there are a number of possibilities. More information would be needed to focus on the actual function of this machine.

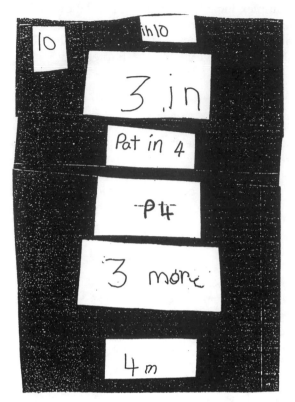

Figure 4.3 The children's function machine instructions
Source: Gifford 1990

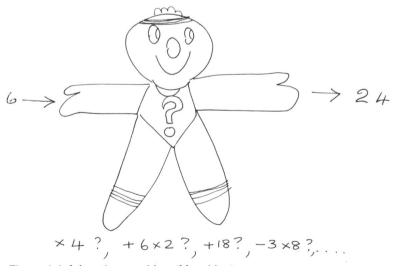

Figure 4.4 A function machine: 'Manchine'

Shape and space

We have chosen what we believe are the most important two-dimensional and three-dimensional shapes for children to get to know. If we add to this a knowledge of angle and position and symmetry these are the keys to a study of shape and space.

Two-dimensional and three-dimensional shapes

It can be argued that school discussion should begin with three-dimensional shapes, because 'the real world' is three-dimensional. We would favour a preliminary treatment of three-dimensional shapes, so that children can 'match', for example, an unsharpened pencil and a baked bean can, or a cereal pack and a chocolate box. Once they can recognise, match and group they will want to name their sets and talk about the attributes of shapes in the set. It is then appropriate to talk about the shapes of 'faces', of corners and edges and an understanding of 'flat' two-dimensional shapes is then necessary. Notice that the mathematical vocabulary can be given when the children need it. Merely telling children 'this is a square and it has four sides all the same and four corners all the same' is rote learning and does not support children's exploration of these observable features. There are five three-dimensional shapes that we think are particularly important as they are all common in the built and manufactured environment. They are cuboid, cube, cylinder, pyramid and prism. Children can begin to have an idea of what these shapes might look like if opened out flat. We call these nets. Nets are linked to networks like the maps we see on the underground, and in computer maze games.

There are four two-dimensional shapes that are the most important ones for young children to learn about. We have chosen them because there exist only five regular[4] solid shapes and these can all be made from our 'short-list' of two-dimensional shapes. These are triangle, square (which is a special case of a rectangle) and pentagon. We have also included circle, for it may already be familiar to children, it is needed in discussions about cylinders, and it features in discussion of angle and rotation.

Angle and position

The important idea to give children about angle is that it is representative of a snapshot of movement. Thus we can begin with their own movements, bending knees and putting arms up, include things like opening the door, closing a book and folding spectacles. Angles are parts of a complete rotation. We apply the idea of part rotations when we talk of the north wind veering westerly, and in the design of clock faces. If we rotate a shape through a part or whole rotation it still remains the same shape; it has simply changed its orientation. If we make a pattern by drawing or laying down a shape, and then changing its position to make a repeat pattern, this is called translation. We can describe position in mathematics using the idea of co-ordinates. An everyday application of this idea is in maps.

Symmetry

Though an abstract idea this is best demonstrated to children through its application in pattern. Examples of reflective and rotational symmetry can be found in artistry from a variety of cultures, and in the natural world. Let the children look at, for example, butterflies and beetles, pictures of big cats, elevations of buildings, and at flags and logos.

Applications

The applications of fundamental mathematics concepts are apparent in every part of our lives. In Table 4.2 those we have designated length, area and perimeter, time, 'mass', and volume we have grouped together here as measures. The other applications are discussed under money, movement and direction, pattern, shapes, and fairness and likelihood.

Measures

The important aspects of measurement for children to grasp have to do with comparison and approximation. We talk about Marcus being taller than Annabel, the small car that does more miles to the gallon than the big one, the oldest tree in the school grounds, who drank most milk, whether we get more apples or oranges to the pound, whether the route round the block to the post office is shorter when we turn right outside the front door and go that way or when we turn left. We make measurement comparisons all the time. All measures are approximate. If we pace out the playground and say it is 51 paces, this is approximate. If we measure it with a trundle wheel or metre sticks as 36 and a bit metres this too is an approximation, albeit with a greater degree of accuracy. The idea of degrees of accuracy and making use of appropriate measuring tools and units is important. We would not use letter scales to weigh potatoes or seconds to measure how long a television programme was. To be skilled at measuring means being able to choose the appropriate measuring tool and units of measurement. Non-standard measures are where we let children begin, for several reasons. These include the fact that children can practise how to do measurement using their own feet and hands, and they do not need to learn much new vocabulary or how to use new tools. Also they can experience what we mean by 'units' by, for example, making a water clock and deciding what can be done in ten drops, 20 drops and so on.

The children can begin to appreciate that we can measure straight and 'bumpy' things, that volume is about space taken up and capacity is how much will go in a box, jug or other container; that when we weigh using a balance we measure 'mass', and that Newtons are a measure of weight; that we can measure the passing of time or say 'it is 10.30, time to go out to play'.

Money

Even the youngest children have some idea that money is a medium of exchange. The crucial concepts are to do with conservation and equivalence of value. The class shop is a deservedly popular feature of many classrooms as it offers opportunities for the use of money and all that means in respect of 'value' and 'fairness'. The shop also offers a wide range of measuring possibilities such as weight, length and the use of numbers to identify quantities. See Clemson and Clemson (1992) for some play shop and post office ideas. Coins are also good resources for showing ideas like multiplication as repeated addition, and rows of two pence toy mice, five pence toy hedgehogs and ten pence toy frogs along with accompanying rows of coins demonstrate these admirably. 'Ways of spending ten pence' are also helping children with the idea of some of the number bonds to ten.

Patterns

As we suggested above, when algebraic ideas are displayed as patterns they take on a fascination much more potent than the idea of a 'general statement'. We can immerse children in a wide variety of experiences which will help them recognise and delight in patterns everywhere. They can, for example, paint, draw, print, make music, thread beads, line up, set out equipment, or create a dance in order to display pattern (Clemson and Clemson 1992). They can also pore over wallpaper and fabric samples, books of abstract art, pictures of ancient and modern tile patterns and mosaics, architectural relief patterns, pictures of creatures and plants and so on.

Movement and direction

In application, we talk of clockwise and anti-clockwise, using work in dance, physical education and time-telling. We use the points of a compass and make and read maps of the local environment. Programmable robots can be used to navigate obstacle courses set out in the hall or to carry out a sequence of moves which describe a predetermined pattern or shape.

Shape

We can use the natural, built and manufactured environment here. A shape trail around the school, the classroom or the local streets can be developed by the children and offered to other classes – photographs and drawings as well as a map could be used. Rubbings of objects from coins to manhole covers could be part of this exploration. We would include here shapes such as the hexagon and octagon as they are shapes which can be derived from equilateral triangles. Naturally occurring irregular shapes can be identified and contrasted with regular ones in order to underline the idea of characteristics. Shape and pattern are often inextricably linked.

Fairness and likelihood

These are the important first ideas that children need to get to know in the area of probability and chance. We can let them play dice games like snakes and ladders and strategy games like dominoes. Through playing they can assess their own notions about luck against the evidence. 'It is not fair' is an expression all children seem to use, and which is important to them. Fairness in game-playing is an appropriate arena for what we mean by 'fair'.

Data

Our curriculum content list omits anything overtly about ways of representing mathematical data. Pictures, tallies, pictograms, block graphs and so on have been omitted because they can be used to depict ideas as well as applications. We can record in picture form the numbers of sides and corners plane shapes have. We can depict the shapes found on pencil boxes in the classroom. We can regard these ways of communicating ideas and information as techniques and skills which can be given to children when they need them, and in the same way as we show them how to write a '2' or the word 'angle'. This means that we need to see data handling and pictorial representation as being embedded within and throughout the curriculum and not amenable to separation.

Ways of presenting content

We have said that this content can be tackled in any order. Clearly individual children have different ranges of knowledge and experience, and it may therefore be that some items are redundant or unattainable by some children as part of their learning programme. However, we do believe that whatever the children's current mathematical understanding, arranging their future learning involves some kind of framework and plan. It is for the teacher to remould our suggestions to tie in with what is considered optimum for the children in the class. Some teachers, however, may wish to examine and consider a number of example treatments of the content. We have devised two such examples. The first is a 'course' which could be worked on as a school year programme. There are three lists of items. The first is about number and applications, the second algebra and applications, and the third shape and space and applications. In subsequent school years the programme would be repeated, taking a new look at each section of the course. Part of the 'course' for a class in their first year is set out in Table 4.3. The course is not intended to be treated in linear fashion. We see mental methods and the acquisition of number bonds as being supported throughout the year. During every school day teachers create and exploit opportunities for children to work on number, algebra and shape. Here are a few situations showing where mathematical opportunities can be seized:

— *'Showing time'*. Phil and Katrina bring small toys like dolls' furniture, Action Man and Barbie in to show their friends. The discussion leads into a comparison of size (to begin children's thinking about the idea of scale). A play tent and camping gear can be set up in the 'home corner'. If the teacher sees this as appropriate just for the day, the children can create an impromptu tent from a sheet and use the play house cups and equipment. A tent and camping gear suitable for the dolls can be put on a display table.

— *'Interest table'*. Make the stimulus display sometimes have mathematical possibilities. For example, a box of ribbons and string, along with parcels, a laced shoe and soft toys may have challenges added, giving children chances to tie knots and bows. They can also estimate how much string is needed to tie a parcel, how much ribbon to make a bow round a soft toy, how long a shoelace needs to be and so on. If they mark their estimates on a sheet of paper, some of the lengths can be cut and tried out. The children may come up with their own ideas about taking the 'how long does it need to be' discussion further.

— *'News'*. When the children tell of happenings in their families this can be a springboard for mathematical discussion about time, sequencing, measures and so on. For example, a discussion about new shoes could lead to talk about pairs, kinds of shops (sets), matching footwear for a purpose or to their owner (two to one correspondence), the sequence of events from animal hide to shoes on our feet, foot and shoe size, and money.

— *'School events'*. Having the decorators in, getting new apparatus, even having a leaking roof can be the starting point for discussions of sizes and quantities.

The curriculum is a seamless web – in concentrating our efforts on

Table 4.3 Part of a three-term 'course' in mathematics

	This plan is for a year group class in their first year of school	
Number and applications	Algebra and applications	Shape and space and applications
Counting without recording	Singing/counting patterns Drawing/painting patterns	Matching shapes
Notation	Sets	Shape vocabulary – talk about/name quadrilaterals rectangle square triangle pentagon circle cuboid cube cylinder pyramid prism
Ordinal number		
Number line		
Practical addition		
Practical subtraction		
Mental addition/subtraction		Movement in dance and games
Record addition/subtraction	Function machines	
Introduction to money		Angle
Zero on number line		
Recognising symbols for numbers in the environment – next postal collection/speed limit/house numbers/birthday cards/clocks	Patterns of number Odds and evens	Shapes in the environment, classroom and school
Estimate, approximate, compare using non-standard measures	Patterns in shape and movement	Symmetry in patterns children make and from a variety of cultures – idea of rotation/reflection. Clockwise
	Patterns in fabrics and toys such as mosaics	Hexagons octagons
Track games, computation games 'Fair'/chance		Shape games 'Fair'/chance

particular parts of it we need to remain conscious of the links and connections that will help children to gain a satisfactory and satisfying grasp of the whole.

The second example shows how mathematics topics can yield activities to cover the content of the curriculum. We have set out topic webs, to show that programmes of work covering a wide array of ideas or focused study can be the subject of a topic approach. 'Numbers and me' has infinite possibilities. Triangles is more focused. The topic webs appear in Figures 4.5 and 4.6. Either topic could be used with children in any of the first three years of schooling. It is possible to imagine topic webs similar to 'numbers and me' with titles like 'finding out about pattern' or 'shapes around me'. Using 'triangles' as a model topic there could be more, called, for example, 'rectangles' or 'all about five'. 'Games' (shown in Figure 4.7) involves work which extends beyond the infant years, though parts of it could be taken on and expanded for young children. A study of beetle drive, dominoes or maze games is well within their ambit.

A CRITIQUE OF A CURRENT CURRICULUM: THE NATIONAL CURRICULUM (ENGLAND AND WALES)

Mathematics in the National Curriculum (England and Wales) has been widely criticised on a number of grounds, including the utilitarian notions on which it is based and its overspecification of content and ways of assessment. We shall focus on its content and teaching implications.

Curriculum content

The National Curriculum comprises five main areas of study, arranged into Attainment Targets, named as follows:

- Using and applying mathematics (in practice this is not discrete and separate, but permeates all the other areas of study)
- Number
- Algebra
- Shape and space
- Handling data

Breadth

The content does represent an attempt to enable children to learn a body of mathematical knowledge and ways of applying that knowledge; it is an attempt at a broad curriculum. However, it is clear that the curriculum compilers did conceive of a body of knowledge to be assimilated by the oldest and ablest children, and then worked down from there to the very

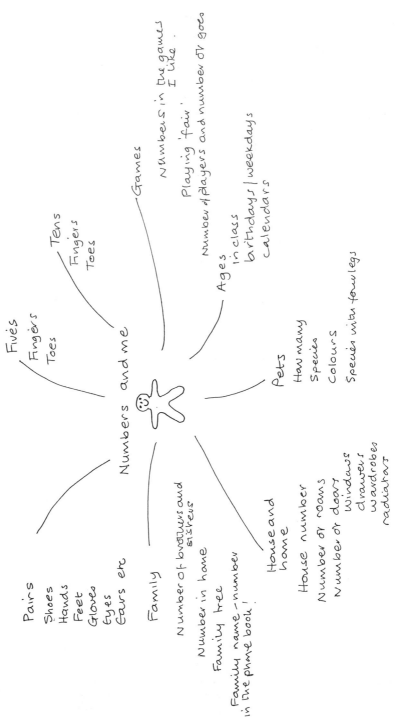

Figure 4.5 Topic web: numbers and me

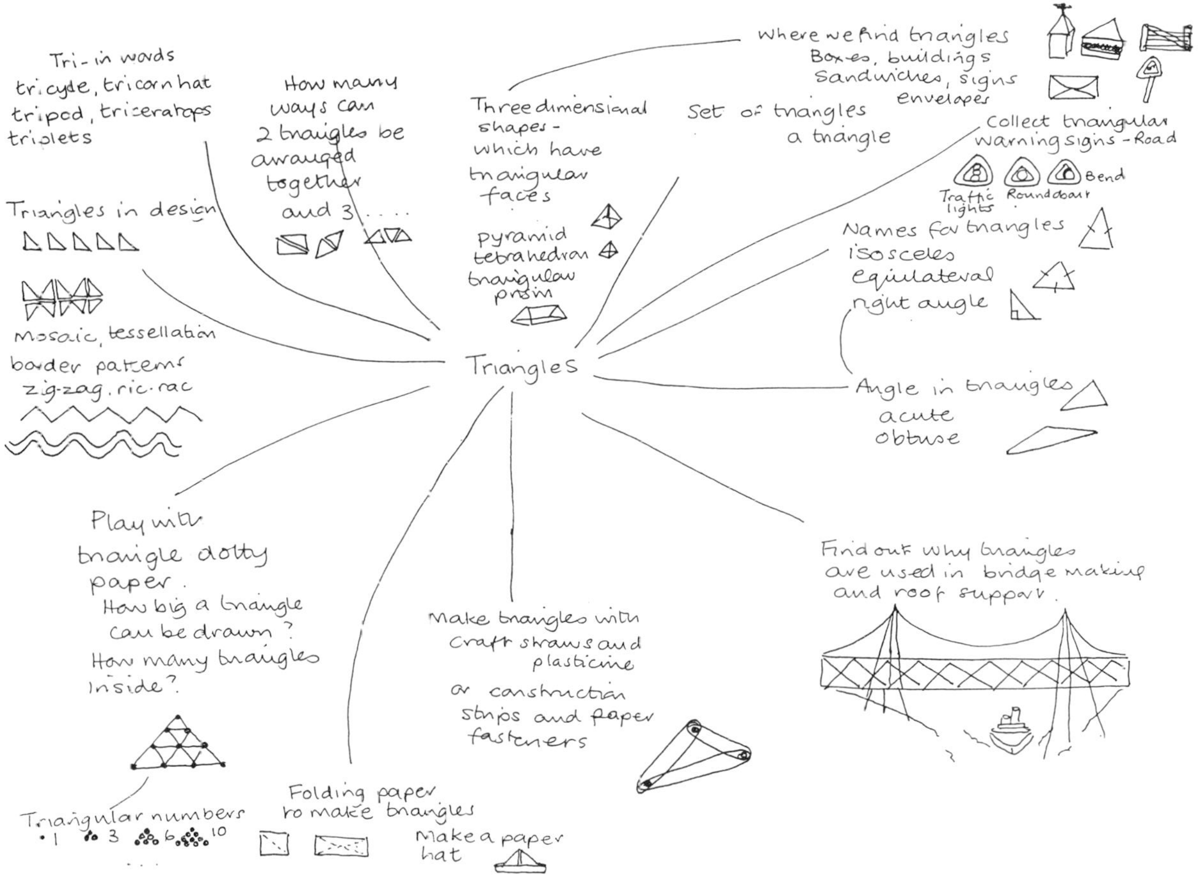

This is a hand-drawn mind map / topic web diagram centered on "Triangles".

Where we find triangles
Boxes, buildings
Sandwiches, signs
envelopes

Collect triangular
warning signs - Road

Set of triangles in
a triangle

Names for triangles
isosceles
equilateral
right angle

Traffic
lights

Bend
Roundabout

Angle in triangles
acute
obtuse

Find out why triangles
are used in bridge making
and roof supports

**Three-dimensional
shapes -
which have
triangular
faces**
Pyramid
tetrahedron
triangular
prism

Triangles

Make triangles with
craft straws and plasticine
or construction
strips and paper
fasteners

Folding paper
to make triangles
make a paper
hat

Tri- in words
tricycle, tricorn hat
tripod, triceratops
triplets

Triangles in design

mosaic, tessellation

border patterns
zigzag, ric rac

**How many
ways can
2 triangles be
arranged
together**
2 and 3 ......

Play with
triangle dotty
paper
How big a triangle
can be drawn?
How many triangles
inside?

Triangular numbers
.1 .·. 3 .·. 6 .·. 10

Figure 4.6 Topic web: triangles

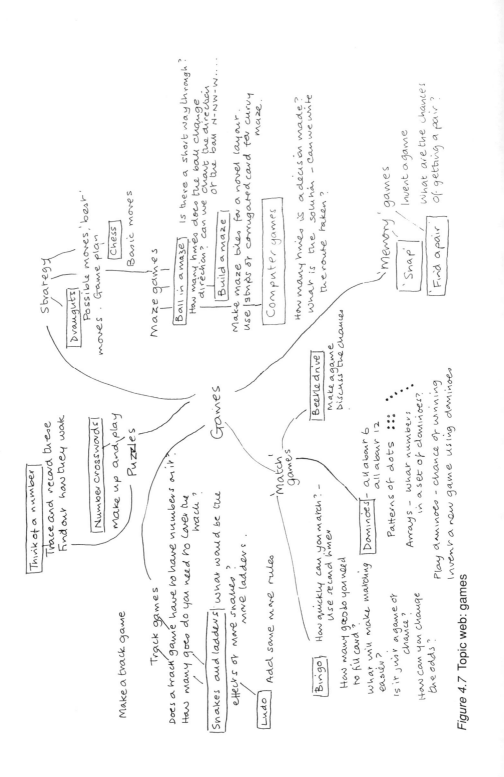

Figure 4.7 Topic web: games

youngest at the bottom! This is contrary to all that is suggested in current theories of learning. It also goes against what we know about mathematics. Arbitrary partitioning of knowledge for children at different points in their school career destroys the possibility of coherent connections and creative thinking. The list becomes reductionist rather than expansive and allowing of breadth of study.

Continuity and progression

The areas for study have been compiled as knowledge item lists (except in Using and applying mathematics, where the focus is on skills). The idea that children should benefit from a curriculum that gets increasingly conceptually complex is attempted by dividing the lists of knowledge items. The lists are subdivided into levels, placing the first items to be learned in Level one, the next in Level two and so on until Level ten is reached. It is assumed by the compilers of the National Curriculum that individual children will reach somewhere from Levels one to three while they are in the infant department or school. This is cause for great concern. The levels of the National Curriculum have quickly become aspirations for teaching and learning. They look like limits, not opportunities. If this continues to be the case levels could actually lower the very standards they were devised to raise. The curriculum attempts to accommodate continuity by allowing all levels to be available to all teachers at all stages of a child's school career. Thus school internal and hand-on records can be entirely consistent. However, levels have become aligned with the parts of children's school careers. Thus the assessment point at the end of the infant years, called Key Stage one, has entered the culture of the school as a ceiling, a schism in educational provision. This mitigates against continuity across infant, junior and secondary phases.

Aims and objectives

The curriculum prescribes the content of learning and makes use of an objectives approach. However, when we look closely at the content of the mathematics curriculum it is couched in terms which make its overarching aims unclear. By aims we mean the ultimate goals teachers should have sight of, and by objectives we mean the 'smaller scale' detailed items to be achieved. If we apply these terms to what is officially set down we think it appropriate that infant teachers may have as an aim: that children should be able to count, order, and work with natural numbers. The objectives to achieve this would list a range of experiences the children should have. Note that our suggestions which follow are intended to be neither comprehensive nor prescriptive, but merely examples:

— Count using aids, tallying, one to one correspondence;

— Put things in order and identify first, second, and so on;
— Add and subtract, using aids and then symbolically.

To achieve these objectives teachers would need to devise a wide range of activities, including the following:

— Play at setting down rows of toys, books and other things found in school and counting them aloud;
— Play at counting beads, pencils and other equipment when putting them away;
— Place some toys in order of height, and children in order of age;
— Count a set and say what 'one more' would make;
— Work out how many customers visit the cake shop if all five cakes are sold;
— Sing and invent counting songs and rhymes;
— Record number bonds to ten in a workbook.

Incidentally these seem to be very much in accord with some of the suggestions made by The Early Years Curriculum Group (1989). If we compare the kind of analysis we have done with what is in official documentation, it appears that a clear indication of goals has not been achieved there. Let us look, for example, at the following statements:

Giving and understanding instructions for movement along a route.

Follow or give instructions related to movement and position.

Follow directions in a PE lesson, or on an errand around school.
(DES 1991: 14)

They are from Attainment Target 4: Shape and space. There is an element from the Programme of Study, a Statement of Attainment and a non-statutory example. They none of them express an aim, nor do they present suggestions for detailed activities. They all seem to fall into our objectives category and all express the same objective.

The Curriculum in action

There were originally no strictures in the National Curriculum as to how the subject matter should be taught. In fact the way the content is couched does permit teachers to allow investigation and exploration. There are also assumptions about teaching for meaning (which was propounded in the so-called 'new' mathematics of the 1950s) rather than the rote learning common before that time (St John-Brooks 1992). It seems now that there may be some official prescriptions regarding class teaching and placing children in ability groups which may erode what flexibility remains in the hands of teachers. For the moment however, Ernest's ideas can be carried through.

There is no statutory control over the teaching approach adopted. This leaves open a 'window of opportunity'. For a problem posing pedagogy, based on an appropriate philosophy of mathematics, can fulfil the statutory obligations in terms of content and assessment and yet still be emancipatory ... the pedagogical suggestions that accompany the National Curriculum in mathematics ... promote a problem solving approach. Thus an invitation to use an inquiry orientated teaching approach, which allows the deployment of a problem posing pedagogy, is built into the system.

(1991: 294–5)

REVIEW

The essential point is that in carrying through a mathematics curriculum we have to be mindful of the possible tension between the ideology held by its designers and our own beliefs. Additionally, in relation specifically to mathematics, we can review the purposes of mathematics education, as seen by those writing the curriculum. For example, as we have seen, those adopting a utilitarian ideology would tend to eschew any mathematics that did not seem directly 'useful'. Hardy (1940, 1992) would argue that it is not sufficient to devote oneself to the applicable, but rather that we need to offer children the opportunity to see the beauty of mathematics and its true links with human knowledge and experience. An emphasis on simple utility trivialises mathematics. Inevitably in a discussion of 'what' is to be taught, we have begun to raise issues about the 'how to go about it'. This, and ideas about how we know when we have efficaciously presented a mathematics curriculum, that is, 'we have done it ... we have got there' will emerge in the sections of the book that are to come.

NOTES

1 See, for example, Pound et al. 1992, and Early Years Curriculum Group 1989.
2 For those wishing to pursue ideas to do with ideology and culture, Ernest's book provides a very thorough and detailed analysis. See also, for example, Skilbeck 1976, Reynolds and Skilbeck 1976 and Lawton 1983.
3 Payment by results was abolished in 1897 but it has become part of the professional memory of all teachers. At the time of writing we seem to be witnessing a form of payment by results once again. This time it has two targets: the whole school performance and the performance of individual teachers (performance-related pay).
4 Regular means the faces are all equal polygons. The five regular solids are cube – square faces, tetrahedron – triangular faces, octahedron – triangular faces, icosahedron – triangular faces and dodecahedron – pentagonal faces. Note the importance of the triangle.

Chapter 5

Mathematics and language

INTRODUCTION

Both language and mathematics are about conveying the meaning of ideas. We mull over these meanings when we quite literally 'think to ourselves'. We communicate them to other people when we talk and write. One of the key differences between language and mathematics is that the latter, appropriately expressed, does not require meanings to be 'worked out' or 'negotiated'. It is direct and unequivocal. Cockcroft explains the importance that most people give to mathematics as due to 'the fact that mathematics provides a means of communication which is powerful, concise and unambiguous' (1982: 1). There is much discussion as to whether mathematics is itself a language. Some writers view it as being a 'full-blown' language in its own right. By others it is seen as a *part* of English, Welsh or any other language; and yet others view it as a kind of 'condensed' language with international currency. It is, at least partly, a language of symbols which transcend words, for people whose native tongues are different can 'write' and 'read' the mathematics. However, when they think about mathematics, and talk, read and write about it, they do use their 'word languages'.

This debate about whether mathematics can be compared with and assigned the attributes of a language is important to teachers because it alerts us to some of the difficulties we encounter in teaching and learning. All subjects in infant classrooms in the UK are taught using English (or Welsh). Some subjects have 'jargon' words that have special meanings, and some take on everyday words and assign them special meanings. For example, a 'pass' in PE, a 'round' in music, a 'line' of poetry, a 'key' in science or geography are all 'special' meanings given to everyday words. In all these respects mathematics is like other subjects. In infant schools mathematics is different from other subjects in one important respect. It has a powerful symbol system which we expect *all* young children to learn. Other subjects have symbols, but most are not introduced to children until they are older. Some schools may have music teachers who introduce infants to musical notation, but we do not regard it as mandatory that they all do it. Teachers do not usually tell children of infant age that salt can be written NaCl or how to read isobars on a weather map. But we do expect every child to recognise, for example, '=' and '6' and to adopt common conventions used in setting down mathematical expressions.

This chapter is devoted to a discussion of problems arising when we 'talk mathematics' and 'write mathematics', and when children 'read mathematics' in the infant classroom. It is our contention that there are three main causes for problems in teaching and learning mathematics. They are to do with the early imposition on children of the symbol system of mathematics; the use of words which have both mathematical meanings and other quite different everyday meanings; and to do with the ways we use words both in speech and print as the vehicle for teaching children. It is vital, then, that as teachers we take account of these possible sources of misunderstanding and confusion. To highlight some of the difficulties we shall look at the following:

— the language of mathematics; that is, mathematical symbols and mathematical words;
— language as the vehicle for mathematical education.

MATHEMATICAL SYMBOLS

The Collins (1987) dictionary definition of a symbol in mathematics is 'a letter, figure, or sign used ... to represent a quantity, phenomenon, operation, function etc.'. There is a long list of such symbols which children in infant school are required to learn. If we take the view that when we use symbols alone we are doing a kind of shorthand, we can press this analogy further. To do shorthand we need to know which squiggles signify each word or phrase being said. But we can then take down, and translate into longhand, messages which have no meaning for us. In mathematics we can learn to write and put into words the symbols but this does not mean that we understand them. Thus as teachers we cannot let children substitute the mechanics of mathematics symbolism for a real understanding of the ideas conveyed by those symbols.

There is another important feature of symbolism which we can explain to children. That is that a symbol is an abstraction. It can be applied without taking account of what is in the 'real' world. If we write 2, this means 2 of absolutely anything from bacteria to universes. In describing school mathematics Hughes refers to it as 'like a secret code'. He goes on to say that the code 'contains a number of features which distinguish it from the informal mathematics which children acquire before school' (1986: 168). Among these features are the ideas that it is 'context-free' and that 'it rests heavily on written symbolism'. According to Hughes it is the inadequate induction into the features of the code and the reasons why we use it that cause children problems with school mathematics. For example, writing an addition sum using symbols does not help a child who cannot make the addition using oranges or bricks or other concrete objects. Thus we need to be careful to give children the chance to move from context bound 'informal mathematics' to formal mathematics which is free of context. The fact that the symbols are context free offers a kind of precision in use. Pimm states:

> the symbol system acts as a kind of filter, dispensing with all but the essential elements involved, as by no means all the relationships among the ideas can be simultaneously represented. The pupils must therefore come to understand this filtering process and become confident users of it.
>
> (1981: 139)

Writing symbols

Pimm (1981) argues that confusion can arise in mathematical language itself, that is in the ways we set down mathematical symbols. Simple examples include 6 and 9, which are different only in the way they appear on the page, and the 7 in 74 which is not the same as the 7 in 47.

To examine whether there are a number of ways of setting down symbols in current use we have asked teachers undertaking in-service courses in mathematics education to show us how they set out computations. Even for what might be seen as the simple addition of forty-seven and eight there were a variety of presentations. It is interesting to see how the computations were written, and how the teachers actually solved the 'sum'. These are the ways they set them on the page:

$$47 \atop + \, 8 \qquad\qquad 47+ \atop \underline{8} \qquad\qquad 47 + 8 =$$

Some of the teachers decided to set out the sum down rather than across the page because they saw it as 'more difficult' than an across-the-page sum. They anticipated the need to develop a staged process for solution of the problem. Where they put the addition sign seems to be based on either a school policy or the scheme used or the teacher's own experience of learning to do addition sums. Many of these teachers were strong in their promotion of one way (and asserting that this was the one right way) of setting out computations. But going further with these same teachers to the actual methods used in solving the sum offered further revealing information. Different methods of solution were being employed – often through conversations 'in their heads'. For example, some teachers did carry out a method, often seen as standard, which is to add the seven and eight to make fifteen and then add the forty to produce fifty-five. Others, made the forty-seven up to fifty and then subtracted the three required from the eight to leave five. Fifty and five then produced the solution. Some teachers just experienced the answer popping into their minds, presumably through a close familiarity with the number bonds involved in the sum.

What is interesting is that these teachers have adopted a variety of ways of setting down and solving. Because they were on an adult maths course we can assume that, though they may not have met all the presentations and methods during their schooldays, they will by now have had a 'wide' exposure, and have known a variety of methods to choose from. These teachers had not all plumped for the same *best way* of doing the sum. Different strategies seem to be the best for different people. This variation in approaches is supported by Cockcroft, who says:

> It is now a . . . well established fact that those who are mathematically effective in everyday life seldom make use 'in their heads' of the standard written methods which are taught in the classroom, but either adapt them in a personal way or make use of methods which are highly idiosyncratic.
>
> (1982: 75)

So, if there is a range of 'best' methods of setting out, and a range of 'best' methods for solution among people who have a choice, we should offer children choices in order to facilitate their acquisition of the skills necessary to solve this and other computations and find *their own* best way.

To show that children as young as 5 can find ways of representing their maths, Gifford reports on an incident recalled by Pugh, who (following an experiment conducted by Hughes) gave children the opportunity to show how many counters had secretly been removed from or added to a pot (see Figure 5.1).

> Jamie, aged five, devised a system for showing addition and subtraction, without the use of symbols. . . . He simply drew the pot, with the counters taken away shown at a distance, or the counters added shown in the pot. This record is very economical and within the familiar context, needs little or no explanation.
>
> (Gifford 1990: 68)

Gifford goes on to give another example, 6 year old Asif (see Figure 5.2):

> He invented . . . his own number sentence form. He was finding numbers that could be made with any combination of twos and fives, using colourfactor rods, and . . . [was encouraged] to record his results in his own way with the purpose of discussing them with his teacher and classmates later. He simply wrote down all the numbers used, then '+', then the total. He told me that he had written 'Two, two, plus, four.'
>
> When I asked him what 'plus' meant, he explained, 'two numbers put

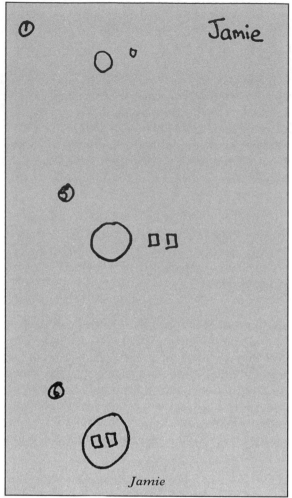

Figure 5.1 Jamie's work
Source: Gifford 1990

together,' (implying that the plus sign showed what you had to do with the whole list of numbers). He clearly understood his invented system, which was far more economical than the standard number sentence, and quite appropriate for the context.

(1990: 68)

Plunkett suggests that, in the context of the use of standard written algorithms,[1] 'One of the most remarkable things about these methods is that *they are used so little*' (1979: 4). He goes on to argue that we should see the teaching of elementary arithmetic as involving three techniques. Children should, he suggests, develop:

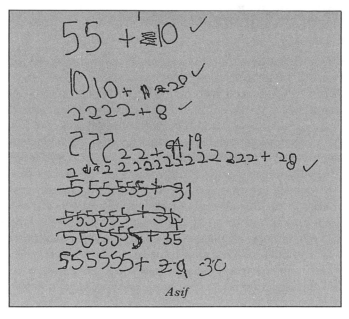

Figure 5.2 Asif's work
Source: Gifford 1990

— mental methods using number bond work for simple calculations;
— the use of the calculator to do computations that 'on the whole few people would want to, or need to';
— some casual written methods.

Plunkett's ideas further support the suggestion that we should allow children to develop methods of their own in order to do mathematics involving symbols.

MATHEMATICAL WORDS

There are accepted ways of writing down symbols when we want to make mathematical statements. However, we have more choice about how to express mathematical ideas when we use words. We have to translate the symbols we see into a framework for 'reading'. For example, the symbol '=' is commonly read as 'equals' and/or 'the same as'. The symbol '−' is referred to as 'minus', 'take away', and 'subtract'. The digit '0' is commonly read or talked about as 'nought', 'zero', or 'nil'. When we do oral number work with children we may say things such as the following:

— 'what is six add two?'
— 'can you add two to six?'

— 'seven take away five?'
— 'take five from seven'
— 'what is the difference between seven and five?'

Notice that we not only use a variety of words to explain what to do with the numbers but we also change the order of the numbers in the sentence. Pimm (1981) spells out some of these ways of presenting basic operations.

Does it matter that we can say and write a number operation in a variety of ways? It certainly does matter that children learn what we mean by all these ways of expressing what we want them to do. There is also the temptation to try to limit the number of ways of describing number operations, in the hope that this might limit children's confusion. This could lead to children coming to believe that computation can only be done in one direction. For example, subtraction is traditionally laid out as being to do with 'taking' the smaller number away from the larger. But if we consider what happens when we go shopping the assistant commonly works out the change by counting on from the actual price to the total tendered. This may be in the children's everyday experience, so it needs to be added to the repertoire of strategies worked on in school. Rather than restricting the ways we describe subtraction many possible ways of talking through the processes should be available to the children. This raises serious questions about the use of standard algorithms[1] in mathematics work.

There are everyday words that are assigned special meanings when they are used in mathematics. Teachers and children need to learn what these are, their meanings in everyday usage, and the specific meanings they acquire when used mathematically. To find some examples of such words we looked at Mathematics in the National Curriculum (England and Wales) (DES 1991) and have listed some we found in Levels 1–3 (that is those levels accessed by teachers and children in all infant classrooms). Table 5.1 presents each word, a suggested everyday context and a 'mathematical meaning'. Some words do have a variety of meanings even in everyday use. In these cases we have chosen one of the contexts in which the meaning is quite different from the mathematical one. These are not strict technical definitions, for such definitions are often wordy and would perhaps have clouded the point we want to make. They are simply meant to give the 'flavour' of some of the misunderstandings that can arise.

There may be some words in this list that we have slipped into using in a variety of contexts, including mathematical ones, without reflecting that they may cause some children problems. There is evidence that they can. For example, Orton (1987) tells of children thinking that 'volume' means the knob on the television and that 'axes' are for chopping wood. Amy, reading aloud from the side of the cereal packet, told us that of course the flakes had to be sold by weight and not volume. After all, when they are still and in the packet they do not make a noise!

Table 5.1 Everyday words found in mathematics Levels 1–3

Word	Everyday use	Mathematical meaning
check	a check shirt	re-work to try and ensure the correct answer
record	make a 'tape' or disc	write down
odd	unusual, peculiar	counting numbers ending in 1,3,5,7,9, etc.
even	make things the same on both sides	numbers ending in 0,2,4,6,8, etc.
ordering	write down something to buy that has to be sent for	arrange things or information
difference	a feature that is not similar in two things	'difference between' – a way of describing subtraction
left	that side! or discarded	remaining
value	importance, expense	magnitude
some/sum	a collection	addition
set	matching parts to make a whole	collection having one feature the same
block	obstruct or toy for building models	'block' graph – to denote magnitudes
table	to sit at	a drawing of ordered information
tree	a growing plant	a pattern of pathways where each path splits again and again
enter	go in	write in some information or put into a computer
place	location	'place' value – change in magnitude with place on page
fair	just	takes account of and eliminates all variation except the one variable to be considered
volume	level of noise	amount of space taken up
mass	huge amount	any amount when 'weighed'
net	for fish	plane (2D) shape which cut and folded makes 3D shape
face	front of head	flat side of 3D shape
plane	flying machine	flat
figure	body shape	number or line diagram

LANGUAGE IN TEACHING AND LEARNING MATHEMATICS

When we try to describe the nature of our own thinking we say that we seem to think in words and pictures. Our thinking about the pictures is in words, so it could be argued that words, that is 'language', are essential to thinking. However, Foss (1969: 47) draws on earlier work with deaf people which demonstrated that they were quite capable of 'many advanced forms of thinking' despite being handicapped in the number of words and ways of expressing ideas available to them. Foss also points out that 'there is little positive evidence' that people who speak different languages think differently. He goes on to imply that it is possible that language might undermine some thinking! There are still however, strong arguments for making language pivotal in our discussion about mathematics education, because words are the 'currency' of teaching and learning. The knowledge that mathematics can be communicated in part without words does not prevent us from requiring teachers and children to speak and listen, and read and write, in the course of their mathematics.

Teachers speaking and listening

In classrooms of the past, speaking was what the teacher did while the children listened. Now that 'speaking and listening' has been legitimised by its addition to the UK language curriculum, those teachers who always let children talk about their tasks no longer feel defensive, and those who favoured a silent group of children while they themselves did all the talking are modifying their modes of working. Despite our impressions to the contrary, it is still the case, however, that the teacher talks more than any of the children.[2] Teacher talk can be of various kinds. Brissenden provides a useful list:

> Exposition
> Question asking
> Praising or encouraging
> Controlling pupils in various ways
> Discussion with pupils.
>
> (1988: 11)

It could be argued that all of these factors are potentially in use in mathematics sessions. In thinking about the teacher's oral and aural contribution to the class the important issues include not only what is said, but the way it is said, and what teachers are listening out for.

HMI reported on the importance of 'the quality of the language used by the teacher in questioning and discussion' (DES 1989: 31). They describe 'good work' in relation to discussion done in classes of 4 and 5 year olds:

Most teachers of young children made time in the day for discussion with the whole class. These sessions offered excellent opportunities for pupils to learn more about mathematical ideas and incorporate relevant mathematical terminology in their use of language. Discussion with the teacher enabled ideas to be refined and for the children to begin to recognise the need for precision in the use of mathematical language.

(DES 1989: 28)

This is what The Mathematical Association (1987a) call 'teacher led'. They cite it as 'particularly appropriate to the introduction of new ideas and skills'.

There has developed in many infant classrooms a preference for informal approaches, where the teacher is 'helping' by strategic intervention rather than more formal strategies which involve 'telling' children about what they are doing. Teachers have tried to supply children with questions rather than answers. According to Alexander, this approach is not always successful.

A common tendency . . . was for some teachers to ask questions rather than make statements or give instructions. In some circumstances this remained true even in straightforward administrative interactions where strings of questions about what was going to happen next sometimes led to complicated and unproductive guessing games.

(1992b: 78)

We are reminded of an opening session to a day where a teacher held up a birthday card to show her class of reception children. The children were asked to say who it was from and allowed wild guesses which got more and more far-fetched, including a ghost, a budgie and a horse. This went on for about ten minutes, with no focused questioning from the teacher to either give clues or extend the range of what was being discussed (to perhaps include who the card was for, what the numeral on the front signified, what was being celebrated, other times we send cards, what happens to a card when it is posted, and so on). Alexander calls 'for a more discriminating balance of questions, statements and instructions; for fewer pseudo-questions and more questions of a kind which encourage children to reason and speculate' (1992b: 144).

There needs to be an understanding of how we might identify the latter. Duffin (1987: 48) says, 'Most of us know the value of teaching through asking questions', but then asks, 'How often in the classroom do teachers ask a question with a 'correct' answer in mind which causes them to reject an answer from a child which does not accord with a 'correct' answer?'. Duffin goes on to say that this is not a feature of real discussion where understandings are exchanged.[3] This point is echoed in *Maths Talk* (Mathematical Association 1987a: 24) where the suggestion is that 'children may search for responses which please the teacher, rather than focus on the thread of the argument; responses of this type can be misleading because children seem to have understood when they have not.' As Pollard and Tann suggest, we need to reflect on the following:

> Why are the children so keen to get the answer 'right'? Do we mostly set up situations where we ask testing questions which have one right answer? How often do we create opportunities for exploring issues, where questions are genuinely aimed at finding out individual views and experiences: a situation in which every response can be valued?
>
> (1987: 149)

It is not possible for children to please the teacher or address the argument if the teacher makes discouraging remarks. A visiting teacher was sitting with a group of children from a reception class recently. The children had been doing some sorting activities.

TEACHER: May I sort the things out now, and you see if you can tell how I have decided what to put in the set? (Teacher starts putting some objects together.)

SUE: No, no, not like that. You aren't doing very well are you?

It is no easier to take this kind of remark if you are a teacher than it is if you are a child. This is just the kind of interjection that stifles thinking, and is therefore for teachers to avoid. So what sorts of remarks promote thinking? The Mathematical Association (1987a) makes suggestions that might fit our 'stifles thinking' category and some that promote thinking. We have tried setting some of their examples alongside one another to point up the contrast:

Stifle	Promote
That's right.	Tell John how it works.
Good boy!	Go on . . .
You're not quite right there.	Where did the 8 come from?
This is the way to do it.	Show me!

To be able to interject in encouraging ways demands that we really listen to children and concentrate. We ourselves have found that tape recordings of sessions we have carried through with children reveal that it can be the teacher who does not listen to all that is important! We hear children complaining that no one listens to them and that they do not get a 'fair hearing'. We have argued elsewhere (Clemson and Clemson 1990) that listening takes effort and practice. Forgive the pun, but listening *intently* is not as easy as it sounds. 'Really focusing your listening is a skill. Many teachers (and many children) cultivate the image that they are good listeners, while their thoughts are elsewhere' (Clemson and Clemson 1991: 52–3). Listening is especially important for teachers as it can be an aid to assessment and evaluation. Pimm puts in a plea: 'teachers of mathematics ... listen with an open ear for what your children are trying to say. It is surprising how often there is a comprehensible basis for mistakes and misunderstandings and one which has a linguistic origin' (1981: 149).

Children speaking and listening

Brissenden (1988) has worked up a list of 'competences' which children can acquire through the adoption of oral strategies in mathematics. They are as follows:

— articulating and presenting an idea publicly, in a clear and intelligible way;
— explaining a method;
— arguing logically in support of an idea;
— criticising an argument logically, including one's own;
— evaluating the correctness of an idea, or its potential in attacking a problem;
— speculating, conjecturing, entertaining an idea provisionally;
— accepting an idea provisionally and examining the consequences, keeping track of a discussion, reviewing;
— coping with being stuck, supporting others in difficulty;
— drawing others out, using 'Show me . . .' or 'How did you get that . . .?!'
— acting as spokesperson for a group's ideas.

This is a formidable list and we would not pretend that they may all come within the range of experience of children in the infant school. However, they do provide pointers about where our 'oral ambitions' set in the infant class might lie. We can certainly think of children we have taught who exhibited half of these competences, even without the conscious introduction of a programme of work such as that envisaged by Brissenden.

If we deem talking about mathematics important, the matter for debate is how much of children's time spent on mathematics in school should be 'talk time'. There is a common assumption that there is more talk time in infant classrooms than in junior ones. Alexander's study (1992b) across the primary sector shows that, in mathematics, children spent only 23 per cent of their time listening and looking, collaborating and talking to the teacher. Perhaps this is adequate, but if we contrast this with 55 per cent of the time writing and 42 per cent reading there does seem to be an imbalance in favour of silent work. We do expect that there would be a shift in these proportions if Alexander had reported on infant classes separately; however, there is food for thought here.

We can speculate on the proportion of all their time in school that children spend really listening. In our experience adults constantly complain that children no longer listen. Rather than focus on the children's 'lack of staying power' we should perhaps be looking at what it is that they are listening to. When children have been asked about what makes a good teacher, there are consistent results over 60 years of studies.[4] Tops is the ability to explain things clearly. This judgement is from children older than infants but it indicates that children have an eye to the efficacy of what they listen to. The important message for teachers of mathematics may be that children's listening skills can be tapped and enhanced if what the teacher says is readily understood. Orton (1987: 125) cites Barnes who argues that teachers are alerted to the correct use of mathematical terms but are less aware of problems in communicating the meaning of concepts and processes. Certainly Shuard and Rothery point to the vocabulary of mathematics as important in the eyes of teachers of the young. As a result of a small research study done by the Language and Reading in Mathematics Group, they report:

> The infant teachers . . . concentrated on oral discussion of practical work, written work not being appropriate to their style of teaching. [They] saw their most important language task in teaching mathematics to be the development of mathematical vocabulary.
>
> (1984: 137)

If we are to enable children to think mathematically and talk about their mathematising, giving them symbols and the vocabulary of mathematics may not be enough. The indications are that teachers who cultivate their own mathematics speaking and listening skills may best promote them in children.

Children reading and writing

A teacher visitor introduced herself to a group of children in a reception class:

TEACHER: I asked your class teacher if you could help me with my maths.
MARGOT: We can help you with the maths but you'll have to help us with the reading!

Four-year-old Margot says it all. Of course she was telling the visitor that the group had not yet learned to read proficiently. Her remark also shows that in her first term in school she had already established that mathematics requires reading but has some aspects that are separate from reading, and that you do not need to 'read' to do those. The reading necessary to mathematics can give us problems, though, even after we have learned to read. Pimm (1981: 149) concurs with this: 'Many children's difficulties with mathematics may be due more to the complexity of wording of written material, rather than the mathematical task being requested.'

In order to help teachers assess the reading skills necessary to use particular texts, 'readability' measures have been devised. Orton lists some of them:

> The Dale-Chall formula is based only on percentage of words not included in a set list of common words and the average number of words in a sentence. The FOG formula is based only on the average number of words in a sentence and the percentage of words with three or more syllables. The Flesch formula is based on the average number of syllables per 100 words and the average number of words per sentence. The Fry procedure is based on the number of syllables and the number of sentences in a 100 word passage. And the 'cloze' procedure is based on the ability of the reader to fill in missing words in text.
>
> (1987: 128)

A consideration of texts we use with infants may lead us to feel that general readability measures are unsuitable. If we look at texts for infant children to work on we may see words such as sum, share, total, match, count, minus, equals, subtract, sets, alike, sort, result, take away, lots of, left, etc. None of these words has many syllables, and many of them are common words, yet the mathematical concepts conveyed by them can be quite complex. Orton (1987) also suggests that measures need to be devised that are specific to parts of the world. A formula devised in the USA may not be useful in Britain. He recommends that teachers make their own judgements about whether a written text is appropriate, on the basis of a range of information. These include 'general attractiveness and appeal', 'style and layout', 'the relationship between text to be read and sections to provide active involvement', 'vocabulary, length of words and length and structure of sentences', 'flow-of-meaning' (1987: 131), and sequencing and pacing . These are important factors to consider when choosing scheme materials.

Managing text may demand more skills on the part of children than we allow when we assess whether they can read the text or not. Let us consider a common pattern of mathematics tasks given to children in class. Initially we give children straightforward practice of a basic concept. Then we ask the children to apply this concept in a number of examples. Finally we give them what we call 'problems'. The thinking behind this three-stage process is that to 'act on' what they know by solving 'problems' means they do not just need reading skill and knowledge of concepts. They may also need to demonstrate some strategies for logical thinking. It may be that this is what Petrova managed to develop in children.[5] The work, undertaken in Russia in the 1950s, may have implications for the teaching of mathematics today. In the experiments young children were able to solve mathematics problems set down in words correctly and without help. This was done by using the following strategies:

— emphasising the importance of every word, no matter how small;
— getting children to read problems aloud;
— deliberately extending the vocabulary of the children (including words for abstract concepts like quantities);
— asking for precise detailed answers to questions relating to the way the problems could be solved.

This research would seem to indicate that children need to achieve reading competence in order to solve mathematical problems, but that talking through the wording and possible ways of solving problems are extremely important too.

It is important that young children should acquire the skills of holding and wielding a pencil, crayon, chalk, felt-tip pen and brush, and that in due course they should be able to write numerals to record their mathematics operations, to write words in mathematics problems, and draw shapes. The problem is that mastery of the skills can be used by teachers as an excuse to limit children's mathematical diet. We do not wait until children can write poetry or stories before we let them listen, learn, play with words, make up rhymes, and solve word puzzles. We may tend to be more restrictive about exposing children to the whole gamut of mathematical experiences. Just as children's oral and practical language repertoire includes all the kinds of language usage (that is stories, rhymes, reports, diaries, true and imaginary, poetry, and so on) before they are competent readers and writers, so too in mathematics, there is no reason why they cannot meet numbers, shapes, patterns, ways of handling number, 'everyday' numbers, problems, puzzles, investigations, and so on before they are competent readers and writers of mathematics.

What is written down in school is widely seen as the most acceptable evidence of learning by a whole range of people, including parents, children and even teachers. The links between knowing, telling and being able to write something down are complex. On the whole we judge teaching on what is said and learning on what is written. As we know this is not wholly reliable and certainly not fair. Even in experiments where children have been asked to demonstrate evidence of what they know by telling, it is still not clear what the relationship is between knowing and being able to tell. Dickson *et al.* report the work of Siegel, who offered mathematics tasks to children:

> In this case the children's ability to *produce* the relevant language lags well behind their ability to attain the concept. The question of whether or not the ability to *understand* develops after or in parallel with attainment of the concept is less clear.
>
> (1984: 333)

We might extend the argument by saying that it can be even more difficult to write about our understanding than to talk about it. This is an important idea when we consider that the predominant way of testing learning seems to be what children can write down. The recent introduction of national tests for children in their infant years has given written evidence of learning validity which may be entirely unfounded. However, despite the knowledge that words, and particularly written words do not encompass all there is in learning, we do still get children to do a lot of writing when they are learning mathematics.

REVIEW

So why does mathematics present difficulties for children? Orton points to the vocabulary, the symbols and the reading that takes place in the classroom.

> Even if the vocabulary is appropriate there might be problems because children do not always interpret statements literally, but sometimes appear to change the meaning into what they think the teacher intended to say. The special symbols of mathematics, as an extension to the language of the mathematics classroom, cause additional problems. Reading mathematics is different from reading literature, or even from reading texts in other subjects.
>
> (1987: 125)

There is a prodigious range of skills required of the teacher, in managing appropriate interactions with children, in encouraging children to master and use mathematics symbols and words, in telling about their mathematics as well as reading and writing down. The underlying message has been about viewing mathematics as open and exploratory, requiring a variety of approaches and creative thinking, rather than a closed and fixed subject best taught by telling and demonstrated as learned by writing.

It is important that as teachers we can review the recording that we ask of children and try to achieve a balance between writing and talking in mathematics. Bird (1992: 167) poses a list of questions for teachers to ask themselves including the following: 'How can I stop myself simply asking children to 'write it down'? How might they be encouraged to feel a need to write or talk?' In addition to the balance of writing and talk there are important considerations in how we get children to record. We teach children ways of setting down computations and layouts for data, but we should also be helping them to understand two important points. The first is, as we have shown earlier in this chapter, that there is rarely a single 'best' way of recording. The second point is that writing down is a way of letting other people know what we have done, and layout can help or hinder that communication. Rather than impose 'rules for writing' on children the question for teachers to ask themselves is, according to Bird

(1992), 'Can any comments about the importance of being careful how thoughts and calculations are recorded come as a result of children actually experiencing the importance themselves?'

NOTES

1 An algorithm is 'a mechanical procedure for solving a problem in a finite number of steps (a mechanical procedure is one that requires no ingenuity)' (Daintith and Nelson 1989: 14).
2 Brissenden says, 'there is a serious imbalance between teacher and pupil talk in mathematics, in favour of the former' (1988: 12). See also Galton *et al.* (1980) who found in the ORACLE study that a 'typical' teacher talked about 80 per cent of the time.
3 Brissenden (1980) provides a detailed analysis of discussion in mathematics.
4 Wragg (1991) cites a study in 1935 when 8,000 Birmingham children placed in order a number of statements about good teachers. They gave top rating to the ability to explain things. In a similar recent study (date not known) Wragg obtained the same result.
5 See, for example, Kilpatrick in Floyd (1981) and Shuard and Rothery (1984) for a discussion of the work of V.D. Petrova.

Part III

Managing mathematics

GENERAL INTRODUCTION

The vocabulary of business management is increasingly being applied to education. Rather than take on that jargon 'wholesale' we can adopt and implement those aspects that serve to illuminate the roles of teacher and learner. Teachers *are* managers. Plans and strategic organisation are as important to them as to a manager in business. However, it would, in our view, be inappropriate to talk of school children as 'clients' or outcomes of teaching and learning as 'products'. Besides, what goes on in schools involves a complex set of processes and variables. Teachers work in a setting where all aspects are subject to constant change. No single moment is like the next, no child is like the next, no teaching or learning episode is an exact replica of any other, and even the content of the curriculum is currently undergoing rapid change and review.

In these circumstances even the best management advice cannot be definitive. We cannot produce a 'manual' that will be applicable to all infant schools and all teachers of infants. What we can do is to raise the major issues. When teachers talk of 'good practice', included in the discussion is effective and purposeful planning associated with organisational structures that support the implementation of plans. In 1978 HMI made clear the importance of these management factors and OFSTED (1993) continues to underline appropriate planning as a major ingredient.

Our own experience as teachers has also convinced us that planning of teaching is one of the keys to the efficient management of learning. It is not a view held by all the teachers we have worked with. This seems to be either because they feel the organic nature of classroom life is lost if outcomes are pre-set, or they feel confident that details of plans are better held in their heads than on paper. Neither reason really stands up to scrutiny. Without objectives time can be wasted in unanticipated directions, plans across the school cannot be made coherent without a contribution from all the teachers, and reliance on our memories in the mêlée of classroom talk and activity is inevitably going to lead to some items being overlooked. The presence of a National Curriculum does not remove the importance of planning. If anything it sharpens it, for the requirements by law are now exacting.

One of our ultimate aims in teaching is that through learning children will acquire knowledge, hone skills, and develop their intellects. Because teachers are engaged in this process they include this aim for themselves too. Thus education brings about change in people, and teaching is about the management of that change. To begin this process we need to establish what is the present state of affairs. Thus, when they are thinking about mathematics, head teachers and their staff need to take cognisance of current practice at both school and class level. Only then can they plan for change. We have highlighted the major issues in planning and implementation for schools in Chapter 6, beginning with a discussion about the major resource in schools, published mathematics schemes. This is then related to a school programme of work, and the effects of the whole school imperatives on teachers and children. In Chapter 7 we discuss the demands on the class teacher as manager, raising questions about resources, teaching approaches, planned learning opportunities and the use of classroom time.

Chapter 6

School plans

INTRODUCTION

Head teachers and their staff are responsible for the offering of a whole curriculum in school. However, as teachers know, they are not accorded ideal conditions to carry this through. For example, they are expected to offer children a broad range of subjects and experiences, as set down in a general school plan, without guidance as to how to make the material manageable. They are urged to 'raise standards' in subjects in which the teachers themselves lack confidence, knowledge and sustained development possibilities. They are each expected, alone, to supply the learning needs of a class of children. There are sometimes more than 30 children in a class, and the teacher has to try to guarantee optimum progress and achievement for all those children.

It is in these conditions that, despite all the difficulties, teachers have, for many years, worked hard and devoted a good deal of time and effort to parts of the mathematics curriculum. School decisions have been made to seek out mathematics resources which will support teachers, fill gaps in what they feel they know about what can be done with children, and 'do' some of the work for the teacher (like the preparation of workbooks, and record sheets). This need for resources has been filled by educational publishers. Mathematics is seen as amenable to a 'whole package' approach. Thus there is a plethora of published materials for which claims are made about their coverage of school mathematics. Teachers must find them extremely useful, for 'bought in' commercial mathematics schemes are in use in most schools (DFE 1992). We have yet to find a school in which there are no published scheme materials at all. We have therefore decided to approach some of the issues for 'whole school mathematics' with the idea that scheme materials form the major mathematics resource. We shall take a close look at the common features of published schemes themselves, and point up some of their strengths and shortcomings. Then we shall examine the whole school issues in the provision of the substance of the curriculum. The final parts of the chapter are about how school plans can affect teachers and children at work in mathematics.

PUBLISHED SCHEMES

Schemes have been with us for many years and some have become well known and popular enough to give their names to mathematics sessions in school. If we describe the typical characteristics of many schemes this will help to highlight some of their advantages and disadvantages.

The characteristics of schemes

Schemes come in parts which 'fit' together 'end on'; for example, one book will follow another on the basis of year or level. There is commonly a teacher's book which has some kind of introduction or statement of purpose, so that teachers have a vision of what constitutes the whole mathematics course. Such handbooks usually contain advice on the children's activities and ideas for extension or practice. Children are presented with tasks in isolation; for example, on worksheets or in work books. It is common to find that there are starter or core tasks and 'add ons' for extending abler children or giving children further opportunities to apply basic ideas. The tasks are often arranged so that children do 'a little bit of this and then a little bit of that'. There may, for example, be two or three pages about addition, followed by some work on three-dimensional shapes. In choosing a mathematics scheme teachers are concerned about the scheme's coverage, the way children's progress is approached and assessed, and the resourcing demands that a scheme might bring.

All modern mathematics schemes offer coverage of number, algebra, shape and space and measures, and most give clear opportunities for developing data handling ideas and the employment of methods for pictorial representation. However, they do differ in the amounts of time and space devoted to each of these, the advocacy of particular methods, skills and techniques, and the order in which topics are arranged. They also differ in respect of the extent to which the core scheme offers coverage and the amount of directly linked 'optional' material that is available. These differences demonstrate the ways in which mathematics is viewed by the authors of the scheme and the way in which it is necessary for the teacher to operate in order to make most effective use of the scheme. In making a decision, therefore, about the adoption of a school-wide scheme, there are implications for teaching approaches and school mathematics curriculum statements.

Schemes as a resource

In reviewing school resources teachers need to make a positive decision about the adoption of scheme materials as *resources for learning* rather than as a kit providing all that is required for teaching and learning. In addition to regarding the scheme books and worksheets as resources to 'choose and use', there are counting aids and so on that may be specified within the scheme, and these of course are then essential. To this basic stock 'found' resources can be collected by individual teachers (there is more in Chapter 7 about this). Additional items requiring capital expenditure have to be decided upon at school level. Computer programs, calculators and books about pattern are items that fit this category.

Advantages and disadvantages of schemes

It can be seen that similar features emerge as both advantages and disadvantages of schemes. They are listed in Table 6.1 and will be discussed in turn.

Table 6.1 Advantages and disadvantages of mathematics schemes

Advantages	Disadvantages
1 Objectives are sometimes clearly stated	1 Sometimes the objectives are unclear
2 Give teachers confidence	2 Do little or nothing to help teachers improve their knowledge of mathematics
3 Highly structured and unequivocal in presentation	3 Tasks presented in linear, hierarchical and cumulative fashion
4 Provide 'ready-made' games and worksheets	4 Games and worksheets are generic
5 Often carry assessment suggestions related to specific items or activities within the scheme	5 Assessment tasks are closed and inflexible
6 Layouts of children's tasks are often consistent	6 Consistency of layout can limit children's confidence, or it can lose appeal
7 Offer a variety of things for children to do	7 Variety of tasks is often within a framework of what is possible using written closed activities

1 Objectives

Even if the objectives are clearly expressed, they have more to do with standard methods and 'facts' than developing mathematical thinking in children. Commonality in objectives can have a positive effect in enabling teachers in a school to have the assurance that they are working on a group enterprise. However, evidence in schemes that objectives are based on clearly articulated aims is absent, as Harling and Roberts indicate:

Despite the stress, by the publishers and authors in their introductions to the schemes and in the promotional literature, on the universal validity of their materials and their apparent belief that they have produced the definitive mathematics scheme, none of the schemes in fact provides evidence properly to substantiate their suggested approach to teaching and learning.

(1988: 57)

2 Confidence

Teachers' lack of confidence in mathematics is well documented.[1] Harling and Roberts (1988) point to press reports criticising mathematics standards and teaching as adding to these feelings. Reynolds discusses a consequence of underconfidence:

Many teachers . . . would never consider 'challenging' the experts who have written the published material. . . . Whilst it is unlikely that a particular text-book (published at a particular time, tested with particular pupils and designed for a particular purpose) will be equally appropriate for all pupils in all schools, that is what some publishers claim. It is what many teachers believe.

(1982: 20)

Though having a teacher's book to hand may help some teachers plan their classroom mathematics, it is an insufficient resource to ensure appropriate teaching and learning for every child, and it does little to enhance the teacher's real expertise. By this we mean a sufficient knowledge of the subject to be able to justify the decisions made in planning and task allocation. This could only be gleaned by further study, which may mean the teacher has to go on a course, but it could be enough to involve the teacher in 'doing' mathematics. We have not seen schemes that say, 'do these tasks before you let the children try them'.

3 Presentation

Though some aspects of schemes may be unavoidable (such as, for example, the 'end on' nature of the books) what turns out is a presentation of tasks in a linear, hierarchical and cumulative fashion. This may have the advantage of giving teachers a view of the direction of the mathematics 'course', and help them if faced with questions about accountability. However, the structure that seems universal in schemes does not reflect how we believe humans learn, nor is it how mathematics should be conceived.

Scheme presentation can also have the effect that children liken school mathematics to a 'race track'. In Desforges and Cockburn's study in infant schools 'The children toiled eagerly on their paper work. They appeared embroiled in a race to get through the scheme as fast as possible or at least to stay in contention with their chosen rivals' (1987: 102).

We know of parents who constantly quiz their children on which page of the scheme book they have reached, and who coach their children at home using the selfsame scheme book as the child uses every day in school. It is like trying to impart English exclusively through a reading scheme. We also know children like Mary and Amelia who weep when they have not done the 'As', 'Bs' and 'Cs' on the set page in the lesson time.

4 Games and worksheets

The problems here seem to be that though these resources may be colourful and appealing, they do need a well articulated rationale to be used to good effect, and they are not geared to the needs of individual children. It is also the case that 'games' are often seen as recreational and, even where an integral part of a scheme, are deemed as being less important than the 'real' work. Games can also be rejected by the children as being 'not real maths' and some, if accustomed to the structure of a scheme, can feel insecure when there is the possibility of more open-ended activity.

5 Assessment

As a resource for teacher assessments, tasks in a scheme are fine, so long as it is clear what exactly is being assessed. Inevitably the tasks will need modification to fit particular children in real classrooms. However, the way scheme work assessment is handled by teachers can give children important messages about what mathematics is. Desforges and Cockburn state in their study that because work done in commercial schemes was 'the only overtly assessed part of the mathematics curriculum', commercial schemes were 'taken to be the whole of what was meant by mathematics' (1987: 102).

6 Layout

A standard, often uniform, layout can give many children a strong sense of security. They know where they are in relation to the scope of the task – finish the page – and they know the 'kit' inside out – when I reach this bit I have to get a card. But a uniform layout can mean children are then underconfident when given any other kind of approach, or it can de-motivate children and begin to look repetitive and boring.

7 Variety of tasks

The authoritative 'right answer' appeal of a textbook approach means that there is a predominance in schemes of tasks that are not open-ended. There is also an over reliance on reading and written work over oral work, which means that reading and writing skills will determine children's chances of making progress in mathematics.

MANAGING MATHEMATICS THROUGH THE SCHOOL

Though the pros and cons of using particular scheme materials can alert us to the need for school plans to supplement what they provide, or offset their shortcomings, there are also some general ideas prevalent in current discussion about the curriculum, which are important in school planning. They are twofold. First, schools should have a written programme of work (including mathematics). Second, the school curriculum (including mathematics) should offer children breadth, balance and depth, and continuity and progression.

Creating a school programme of work

A published 'through school' mathematics scheme does not constitute a school plan or programme of work. It may be that in some schools, implementation of the school plan has come to mean distributing and using the appropriate books from a published scheme. According to Reynolds, 'such action almost amounts to dereliction of duty' (1982: 20). Critical of published schemes, he advises teachers to 'look more widely for guidance and inspiration as to how to make the best use of a school's resources of staff, rooms, equipment and for the special needs of the pupils in that school' (1982: 21). This includes the use of local authority guidelines. The latter may be seen to be rendered redundant where there are national curricula, despite the paucity of advice for teachers in some of the national documentation.

School mathematics plans *must* include processes, as well as content. Using investigative approaches, and getting children to think about and use what they know, in a variety of settings, in order to embark on new learning, should be characteristic of work in the first school. It is regrettable that these approaches, which seem to promote confidence and foster positive feelings about mathematics, are not generally the mainspring of published schemes. Thus school plans, whether or not they envisage the use of scheme materials, need to make explicit the variety of approaches available to staff, and the ways in which such strategies can be carried through within the school. Proudfoot (1992), herself a teacher, says that schemes make mathematics boring. Some of the things lacking in many schemes are made evident by her reasons for using investigations. These include the power they have in reinforcing children's skills in novel ways, helping in identifying difficulties, providing 'starting points' for children's exploration, stopping 'maths just being about right and wrong', making maths fun and emphasising 'children's own methods' (1992: 132).

Breadth, balance and depth

With regard to curriculum breadth in the current debate on primary education, there is much being said about curriculum overload. For example, in the National Curriculum (England and Wales) there is so much work to do in so many subjects, that many teachers feel the content demands are overwhelming. The National Curriculum Council has called for 'reducing the primary curriculum to make it more manageable'.[2] A leader writer in a national newspaper reports that the NCC is saying that 'the curriculum is too prescriptive and unrealistically encyclopaedic. Depth is being sacrificed in the pursuit of breadth'.[3] It is difficult to tell to what extent mathematics work is suffering due to pressures from other subjects. The DFE, reporting on work in schools in the year 1990–1, found:

> no evidence of any marked improvement or decline in general stan-
> dards . . . in Year 1, about three-quarters of the work was satisfactory . . .
> in Year 2. Sometimes the work was too narrow . . . [with] . . . important
> aspects such as . . . estimation and approximation left out.
>
> (1992: 1)

Teachers whom we have talked to have vociferously complained that there is too much work to cover (though not specifically in mathematics). They do voice problems in covering work related to mathematics skills (like those set out in Attainment Target 1 of the National Curriculum for England and Wales), but the problems may relate more to 'how to tackle it' rather than 'how to fit it in'.

There would seem to be two possible responses to the suggestion that there is too much to do in mathematics. They are to reduce the demand, or to explore ways in which the demand can be better managed – both reactively and proactively. Despite the support for the former from policy makers in the UK, we are of the view that this approach is fundamentally flawed. The reduction of demand, in this case, is about teacher workload and not about children's rights to a full and enlightened mathematics curriculum. The issue of teacher workload is not really addressed by a reductionist approach. There is no guarantee that doing less means doing better. Any reduction may turn out to be a paper exercise – teachers having to provide 'hidden' content in order to offer a full mathematics curriculum. The amount of the mathematics iceberg that is hidden is irrelevant only to those who do not have to acknowledge its actual size! We therefore favour what might be termed a management approach. The issue is not to do less but to offer what is necessary effectively, efficiently and completely. We know that there are resource issues that are not all within the ambit of the individual school – but we do believe that force of argument about need for resources can only be enhanced by clear planning.

In addition to breadth and balance in the whole curriculum and in mathematics, there is also a need for depth in mathematics. It is tempting for schools, in addition to providing a scheme, to take just one main initiative – to 'timetable' sufficient mathematics hours. Campbell (1992) looked at the amount of time infant teachers spent on each subject. Of 18 hours' teaching time each week, 18 per cent was spent on mathematics. This amounted to 6.7 hours, for sometimes mathematics was combined with other subjects. Cockcroft recommends between four and five hours a week being designated mathematics time, for 'children may do quite a lot of mathematics outside the time allocated to it' (1982, para 104: 353). The idea has taken hold that the more timetable time is spent on a subject, the more children learn (that is, 'depth' of learning is allowed for). This is the reason why compilers of the National Curriculum (England and Wales) have arrived at percentages of time children should spend on each of the core subjects, mathematics, English and science. Alexander's evidence would refute this idea.

> The large amounts of time allocated to language and mathematics were the least efficiently used, since children spent less of their time working and more of their time distracted in these subjects than in other areas given far less time. This somewhat undermines the conventional allocations of curriculum time in primary classrooms, and indeed the assumption . . . that the quality of curriculum delivery depends directly on the amount of time allocated.
>
> (1992b: 41)

It is what happens to time in class that is within the teacher's control and will be discussed when we look at what teachers actually do, in Chapter 7.

To ensure breadth, balance and depth it is necessary to consider much more than global time and the contents of a given scheme. We need to look at:

- the range of mathematical activities within classes and across years
- the ways in which topics are revisited through the school
- the proportion of time spent on each facet of mathematics [4]

In order to secure depth we need to consider:

- the opportunities to persist with a topic before moving to a new 'page'
- ways in which schemes support depth
- the interface between the phases offered through the school; for

example, if a scheme book is planned for use in class 2, can it also be available to children in class 1 if they need it?

Continuity and progression

In order to evaluate continuity we need to consider:

- the relationship that proposed new learning has with previous experience through the school, across schools and within classes
- the ways in which children are given information enabling them to see the pattern in their own learning
- the links to be forged between items of knowledge under a set of overarching mathematical concepts

Progression is a term which seems to have two connotations. When associated with continuity it is often used to refer to transition between different sectors; for example, between infant and junior departments or schools. It is also used to describe progression within a subject or topic within a subject. In this usage it is linked with formative and diagnostic assessment. In planning the mathematics curriculum the idea of progression must be handled in both respects. School aims need to secure the progress of individual children as well as the progression of groups of children.

> The overall aim must be the creation of a school learning culture which is reflected in every individual classroom. Only then can continuity and progression in pupil learning and experience be adequately achieved.
> (Bennett 1992: 24)

SCHOOL PLANS AND TEACHERS

In making school plans for mathematics the key questions regarding the staff are as follows:

— What is the knowledge and experience of the teachers and if necessary how can they be augmented?
— How can the teachers be deployed?
— How can teachers' efforts be co-ordinated?

We shall deal with each of these in turn.

Knowledge and experience

We are concerned that teachers become knowledgeable about mathematics education. They cannot do that through using only a scheme. In fact the ways scheme materials are presented sometimes make it difficult for teachers actually to become engaged with the mathematics. It is essential that mathematical work in the classroom is not confined by teachers' lack of understanding. Teachers gain some knowledge in their initial teacher education but there is a continuing need for in-service education – and this should be about augmenting teachers' own knowledge rather than about the ways to implement scheme materials. Mathematics education for teachers should be a component in the school in-service plan. Strategies for the sharing of individual experiences with the staff team should be devised and acted out regularly. There is a series of staff development strategies that we can employ.

Teacher development and appraisal

It is extraordinary that teachers who understand so well the worst effects on children of things like 'competition' and 'success' or 'failure' are all too ready to apply these judgements to themselves and colleagues. Staff development is not primarily remediation for 'weak' colleagues. Real staff development is negotiated and has to engage with willing participants. The reasons for teachers taking part vary. They may, for example, want to enhance their career prospects; they may have made a personal decision to try to improve their mathematics; or they may be worried about external inspection of their work.[5] A development programme that builds on 'failure' and the application of narrow remedies in a 'deficiency' context would not motivate children and we do not believe it is satisfactory for teachers either. A variety of opportunities need to be available, and they should include the following:

- work with a colleague in one's own school;
- work with a colleague in another school;
- visits to other schools;
- help from advisory teachers[6] and, where available, teacher educators
- participating in, or organising, school-based in-service days on mathematics where these are linked to development activities and are not seen as 'one off' events;
- attending mathematics education courses;[7]
- engaging in personal mathematical activity (rather akin to reading children's books – both enjoyable and useful);
- carrying out research in one's own classroom, often with the support of a higher education institution.

Formal appraisal systems can also be part of a development programme, for they involve head teachers in whole staff profiling considerations, and each teacher in a structured reflection upon their achievements and aspirations. Wragg sees the professional development of teachers as central to the appraisal process (1987: 67). The outcome of appraisal may be that a teacher plans to do any one or several of the items in the development list above, or some which may specifically extend their teaching repertoire; for example, trying a different form of class organisation or moving from a top infant to a reception class.[8]

Deployment

The decisions made at school level about the organisation of teaching provision are a major determinant of how teachers can organise, plan and manage their responsibilities. It therefore has much to do with the efficacy of curriculum delivery. It has long been the case that teachers have been given a class of 30 or more children for whose school day they are responsible. Apart from during assembly and at play times and lunch time, the children in the class may not see another member of staff. The reasoning behind the model was as follows. Children feel more 'secure' with someone they know well. The teacher 'becomes a trusted figure on whom they can rely' (Choat 1980). It is easier to plan and monitor the progress of individual children if one person does it. It 'provides the teacher with a deeper understanding of the child' (Alexander 1992b: 23). One teacher's weak points are offset by another's strengths, and in moving up the school the children will have a variety of experience.

This static one-teacher-own-class model has now been called into question. If we accept that the current mathematics curriculum demands expertise in mathematics education, it seems to make sense to give children the benefit of some of that expertise if it is available in school. For example, let us imagine that Miss Wilkinson, the teacher of the top infants, has mathematics education in her background that the reception class teacher, Mrs McLeish, and the middle infant class teacher, Mrs Harris, lack. Is it wise to wait until children reach Miss Wilkinson's class (if she is still working at the school) for them to have the benefit of her strength? If we are to put knowledge criteria above those of dubious assumptions about 'security', then it clearly is not. As Alexander suggests:

We shall have to confront the question, unpalatable to many in primary education, of the extent to which the generalist class-teacher system is capable of delivering either the professional expertise or the classroom experiences which are required if children's needs and potentialities are to be identified and addressed. Far from vouchsafing special insights into what children are capable of, as is usually claimed, the class-teacher system may sometimes do the exact opposite.

(1992b: 24)

Co-ordination

The job of co-ordinating mathematics is assigned to a class teacher. The mathematics co-ordinator's role is multi-faceted.[9] The major elements of the role are:

- producing the mathematics curriculum plan and associated statements;
- supporting colleagues;
- choosing and organising resources, including the mathematics scheme;
- translating statutory requirements (monitoring work done and assessment and record keeping);
- helping to identify and remedy children's difficulties;
- contributing to staff development and explaining ideas;
- liaising with colleagues in schools the children go on to;
- exemplifying good practice;
- presenting the school mathematics policy to parents and governors.

Co-ordinators are also expected to be agents of change in the ways mathematics works in the school. They can only be effective if there is acceptance of the following: the need for change, the need to provide institutional support and resourcing of the change, and the need to evaluate the effects of change.

SCHOOL PLANS AND CHILDREN

In making school decisions about mathematics it is appropriate to ask ourselves about our aims regarding the children. What is it that we wish children to know and be able to do? An overview of commentary on the 'state of mathematics teaching and learning', indicates to Desforges and Cockburn that:

> children do not need further doses of basic skills training. Rather they appear to need to acquire a 'feel' for number and other mathematical processes, together with a degree of intellectual autonomy which would enable them to go beyond routine calculations and to solve real-life problems involving mathematical thinking. They need to learn to use their skills with flexibility. They need to learn to think with mathematics rather than merely respond with routines.

(1987: 3)

If this is the case we need to consider whether the kinds of situations in which children are expected to work, and the kinds of tasks given them will lead to the desired outcome.

Though there are schools where teachers team-teach, sharing all their duties to a large group of children, this is the exception to a fairly consistent form of organisation. It is more typical for children to be placed in fixed year group classes. Where intake numbers do not amount to a whole class there are mixed age groups in a class. The important point is that the composition of classes tends to be fixed for every session of every day over the school year, and that class allocation is an administrative decision. A further consequence of this decision is that if there is a through-school scheme it may be that only parts of the scheme become available to children in any one class. Though teachers often ability band children *within* their class, these groupings will perforce be related to the spread present in those 30 or so children, and not the whole population of the school. The supposition that being placed in a group within a class is the best way to enable children to learn the kinds of mathematics that Desforges and Cockburn talk about cannot necessarily be sustained, unless we have examined other possible groupings or arrangements and found them less satisfactory. 'Withdrawal' of children from a whole class group has occurred for few children. Our experience is that it is commonly children with reading difficulties who receive this treatment (in addition to those regarded as having special needs). Withdrawal of children having specific difficulties or exceptional skills in mathematics is perhaps not an option considered in schools, for a super-ordinate goal may be to get all children to read. Waters offers another strategy for meeting children's needs:

> Where consideration is given to the needs of a whole school at the same time, children can be placed in ability groups irrespective of age, and for the period of the activity they work with a teacher to achieve maximum development.
>
> (1979: 70)

Though this may sound a good idea there are two major problems. The first relates to the attitudes of the children themselves and their parents. Five year old April and her parents may be quite happy for her to work alongside 9 year old Dean on similar kinds of work in mathematics. Dean and his parents may not be so happy. To spare Dean feelings of failure may require a shift in school ethos towards what could be called a 'grade' system. The idea would be that children are required to reach a certain standard *regardless of age* before going on in their learning or group assignment within the school. In primary schools where groupings have for many years been deliberately of mixed ability but similar age, this would represent a dramatic change in ideology. Being 'labelled' by teachers as failing is known to affect children's future performance in school and being called brains or swot, or more particularly dunce or dummy by other children can make school life an ordeal. The second problem relates to the feasibility of across class provision of learning opportunities in schools as they are currently staffed. The problem becomes one of providing all the other children with educational opportunity while a class teacher is not teaching a class. In England and Wales schools are now managing their own budgets, and decisions may therefore be made about 'strategic staffing' to allow group withdrawal in mathematics.

REVIEW

We have tried to indicate that though published mathematics schemes feature in much of school mathematics they do have shortcomings. If we take on board the findings of HMI (DES 1989) that there is 'little evidence to suggest that heavy reliance on routine sessions of mathematics based on textbooks and published workcards resulted in the most effective learning' (para 74, p. 24), the implication is that school plans should support teachers in preventing children's diet of mathematics from being so narrow.

Breadth, balance and depth, continuity and progression in the mathematics curriculum demand whole school management strategies which involve head teachers and their staff in a consideration of the following:

— school programmes of work that use published schemes as a resource;
— an acknowledgement that teacher development cannot be supported through published mathematics schemes. Schemes do not enrich teachers;
— co-ordination of teachers' efforts, well orchestrated, should have positive effects for teachers' knowledge of mathematics education and children's access to a sound curriculum;
— class allocation should not limit the ways teachers' expertise is used, nor the ways children's learning needs are met.

NOTES

1 See, for example, Walden and Walkerdine (1982).
2 Reported in the *Times Education Supplement* (22 January 1993).
3 Comment column in the *Guardian* (19 January 1993).
4 HMI (DFE 1992: 1) report that number work was being 'unduly emphasised' in top infant classes.
5 See the work of Ausubel (1968), and Chapter 1 where there is some discussion of his work.
6 In the UK there has been a tradition of seconding teachers to a peripatetic advisory unit with the intention of those advisory teachers working alongside teachers in their classrooms. This has had a good level of success but currently there is a diminution of the role of local education authorities allied to the encouragement of opting out of local control by central government. This means that the opportunities for sharing good practice that advisory teachers could grasp are increasingly no longer available.
7 Over the last few years there has been special funding by central government in the UK for '20-day' courses intended to enhance the subject knowledge of primary mathematics teachers. Evaluation of these courses done by the

National Foundation for Educational Research (NFER) indicate that they have been generally very successful for the participants.
8   See Whitaker (1983) for a list of possible outcomes from an appraisal interview.
9   See Cockcroft (1982) for a list of the duties of a mathematics co-ordinator.

Chapter 7

Mathematics in the classroom

INTRODUCTION

Teachers are themselves the managers of their classrooms and their teaching and it is they who can enable children to be managers of their learning. Thus teacher and children are engaged in a group endeavour. We all recall those classes where it took the children half the year to 'get the hang' of what we as teachers were asking of them. We can also remember the classes which, as a whole, seemed to 'do things aright from day one' and lived up to our expectations of them. Part of the explanation for why some classes 'work' better than others is due to the extent to which they can accommodate the management structures set by the teacher. There is a mutuality here. Both teacher and children are important. Between them lies the substance of their endeavour, in this case mathematics. Both teachers and children have to work within the constraints of the resources available and the 'space' they work in. We shall begin by looking at these constraints, following which we take up the theme for this chapter. The focus then is on what teachers actually do. In relation to mathematics they make and review plans about teaching and learning for a term, a week or individual lessons or tasks. In class they choose how they teach and the kinds of groupings appropriate for children and they monitor time spent and the 'pace' of classroom activity.

CLASSROOM CONSTRAINTS

Resources

Sadly, among all the topics for current debate in primary education, the question of resourcing seems very low on the political agenda. HMI (DFE 1992: xi) report, 'The level of resources in schools is generally adequate and in some respects improving'. Teachers cannot therefore assume that all their resource needs, once identified, will be met. Resource needs depend on the kind of curriculum to be provided and the teacher's strategies for provision. Thus if, for example, school plans are such that all children should have access to calculators all the time this would require special resourcing. If the teacher is going to employ 'investigative' approaches to some parts of mathematics unorthodox resources may be required. However, all teachers have to work within some resource constraints.

> In teaching there is a compromise between what you would like to do and what you can do with the facilities and resources at your disposal. It is important to optimize this compromise by considering the resources needed, the way in which they are managed, and how they are used with the children.
>
> (Goodwin 1987: 123)

What counts as a resource? Actually anything and anyone, or pictures or written details about anything or anyone that can be brought into the classroom are potential resources. We choose those we use according to availability, familiarity, and ease of use. When assembling a resource bank we can include people and things, children and adults, bought in manufactured apparatus or found and home-made items, books, tapes, videos, computers and software and so on. 'People resources' can sometimes be the most potent and include the children, teachers, caretaker and lunch time assistants who are about in school every day. Add to these the 'visitors' such as the mathematics adviser, local shopkeeper and helper parents who come in to play mathematics games, assist with art work and do some cooking, and the human resource list becomes extensive. Items such as pencils, crayons, books and rulers are available in all classrooms and can be set aside as mathematics resources for the time that they are needed. Added to these, most schools seem to stock commercially produced apparatus for counting and construction.

If there is a through school scheme in use, the resource list advised in the teacher's notes attached to it is essential. If you are using a variety of scheme materials, or creating your own 'scheme' you will be able to amass your own mathematics resource collection. We have set down a list of some suggested possibilities for a class teacher's resource bank in a resource book for teachers (Clemson and Clemson 1992: vi). The list includes things like those set down under the workshop idea headed 'identifying resource needs' in Chapter 11. We would consider some of these things to be essential. Many of the resources on the list come free or are inexpensive. However, when evaluating our own resourcing there are two prime constraints. The first is the cost of some resources. The second is the storage space available. This brings us to the next major consideration which has to do with access. No matter how many or few the resources, we do need to be able to get at them! We have argued for resources to be assigned to class teachers or teacher-teams and to be held centrally, depending on expendability, extent of use and expense (Clemson and

Clemson 1989). Spare exercise books and pencils may be held in class-rooms (these are expendable, used daily and inexpensive), story books, counting books and squared paper may be held accessible to a teacher-team (books are not expendable; neither specific books nor squared paper is used daily and books are not cheap). Depending on the financial situation of a school, sets of solid shapes, computers, televisions and videos may have to be assigned to central stock and a signing out record kept. The challenge in resourcing is to regard a wide range of things as potential resources and devise novel ways of using them.

Room to learn

The space we have to teach and learn in can affect the quality of that experience. Many writers discuss the merits of particular classroom layouts and types of storage. No best ways to set out the room or store equipment emerge. Dean (1983) talks of arranging furniture to give 'optimum opportunity for the work to be done'; and 'discriminating use of display' to offer 'encouragement and interest', and to 'stimulate and extend knowledge and thinking'. When teaching infants we have always set out the room so that from at least part of it, all the work spaces could be seen, and that was the location which we as teachers held when not at close quarters with a group of children. It also seemed to make sense to us to devise systems for storage and access that were as useful to the children as to ourselves. The systems relied on precepts like clear labelling, low level storage so that children could reach things, and clear strategies for getting items out and putting them away. If the system has relatively stable rules the children can be encouraged to conform to them, and to learn management skills for themselves in the process.

TEACHERS' PLANS

Unlike young children, whose school life is limited to school hours, teachers have much to do away from children in order to make things happen in the classroom. Their chief responsibility has to do with planning and reviewing plans.

The importance of planning

Year plans must be made in consultation with other staff in the school, to ensure continuity and avoid repetition of material already taught. Termly, weekly and daily plans and the review of how well these have been carried through, are part of a class teacher's job. In order to establish where to begin planning, we need to devise efficient ways of establishing what children already know. We would argue that children spend some time in mathematics rehearsing skills they already have and retracing learning they have already mastered. Not only does this sometimes reduce children's motivation and their interest in and willingness to do a task, but it also wastes time which could perhaps be spent in mastering new concepts. It is therefore important that teachers see assessment as part of their everyday work and constantly monitor what children can do. This is no easy task. A teacher's own daily records are vital. To give pointers to the situation in your own classroom it may be helpful to devise a record sheet which gives a mathematics diary summary for a number of children. If the children in your class are grouped you may choose two from each group. Your record, done in a few minutes each day and over as little as a week or two, may indicate the proportions of time children spend learning the new and demonstrating what they know already. We would argue that action to change these proportions involves the kinds of teaching groupings you adopt and the strategies you favour for teaching.

Having argued strongly that planning is an essential component of teaching and learning, we now offer a series of strategies for planning how we convey the subject matter of mathematics. They are:

— 'basic concepts' which we can regard as the prerogative of every child and then 'add-ons' for children who have time to cover them;
— themes within mathematics;
— mathematics and other parts of the curriculum.

We shall spell out each of these in turn.

Plan for the 'basics' plus 'add-ons'

We have set out what we see as a curriculum in mathematics for young children in Chapter 4. Our plans must include, first, what we see or what is nationally prescribed as essential, and then incorporate add-ons for children who have mastered what is 'basic'. This begs the question of what can be conceived as 'basics' for the children we teach. We would suggest that the 'basics' are universal minimums and would not go along with teachers who made exclusions from the basic list for any child. This does appear to be the practice in some schools. For example, Tizard *et al.* discovered in their project schools that there were:

> marked differences between teachers in the items taught ... some reception teachers in the project schools believed that certain 3R curriculum items were too difficult for their children, whereas other teachers did not. But there was no difference between the schools in the range of ability of the children entering these classes. These results suggest that the role of teacher expectations in curriculum design may be an important one. ... If there is a concern to give equal opportunities to all

children ... [we need] to ensure that [teachers'] expectations are sufficiently high to prevent children being held back unnecessarily.

(1988: 41)

Note that these findings related not to individual children but to whole classes. Tizard and her colleagues asked teachers why they had not introduced some items. 'Whilst some teachers answered that these items were too difficult for children of this age, others said they were too difficult for the children in this school' (Tizard *et al.* 1988: 173).

Plans for basics plus add-ons can be relatively long term, for they are based on the content, and should not be dependent on the specific children who happen to be in our present class or in classes we have had recently. They are the kind of plan underlying the layouts of tasks within schemes, and thus point up one of the problems in schemes; namely they cannot 'fit' individual children, only 'pieces of knowledge'. This kind of plan is suitable for mission statements, external scrutiny and coherent plans for whole schools.

Plans for mathematics themes

In identifying mathematics 'themes' we are concerned with a set of linked activities within mathematics which have a clear rationale for the linkages made. We believe that a thematic approach is one that should be part of the mathematics programme and within the repertoire of all teachers. In offering children themes we are extending opportunities which allow for a range of learning styles within our mathematics provision – we are not relying on the single, hierarchical approach which scheme books are likely to offer.

One way of developing themes is to begin with the mathematics content that you wish to offer and then review all the written resources available to you to serve that content. Draw nets to connect the elements that you wish to emphasise and link nets with theme titles. Then plan each theme for a period of a week or so of mathematics and put it into action with the whole class or part of the class. A sample list of themes[1] may go as follows:

— all about ten – counting to ten, numerals to ten, number bonds to ten, sets, tallies, block graphs;
— networks and pathways – journeys to school, characteristics of 3-D shapes, direction, treasure maps, mazes and maze games;
— circles – angles, movement and parts of a circle, shapes incorporating circles like cylinders and cones, circularity in timekeeping and telling;
— plane shapes – plane faces – all about 2-D shapes, cubes, cuboids, prisms, pyramids;
— the right place – place value and location as in map grids;
— balance – weighing, sides of a computation, symmetry.

Nets for additional themes have been drawn in Chapter 4.

Plans for mathematics and other subjects

In our view, if teachers 'do' mathematics in sharply defined sessions predominantly using scheme books, children may come to believe that mathematics is separate from other parts of the school day and from everyday life. To give children a sense of the ubiquitousness of mathematics, and therefore of its range, it may be helpful to deliberately seek out ways of working at mathematics and other subjects together, and to seize mathematical opportunities whenever and wherever they arise in the school day.

Mathematics and English

Ideas about talking about mathematics were raised in Chapter 5. Mathematics talk can satisfy our goals regarding children's speaking and listening skills in English. In addition, other work which many people would label as part of 'English' makes an important contribution to mathematics. This includes stories, rhymes, songs and jokes, the use of information books and writing.

Stories provide children with opportunities for ordering events or ideas (that is sequencing and ordinal number), counting (in stories where an item or person is added to each page) and vocabulary (for example, the relative sizes of Jack and the giant, or the number of wishes). Stories can lead to the exploration of problems of a 'what if' kind and involve deductive thinking. For example, what would have happened if the first two pigs had joined the third in building one big house? Books themselves provide a resource for shape and size comparisons and measurement, discussion of page numbering and odds and evens, and chances to stack, pack and display. Story books can provide the stimulus for puppet plays and children's theatre, where the children can, for example, show their understanding of position words (He's behind you!) and employ counting and sequencing; they could, for example, have a number of puppets running after the gingerbread man and so on.

Rhymes, songs and jokes present children with ideas about order of lines and verses (sequencing and pattern), counting (in rhymes like 'One, two, buckle my shoe') and attributes (such as size and colour of items in the song). Jokes and rhymes give children opportunities to make predictions and play with what is unlikely through to what is impossible. Rhymes, songs and jokes all present ideas for use in drama, where some of the mathematical ideas then become concrete.

Information books are, of course, a source of data to use in mathematical ways. For example, the children could find out the size of their favourite dinosaur and then trace around its shape on the playing field, and compare this with their own size. A wealth of number and shape 'facts' can be made available to children for their mathematics, and these 'facts' can reflect the children's own interests. In writing about their work in mathematics the children can begin to acquire the skills of reporting. With regard to writing Killworth *et al.* note of 3–5 year olds:

> Placing number apparatus on the writing table can prompt children to include maths in their writing. . . . Creating a hairdressers as part of a topic . . . led to some fascinating mathematical writing. Children were able to give their clients appointments in a large appointment book. . . . When the hair was washed, cut, curled and dried, clients were given a bill.
>
> (1992: 61–2)

Mathematics and science and technology

In science and technology the children use mathematical ideas all the time. For example:

- Measures – using non-standard and standard units and a variety of measuring tools having different degrees of accuracy (shadow length can be measured using hands, feet, string rulers and tapes; a study of solubility requires jugs and mugs and calibrated containers; work on the best size of bag for a fruit shop might involve masses and balances; to find the quickest route to the school hall may require timers and clocks).
- Handling data – recording results in words and pictures (frequency charts and tallies, block graphs).
- Constructions and control – building a cart or crane (shape, and movement including rotation)
  – setting an obstacle course for a computer robot (nets, pathways, location, rotation).

Mathematics, history and geography and RE

Mathematical ideas about time and place are the nub of much work in history, geography and RE. Here are some examples of such work:

- Timelines – recording events from past to present (calendars, dates).
- Design in the past – patterns made in ancient and recent times (symmetry, foundations for tessellation, translation, rotation, reflection).
- Picture maps – trails, and knowledge of addresses (shape, direction, location, compass points).
- Weather records – daily chart (handling data)
  – sunshine and rainfall (measures)
  – inventing symbols (concept of a symbol).

Mathematics and art and music

The connections that can be made between mathematical ideas and work in art and music are extensive. We ourselves have taught classes of children where we have increased the number and variety of art opportunities. We found that their achievements in parts of mathematics were enhanced when compared with a parallel class which did not do much art. We can therefore help children to be more confident in mathematics through art. Examples of activities include:

- Collecting and sorting objects – making a collage, or display (handling data)
  – sorting colours or textures (attribute recognition).
- Shape – observational drawing (recognising, matching and replicating shape).
- Pattern – making a mosaic (symmetry, foundations of tessellation)
  – clapping out a rhythm (sequencing and repetition).
- Signs and symbols – a first look at sheet music (symbol systems).

Mathematics and PE

In moving and controlling their bodies, both alone and in work with a partner, young children can demonstrate their perceptions of their body shape, the space it occupies and the space in which it is set. This is important, not only to engender confident mien in the children but also to help them understand about shape and movement. Here are some of the contributions this can make to mathematics:

- Movement and pattern – creating and replicating movements (sequencing, translation, reflection, rotation)
  – giving and responding to instructions about moving in different directions.

Mathematics in cross-curricular topics

Despite the tightening hold of subject specialists on the design of curricula, some teachers of infants are still choosing to plan the children's work around topics, so that the subjects are integrated one with another. In order to rigorously pursue appropriate learning for every child these teachers have to invest much time in creative planning. However, the pay off in terms of enlivened sessions and high motivation is, we believe, worth the effort. Rather than set out examples of the kind of topic that has been relatively common for some while, like 'Ourselves' or 'Pets', we have chosen topics which we hope will be seen as novel. We feel that teachers need stimulus to their teaching as much as children do to their learning.

The intention is to show that topic choice can be as inventive as topic content. We have therefore drawn up nets for topics entitled 'Wrap it up' and 'Books' (see Figures 7.1 and 7.2).

Checklist for action

Here are the main indicators for action drawn from this part of the chapter:

— Review the actual content of the whole mathematics curriculum for your class and school (or the infant department if the school is primary).
— Decide on a strategy or strategies to enable coverage; these will include regular assessment, 'the basics', mathematics themes and mathematics through the curriculum.
— Examine what support is necessary to carry through the planned strategies, including personnel; for example, ancillary or volunteer parent help and appropriate resources and time.
— Put into action.

CLASSROOM ORGANISATION

Teaching styles, grouping the children and time are the three most important management issues.

Teaching styles

Teaching styles, labelled traditional and progressive, have become the totems of protagonists in the 'back to basics' versus 'progressive approaches' debate. Informality in classrooms and its projected outcomes is currently viewed by some as the root cause of 'poor standards'. Bennett's work (1976) was extremely influential in fuelling the 'back to basics' cause. It seemed to indicate that for children in junior schools, formal teaching made for better pupil progress. However, as Boydell (1978) reminds us, the final sample was small, the formal teachers were more experienced, the children's home backgrounds were not explored and the children's familiarity with the styles offered was not established. Added to this the assessment of progress was through pencil and paper tests, which may just by its presentation favour the formally taught. Boydell also points out that 'Large areas of children's learning were left totally unexplored, for instance high-level cognitive concepts' (1978: 63). One of the outcomes of Galton et al.'s work in the Oracle study (1980) was a typology of teacher styles. These are useful to us in that they present us with summary descriptions of teachers against which we can match our own strategies. In brief the teacher styles were:

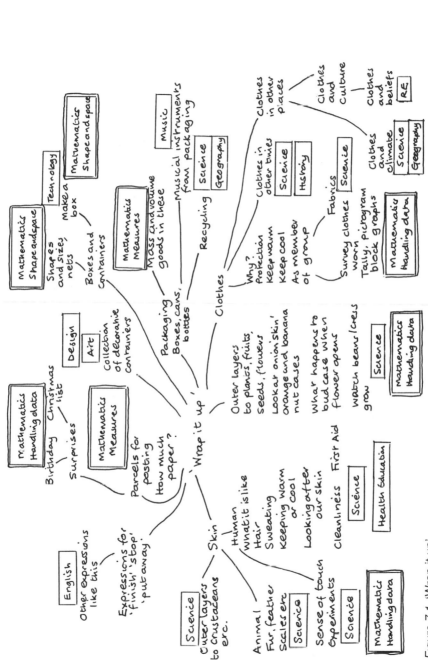

Figure 7.1 'Wrap it up'

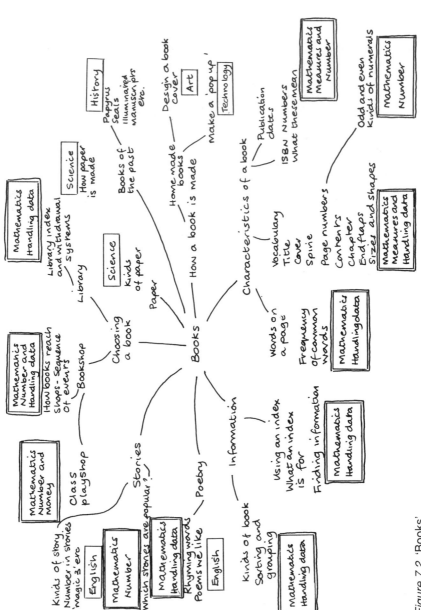

Figure 7.2 'Books'

- Individual monitors – set work individually, monitor such work, high rate of interaction with individual children.
- Class enquirers – used class teaching and questioning and feedback; learning teacher managed.
- Group instructors – children grouped and teacher delivers facts and open questions, less individual attention.
- Style changers – mix of three styles above; infrequent changers changed style gradually over a year, rotating changers worked groups of children moving through a series of activities and habitual changers changed style from individual to class when necessary.

This picture of teachers at work does not match neatly with the idea that they are formal *or* informal. Rather, Galton *et al* (1980) maintain: 'each style can claim to offer advantages and disadvantages to different pupils ... the evidence ... suggests that no one style enjoys an over-all advantage.' However, as Galton and Simon report in *Progress and Performance in the Primary Classroom* (1980: 75), when they gave pupils basic skill tests they found that in mathematics' the *class enquirers* achieved greater gains' for all pupils.

Despite the recent gathering momentum of arguments for an apparent return to more formal teaching, it is widely thought that teachers, particularly in infant classrooms, have continued to adopt and adhere with enthusiasm to informal teaching styles compatible with child centred approaches. This is actually not what has happened. As Alexander *et al.* (1992) point out:

> The ideas and practices connoted by words like 'progressive' and 'informal' had a profound impact in certain schools and LEAs. Elsewhere they were either ignored, or – more damagingly in our view – adopted as so much rhetoric to sustain practice which in visual terms might look attractive and busy but which lacked any serious educational rationale.
>
> (para 20, p.5)

This implies an appearance of informality without the implementation of all the implications. It is regrettable that it appears that the 'progressive approaches' endorsed by the Plowden Report are actually being condemned without trial. It is hard to see whether informal methods have impinged on children's school experience of infant mathematics. We suspect from our own anecdotal evidence that teachers have never let children 'explore' and 'discover' number. They may, however, have viewed shape and 'applied' areas like shopping and time as amenable to 'discovery'. It may be that these are just the areas where children may have received less guidance, less pacing and less challenge. Children playing with water, sand or a classroom shop do not learn mathematics unless there is strategic guidance from the teacher.

The way to use the current debate to good effect is to reflect on and scrutinise the methods in use and to adopt a more eclectic and pragmatic take up of method according to specific objectives. 'A teaching method is "effective" only in relation to a clear view of the educational outcomes to which one's teaching is directed'. (Alexander 1992a). HMI say that in mathematics 'pupils achieved most where teachers used a variety of approaches and achieved a sensible balance within that variety' (DES 1992: 1).

Cockcroft offers a list of the kinds of approaches which should occur within mathematics teaching. They are:

— exposition by the teacher;
— discussion between teacher and pupils and between pupils themselves;
— appropriate practical work;
— consolidation and practice of fundamental skills and routines;
— problem solving, including the application of mathematics to everyday situations;
— investigational work.

(1982: 71)

Cockcroft goes on to say that this list contains nothing new and that in fact all the items had already appeared in papers and reports over many years. He does feel that, at the time of reporting, there were still many classrooms in which even a majority of these approaches were not employed. Predating Cockcroft a little, but making a similar point on the basis of a review of almost a century of writings about classroom mathematics, McIntosh (1977: 95) says that a list setting down the things that should be done to improve primary mathematics includes the following:

1 – Don't start formal work too early.
2 – Use materials and start from practical activities.
3 – Give children problems and freedom initially to find their own methods of solution.
4 – Children must have particular examples from which to generalise.
5 – Go for relevance and the involvement of the child.
6 – Go for reasons and understanding of processes. Never give mechanical rules.
7 – Emphasise and encourage discussion by children.
8 – Follow understanding with practice and applications.

The lists provided by either Cockcroft or McIntosh could form the backbone of a plan for a self-evaluation process in mathematics or indeed an in school in-service education programme.

Organising groups and groupings

Whole class

Whole class teaching is receiving much support from current debate in the UK. This is despite important weaknesses. In whole class teaching there 'is a tendency for the teaching to be pitched too much towards the middle of the ability range, and thus to risk losing the less able and boring the brightest' (Alexander *et al.* 1992). The 'three wise men'[2] go on to say:

> Despite these potential weaknesses whole class teaching is an essential teaching skill, which all primary school teachers should be able to deploy as appropriate. Provided that the teacher has a firm grasp of the subject matter to be taught and the skills to involve the class, pupils' thinking can be advanced very effectively.
>
> (para 92, p.24)

Class teaching is not the predominant method used by many infant teachers when teaching mathematics. They are reluctant to lump together children who may be seen to be demonstrating a difference of two years in terms of performance. Many such teachers do use a whole class setting to introduce sessions, and to draw together the children and the main points of a session at the end.

Criteria for grouping within a class

There has developed in infant classrooms the organisational practice of placing children in groups for their work assignation. These groups are based on a number of criteria which include age, interest, friendship and mixed or similar ability. Teachers often seem to find that 'setting' children according to ability provides work groups which can tackle the same task, either independent of one another or collaboratively. Grouping according to language skill, and reading ability in particular, seems one of the common ways of grouping. This may not prove advantageous to children's progress in mathematics. Reading skills are necessary to use mathematics scheme materials, workbooks and work cards. But there is not necessarily an exact match of ability or progress in mathematics and language for every child at every point in their infant school career.

From the teacher's point of view organising in groups seems to have other purposes. Teachers may want to maximise the use of scarce resources. Only some of the children can use the shape box, if there is only one box of shapes! Also teachers do not have the time to tell every individual child what they would like them to achieve in each session so they tag children by grouping. If, for example, the teacher says 'Squirrel group do their maths busy books this morning' she is assigning individual tasks to a number of children at once. It can also serve as an 'assembling' instruction. If she says, 'Purple group work with me', that may well mean we are going to be engaged on a collaborative effort, or I am going to give you special and separate instruction. Either way it is a signal for the children to physically come together.

Grouping and children

Our reasons for placing a child in a group need to be clear to both teacher and child. From the child's point of view it may be that we hope the chief reason for being in a group can be seen to be one of the following:

— work can be done collaboratively;
— help can be sought from group members as they are doing the same task;
— there is a possibility of learning by looking at what other children in the group are doing.

When we reflect on what really happens in groups, it is the case that children are often engaged on individual tasks. Galton and Simon for example say, 'although seated in groups, we found that, overwhelmingly, the pupils are engaged in individual work; that is the work or tasks set to pupils is largely *individualized*' (1980: 29). As Bennett points out, 'pupils work *in* groups, but not *as* groups' (1992: 18). In mathematics we believe that this is to do with the common pattern of scheme and worksheet use. This is often a matter of an individual child working through a practical task with the scheme page as a stimulus, and doing recording like colouring or completing a written exercise on a worksheet. Whilst it often happens that children sitting together are working on the same task the emphasis is on individual achievement. To foster genuine group work, rather than using groupings as a device for matching individual tasks to children and to enable appropriate seating, we need to widen the repertoire of tasks given to the children. Open-ended challenges in which there is the possibility of alternative solutions offer most chance for group interaction to take place. However, if such work is outside the normal experience of the children then it is likely that dominant individuals will 'take over'.

Individual

Work has to be assigned to individual children where they require a programme different from other children in the class. Though we have all at some time used individual assignments as a strategic measure, as a 'holding activity' when we wish a child to 'move on' in their learning when other children in the class do so, the most justified use of individual tasks is for those children whose progress in mathematics is markedly different from their classmates. This includes those who find mathematics difficult and those who excel.

If we as teachers choose to try to extend the idea of individualised programmes for each of the children in a class, this can present us with management problems. As Galton *et al.* found, teachers who operated as though each child had an individualised programme of work were under pressure. Talk with children was brief: 'prolonged interaction with a pupil is usually prevented by the pressure that results from the demands of other pupils' (1980: 122). Much of the teacher's time is spent monitoring rather than offering challenge and extension to children. How teacher and children spend their class time is another crucial management issue, and the one to which we turn next.

Time for mathematics

What has to be given emphasis in our focusing on timing in mathematics is that the children are enabled to spend the maximum possible time on a task. Though we cannot literally 'save time' we can try to avoid children's exposure during mathematics time to anything that is not connected with the learning of mathematics. Galton *et al.* talk about time on tasks. Though their data are not specifically about mathematics, it is interesting to note that in the junior schools they looked at, children spent only 58.1 per cent of their time actually on tasks. Further time was spent in doing routine activities like 'preparations for task work, discussions about materials . . . waiting for teacher to check over or mark . . . work' (1980: 63). Bennett (1978) draws a distinction between 'curriculum activity' time and 'active' learning time. By these terms are meant the time allocations given to curriculum areas, in this case mathematics, and the time that children spend actually doing mathematics. Studies by Mortimore *et al.* (1988) and Rutter *et al.* (1979) in relation to junior and secondary schools respectively, indicate a positive correlation between achievement and purposeful activity focused on the subject matter in hand – for both teacher and child. There is every reason to believe that active time on tasks enhances achievement for young children.

There is much management assistance that teachers can give to children to avoid wasting time. If we picture a child setting about a mathematics task we need to predict how the session will go. It may be something like this:

— Listen to instructions about task allocation
— Find a place to sit
— Get pencil and book
— Get resources for task

— Listen to what to do, or read what to do
— Try task
— Record findings if necessary
— Put away resources and pencil
— Give book to teacher or put on the teacher's desk

The order of these activities may vary greatly from one assignment to another and one class to another but the basic elements will probably be the same. Following this example sequence the possibilities of time loss include:

— Did not listen, has to ask again what to do
— Cannot sit in usual place or with friend, argument starts
— Book not in tray, not enough sharp pencils
— Enough resources unavailable or broken
— Does not listen, has problems with text
— Unsuccessful at first attempt, has to wait for teacher help
— Does not know how to set out findings, needs teacher help
— Spends time 'playing' with instead of putting away resources
— Does not know where to put book and has to ask teacher

With all these points of distraction it is a wonder children manage any task. There are strategies that can be adopted which would help to reduce the chance of any of the above happening. Some are directly dependent on the teacher. It is for the teacher to attempt to ensure that everyone has listened to and understood instructions, and to monitor the condition and availability of resources for the session. If children have problems with the text or presentation of a task or do not know how to set down their answers the teacher can reflect on whether the task is well 'matched' to the child. All the other sources of time loss relate to generic management skills which can be taught to the children. Where to sit, what to do if you have tried a piece of work and cannot do it, delay in putting away and where to put finished work are all items for a 'child management skills' agenda.

> The study skills that serve children throughout their lives can be begun in the reception class. A child who can decide what they need to do a piece of work, can go and get those resources, use them properly, and then put them away correctly and in good condition at the end of the task, is already a 'student'.

> (Clemson and Clemson 1989: 74)

If resources are ready to hand, accessible to children, appropriately labelled and if children have been shown they are there and how to get them out, they should, with practice, be able to resource themselves. This view is supported by Dean (1983). As Desforges and Cockburn suggest:

> One thing is certain and that is that any deficiencies in the availability or accessibility of materials and any uncertainty as to their relevance or use

is bound to have a damaging effect on the quality of the children's mathematical experience.

(1987: 47)

Teachers can also set up a series of strategies for children to use in lesson time when they cannot get on. A list of such strategies might include some of the following:

— Record what you have done as far as you can
— Leave the task and go on to the next until teacher comes
— Leave the task and go and do another activity (planned by teacher)
— Go and watch someone else who is getting on with the task

If some of the children are not yet readers a picture flowchart like that shown in Figure 7.3 can be made to indicate to them the order of trying these strategies.

Teachers are empowered to create and control the timing in each lesson. This kind of management includes what Pollard and Tann call 'pacing'.

It involves making appropriate judgements about the timing and phasing of the various activities and parts of a session and then taking suitable actions. For instance, the activities have to be introduced: this is often an initial 'motivational phase' where the children's interest is stimulated. . . . Sessions then often enter an 'incubation and development phase' in which children think about the activities, explore ideas and then tackle tasks. From time to time there may be a need for a 'restructuring phase', where objectives and procedures may need to be clarified further. Finally there may be a 'review phase' for reinforcing good effort or for reflecting on overall progress.

(1987: 123)

This is all very well, but we do need to take account of the fact that children who may demonstrate 'similar levels of attainment work at very different speeds' (Desforges and Cockburn 1987) and the teacher's pacing needs to be flexible enough to take account of that.

It may also be that the presence of routines in sessions, which children are induced to conform to, may actually reduce the children's opportunities for demonstrating their own methods, in short for being creative in their mathematics. Desforges and Cockburn tell us about 7-year-old Neil who could do sums in his head but conformed to the procedure the teacher had given him. The ritual of the following:

Introduction to the work, key points or procedures . . . identified . . . pupil–teacher interaction in which key points were exercised, a summary by the teacher of the procedure, a written exercise for the children and finally an assessment of the children's work.

(1987: 58)

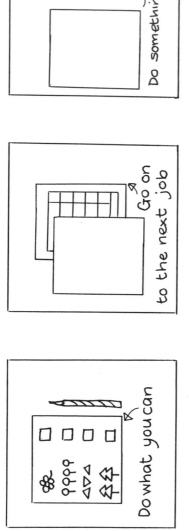

Do what you can

Go on to the next job

Do something else

Watch someone else

Put these pictures on card.
Display those you wish the children to use.

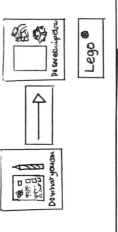

Mathematics   Thursday

Do what you can

Lego ®

Example

Figure 7.3 A picture flowchart

may be training children to follow the teacher's methods and supply 'right' answers in the accepted fashion. This is not enabling children to handle information in novel ways, but more like a rote task.

It is also important to give children time to 'finish'.

> Forms of organisation which require children and their teacher to change their activity after a set period of time inhibit sustained work in mathematics. This is particularly true if the child has been working constructively with material or apparatus and needs an extension of time to complete his task before the equipment is packed away or used again for something else. . . . If it is decided to impose timetabling restrictions these should be interpreted flexibly, bearing in mind the needs of the individual child. Over-fragmentation of the child's day should be avoided.
>
> (DES 1979: 8)

REVIEW

We have tried to identify those elements of management of mathematics teaching that we see as central to the provision of sound and purposeful learning opportunities. Essentially, these elements are concerned with resources, planning, teaching approaches, children's groupings and the use of time.

To be successful in providing children with learning opportunities that will not just get them on to the next phase of a published scheme, teachers need to consider the following:

— the ways in which the resources can be more extensively and creatively used;
— the creation of work space which supports rather than impedes mathematical activity;
— the creation of plans which start where children are and allows a mix of activities which assures children that mathematics is not just 'sums' or 'schemes';
— the adoption of teaching strategies and groupings of children that support the specific kind of work to be undertaken and flexibility to change these when the work demands;
— the need to see that mathematics time is spent on task and that each session requires pacing but not routinisation.

NOTES

1 Ideas for themes and linkages can often be found in the journals of the Association of Teachers of Mathematics and the Mathematical Association.
2 Alexander, Rose and Woodhead who produced a discussion paper for the Department of Education and Science (1992) were dubbed 'the three wise men'.

Part IV

Mathematics in action

GENERAL INTRODUCTION

Children's responses to mathematical situations and opportunities must lead us to question the validity of the tasks that we are setting and to consider ways in which we might gain greater sensitivity and insight into intellectual processes and challenges.

When we talk to and work with children we are constantly struck by the ways in which children repeatedly remind us that they are capable of more than we thought and that it is adults, not children, who have hang-ups about ages and stages, learning steps or 'milestones'. For children experience is continuous, not contrived. They are in life, not part of an experiment. While the skilled teacher needs to be aware of the setting of the learning, if teachers took more account of the flow of experience than the number of sessions in a day or week; there might be more opportunities for children to follow through thinking, implement good ideas, feel satisfied with what they have done and feel more independent as learners. The idea that school life is a continuous experience can also fuel teachers' thinking about how children view what they do in a session. It does not have to look like 'maths' to be mathematical and all kinds of ideas can be brought to bear on the work being done. This is not to say that teachers should withdraw and let children's experience flow on unaided. Judicious intervention furthers the thinking of the children rather than impedes it.

There are those who are all too ready to blame teachers for not listening, using inappropriate language, and giving unsuitable tasks to children. But the reality of classroom life is such that there will always be 'mistakes' and 'mismatches'. A glance at the chapter that follows should convince even the most ardent advocate of subject specialism that teaching mathematics to young children is not easy and its success depends on teachers' willingness continuously to reflect upon their experiences. To suggest that all we need is a knowledge of the subject is to profess no understanding of what is involved.

It is unlikely . . . children [will] become mathematically educated, even if the mathematician is their teacher, for concept attainment is stressed at the expense of concept development and the pupil is passively guided through the logical structure of the subject rather than to the logical structuring of his/her own understanding.

(Blenkin and Kelly 1987: 190)

Chapter 8

Classroom episodes

INTRODUCTION

The purpose of this chapter is to try to convey the importance of really valuing what children do and say, and of listening to and reading what goes on in classroom interactions. We offer some classroom episodes, many in transcript form, in order to encourage the reader to consider and interpret interaction in their own classrooms. We would hope that the power of some of the interactions will lead to the use of tape recording, occasionally, as a means of reflection on what children are really doing in their mathematics work.

There have been two main sources for the contributions that follow. In addition to parts of teaching sessions there are comments made by teachers, advisory teachers and others with a concern for mathematics education. The teaching episodes were obtained through working with groups of children in a range of schools. Where it was possible to tape record discussion with the children, extracts from the conversations are included. Where this was not possible a description of the activity and interaction is given. The teacher comments which appear, generally, at the beginning of each sub-section, are augmented where appropriate by some additional examples from recent research.

We have chosen a number of headings under which to place the episodes and comments. They are these:

— Group work
— Matching tasks to children
— Teacher expectations
— Resourcing activities
— Teacher listens
— Words, signs and mathematics
— Stimuli for mathematics

These headings reflect our own interpretations of the work done with different groups of children. However, it would be perfectly possible and legitimate for these episodes to be interpreted differently and placed under other headings in this list or under new headings. In considering classroom interactions we need to be clear about the subjective nature of our interpretations, whilst appreciating that this does not invalidate the use of recordings and transcripts. At the end of each episode we have set down some of the points which arose in our reflection on the interchanges with children. Again they are merely intended to give some indication of our thoughts, and our hope is that they will provoke further thinking and give support to the strategy of using tape recordings when attempting evaluation. Three other points need to be made: we did not know the children and therefore had to consider the building of relationships in ways that would be different from those of the class teacher; in all cases the class teachers were consulted about and chose the kind of work to be done; and finally, in no sense should the episodes be seen to be exemplary – 'good practice' is far too complex for us to suggest that we could evidence such during these 'special' and brief contacts with children.

GROUP WORK

> It might be anticipated that getting . . . young children to share ideas and learn from each other could create certain problems. . . . The teacher's task is not only to keep discussion to the matter in hand but to sustain progress in learning and help children to render spontaneous contributions meaningful.
>
> (Desforges and Cockburn 1987: 71)

Some top infants were shown some dotty paper (dotty squares). The children were asked if they had seen it before.

RACHEL: It's got spots all over. It's got chicken pox.
KEITH: (looking at the shape of the whole array across the page) It's like a rectangle.

The teacher shows some offset dots (dotty triangles)

TEACHER: What about this one?
RACHEL: It's just the same. Oh no, the spots are in triangles.

Some shapes are drawn on the dotty paper.

KEITH: That's an upside down triangle.
TEACHER: Why do you say it's upside down?
KEITH: Because it's not a right way triangle.
TEACHER: Tell me about a right way triangle. Show me this one as a right way triangle.

These children are very focused, with all talk relating to the task. However, all dialogue is like a series of one to ones with the teacher and they seemed to be unused to operating as a group. Two of the four children present did not speak at all in this interchange. When asked to help one another one child leapt in and did the whole job. They did not use group discussion and when given something to do the children stopped talking. Even if they were playing a game which involved everyone in having a turn, they stayed quiet until their turn, said little and the game continued. We feel that unless there is an 'oral culture' where speaking and listening are valued just as much as doing and writing, the children will find it difficult to respond to a visitor who expects them to talk to each other.

Group work and mathematics

Group work allows an exchange of ideas and is part of the educative process. It is common for children to work individually in mathematics, rather than *as* a group. Children (possibly through the influence of their teachers) sometimes seem to come to view mathematics as 'work that is done by yourself'. So that children are allowed the opportunity to share ideas in mathematics, group work in mathematics requires special encouragement and support. There is, for teachers, a tension between the provision of opportunities for individual progression and collaborative activity, which needs consideration in the planning of classroom sessions.

MATCHING TASKS TO CHILDREN

> 'Some teachers misunderstand how children learn. For example, teaching about castles – children are actually drawing a picture of a castle. Osmosis doesn't work.'
> 'Older children with learning problems in mathematics are being given the same diet even though it failed when they were five.'
> 'Children find time difficult. Telling time really ought to be taught at home.'

A mixed collection of 'two-dimensional' shapes, including squares, rectangles, irregular quadrilaterals, triangles, circles, pentagons and hexagons were placed before some top infant children. They each took a shape from the set and described it, looking at corners, sides and faces.

MAX:	It's a square. It's got four sides. It's got four corners. It's flat.
TEACHER:	Can you tell me something else about the sides?
MAX:	It's got straight sides. It's a 2-D shape.
TEACHER:	What does the 'D' mean?
MAX:	Dimensional.

With another group a game was played involving matching a plane shape with its name and statements about sides and corners. Then the children were shown four triangles which fitted together to make a square. The teacher gave the children two of the triangles.

TEACHER: What shapes can you make?
NADINE: (pushing one triangle forward) That's a triangle.
TEACHER: Yes, but can you put the shapes together to make a shape?
NADINE: Two triangles make one enormous one.
TEACHER: Can you make a shape with four sides?
NADINE: (putting triangle diagonals together) It's a square.

The children went on to make shapes from three and four triangles.

A number of gift-wrapped boxes were set out on the table in front of some 6 and 7 year olds and each child in turn chose one and described it. The collection comprised a cube, cuboids, a cylinder, a pyramid, a cone, and a triangular prism.

TEACHER: I'm going to let you choose one of these shapes each and tell us about it.
AMANDA: Mine's a cone. It's got one face. It's curved around the side and it's got a point.
TEACHER: What is a face?
MORRIS: It's flat.
TEACHER: What about this? (pointing to curve of cone)
MORRIS: That's not flat so it's not a face.
TEACHER: That's interesting. What about you Nadine, what shape would you like to tell us about?
NADINE: It's a square.
TEACHER: Is it?
NADINE: Oops no. It's got eight corners . . . four faces.
TEACHER: You count them for us.
NADINE: 1,2 3,4,5,6 . . . um.
TEACHER: Can you tell us about the faces? (Nadine does not reply so the teacher picks up a cuboid) What about this one? How many corners does this have?
NADINE: Eight.
TEACHER: And how many faces?
NADINE: Six.
TEACHER: So it's like this one isn't it? How is it different?
NADINE: It's longer and flatter.
TEACHER: What do we call this longer flatter shape?
NADINE: A rectangle.

Rickie takes a shape.

RICKIE: It's a pyramid. It's got five faces and five corners.
MORRIS: Four corners and a point.

In the other group:

TEACHER: Keith, you choose one and tell us about it.
KEITH: (chooses a cuboid) It's a rectangle.
TEACHER: What's a rectangle? Show me a rectangle (Keith points to the whole thing)

Keith goes on to identify corners and faces, and a comparison and discussion of rectangles and cuboids ensues.

Clearly there was some confusion about naming the shape of a face and the entire shape. For example, Keith wanted to call a cuboid a rectangle. The cylinder presented dilemmas for all the children, as they could 'see' two faces and were not sure how to deal with the surface between. A cylinder was cut open to reveal what happens when we flatten the surface. At the subsequent session the children were shown the skeleton of a hexagonal prism.

TEACHER: What is this shape?
ALL: Don't know.
TEACHER: (pointing to end face) What's that shape there?
MORRIS: It's a hexagon.
RICKIE: It looks like an octagon.
TEACHER: Let Ann count the sides and then we'll decide.
ANN: 1, 2, 3, 4, 5, 6.
RICKIE: Hexagon.
TEACHER: (pointing to a triangular prism) What do we call this one?
ALL: A triangular prism.
TEACHER: Can you see why it might be called that?
NADINE: Because it's in like a triangle . . . and that's like a hexagon.
TEACHER: So we call it a hexagonal prism.

Work with children from a reception class involved sorting a collection of badges. The teacher tipped out a bag of badges on to the table.

ADELE: I know, why don't we match which ones are big and which ones are small.
TEACHER: All right Adele, you start with that job. What are you going to put in your set? We'll watch and see.
ADELE: The small ones go here. These are the smallest ones, these are the medium-sized ones and these are the biggest ones.
TEACHER: John would like a go now. Tip them all out John and then we can see what you are doing.
GRETA: (watching John) Those don't go together!
ADELE: I know why he has put those together – because they're all birthday ones!
JOHN: No, because they have numbers on.

> TEACHER: Greta's turn now.
> GRETA: Is that a nine?
> TEACHER: It could be a nine, couldn't it?
> JOHN: Or a six.
> GRETA: I think it's a six, I do.
> TEACHER: Now, let's watch what Greta's doing.
> ADELE: I think I know what she is doing.
> TEACHER: What do you think, Adele?
> ADELE: They've all got words on them.
> GRETA: Yes!

Though the children obliged by sorting the badges in a number of ways the challenge may not have been sufficiently complex for them.

Another session had a rather daunting opening when a variety of card shapes were put on the table by the teacher.

> TEACHER: Let Greta have first go. I want you to sort out all the shapes that have four sides. (Greta sorts shapes) . . . Now what have we here?
> ADELE: I know I know. (picks up some shapes) These are all rectangles . . . a sort of another shape (picks up irregular quadrilateral) and two squares.
> TEACHER: (picks up irregular quadrilateral) Is that a rectangle?
> ADELE: No.
> TEACHER: Why not?
> JOHN: Because it's the shape of a boat.
> TEACHER: Does it belong in a set of shapes with four sides?
> JOHN: 1, 2, 3, 4; yes, it does.

John has a turn at sorting a set from all the shapes.

> TEACHER: Can you see them all everybody? Are you happy? What have we got here? . . . A set of . . .?
> CHILDREN: Rectangles.
> TEACHER: How do we know they are rectangles? What can you tell me about them?
> SUE: They have got four sides.
> TEACHER: (holding up a square) This one's got four sides. Does this go in the set?
> SUE: No, because they are long shapes.
> TEACHER: Here's my go. How have I made up my mind what to put in the set? Greta?
> GRETA: They've all got three sides.
> TEACHER: So they are all . . . ?
> CHILDREN: Triangles.

TEACHER:	(holding up a very acute angled triangle from the set) Is this a triangle?
JOHN:	No.
GRETA:	Yes.
TEACHER:	Why do you say that John?
JOHN:	Because this has got a long side, and these (points to 'squatter' triangles) have short sides . . .

Teacher hold up a rectangle.

TEACHER:	What shape do you think this is?
CHILDREN:	Rectangle.
TEACHER:	(cutting off a piece) If I cut a piece off, what shape have I got now?
CHILDREN:	Rectangle.
JOHN:	(picking up cut off piece) This is a rectangle.

As more pieces are cut off the children chorus rectangle each time, until the shape approaches a square when they suddenly call square! The teacher lays out the square and all the pieces together to make a rectangle. She then removes a piece at a time while the children call rectangle–rectangle–rectangle–square!

The idea of a quarter turn was shown to some children and the words angle and right angle were introduced. The children were shown how to make a right angle tester by folding any shape of paper twice. They enjoyed finding right angles on the wrapped gift boxes on the table before them. The shapes included a cube, cuboid, pyramid, and prisms. Some children found right angles in the room around them, including on the table leg, the corner of the display board, a book and a piece of paper. We looked at some drawings of plane shapes and skeletons of 3-D shapes and tried to spot the right angles on the faces of these.

TEACHER:	(looking at one of the corners of an acute angled triangle) Is that a right angle?
MORRIS:	No.
TEACHER:	Why do you think that?
MORRIS:	It's a bit too pointed.
TEACHER:	Rickie, can you see a couple?
RICKIE:	How many?
TEACHER:	Two.

Later:

TEACHER:	I can make a right angle with my arm, at the elbow.
MORRIS:	I can do it with my knee when I sit on the chair.
RICKIE:	I can do it with my finger . . . look.

With another group the children were invited to make their own right angle testers and they did so accurately and enjoyed looking for these on the cube, cuboid, prisms and pyramid set on the table.

> KEITH: I've found one on the table leg . . . does the table corner work? . . . No (the table is octagonal). Puts tester against corner of notice board . . . yes!
>
> MAX: I've got one here (corner of book) and here (corner of sheet of paper).

Match and mathematics

In some classroom sessions there seem to be children who can pick up an idea and 'run with it', take it, make it their own and further develop it. Other children in the same session seem to require direct teaching, even to come to some understanding of what it is that they are required to do. The problem of matching tasks to children is a fraught one, because so many ideas and skills are often brought to bear in a single task that it can be difficult to predict what a child needs to know or is able to do before attempting it. The danger also is in being over-prescriptive. If we 'over–determine' the task there is a danger that the children are precluded from meeting sufficient of what is novel and original to challenge them.

TEACHER EXPECTATIONS

In a reception class a group of children were given a giant's 'pocket' containing a collection of small things. These were its contents: lolly stick, pencil, stickers, badge, toy frog, toy rhino and toy elephant, string, shell, pebble, sticky tape, marble, padlock, clip, toy cup, notebook and pencil sharpener. They were told that the giant has a lot of things in his pocket and there is such a muddle that they really need sorting out. The first child to do the sorting put each item in a separate set. When asked which of all the things might go together the children offered the following suggestions:

— stickers and badge go together;
— pencil and notebook, because 'you could write a story in that book';
— pebble and shell, 'found on the beach';
— Sellotape and stickers, 'because they stick on to things and stick things together';
— small things, 'We could make a set of small things; we have the rhino, elephant and cup' (there may have been the idea that these were miniatures of the real things, though the marble and clip were added).

Given access to the resources but no constraints on their sorting, note that the children did not resort to colour, shape or thickness, or other labellings that a maths lesson might demand. Relative size became a feature, but at the end of the activity.

A teacher was invited in to work with some reception (4 and 5 year old) children on numbers 1 to 10. She declined to be limited to this range but brought a lot of practical resources which would support a lot of counting, ordering and number bond work. One boy, aged 5, helped himself to a carton of pebbles and proceeded to set them out in a long line. After a while he pronounced, with no assistance, that there were 87 pebbles. The visiting teacher asked him how he had achieved this result and he demonstrated, arriving this time at the answer 89. He wrote this on a piece of paper and put the paper next to the pebbles. As a result of some questioning he explained that he did mathematics with his dad, who was out of a job, for fun for both of them. He then demonstrated some computations on paper of the type that he could happily set himself. His teacher had set him off on tracing dots to learn how to write numbers. He was, after two weeks in school, being labelled as disruptive as he would not co-operate in completing his mathematics work.

Teacher expectations and mathematics

It seems to us that teachers have to employ sets of general expectations, because they have both a large number of children to take account of and often also a prescribed curriculum. To avoid work overload in preparation and presentation, teachers employ expectations about what the children can do. However, they also need to be alert to individual differences among children. It is the case that the expectations of teachers can be seen as limitations to children's learning. There is much evidence to indicate that because what the teacher expects is important to children it can influence what children think they can do and indeed what they achieve. It is a daunting thought to know that teachers can boost or depress children's views of their own potential, and one that we feel teachers need to constantly review.

RESOURCING ACTIVITIES

The group of children who so successfully managed a variety of novel sorts in the episode described above created difficulties for the teacher when they were given another task. The children were given a bag of toys to tip on to the table. In the bag was a soft toy duck, a plastic lizard, four soft rabbits and three soft bears.

TEACHER: I'm going to make a set of . . . let's think . . . I need to look at them all don't I? . . a set of animals with four legs.

JOHN: (holding up a duck) I've only got two.

ADELE: (holding up a bear) I've got two legs and two arms.

TEACHER: Let's do a set of animals with two legs and two arms.

The children were still doubtful about putting in all the bears and rabbits, and the lizard did not fit their idea of this set either. The teacher tried again.

TEACHER: Let's have a set of animals with four paws. Has this one got four paws? What do you think, Greta?

Eventually all the rabbits and bears were put in the set, but the children did need to examine every one individually. The children found it easier to sort those that had black eyes, and then those with long tails.

JOHN: Let's do those that's got wings.
TEACHER: OK.

John puts in the duck.

ADELE: Just one?
GRETA: What about if rabbits flew?
TEACHER: If rabbits could fly we could put them in too, couldn't we?

What had seemed to the teacher when collecting her resources to be a straightforward sorting activity quickly became a discussion about how we name parts of animals, anthropomorphism, and discussion about the change in results if rabbits could fly. It is difficult to establish whether teacher or children learned more in this episode.

At the next session the children were shown some cut out features and a face outline, and they took turns at creating a face. The idea was that they should create a 'set' which constituted a complete face.

TEACHER: For the first job, I want you to come and stand by me so that we are all looking the same way. Now what have we got here? (Gets out cut out features for a face, comprising a face outline with a mouth drawn in, two pairs of ears, two pairs of eyes and two noses).
ADELE: Clown face.
TEACHER: Let John have first go. Make a face John.

John tried to fit all the features in to the extent that when he came upon a second pair of eyes he laid them on top of those he had already set down.

TEACHER: I'm going to quickly draw the face that John has made.

Adele has a go.

TEACHER: Is Adele's face different from John's?
CHILDREN: Yes.
TEACHER: How is it different?

Children point out the differences.

GRETA: I was going to do it like that (points to a face).

TEACHER: You have a go now. See if you can do a different one from John's and Adele's.

GRETA: Can't.

TEACHER: Have a try. . . . Would you like next go Sue? See if you can make a face that is different in some way from the two we have done.

JOHN: That's his nose. . . . That's not a mouth.

TEACHER: How is Sue's different from John's? Now Greta have a try. Use a different collection, Greta. Sue has done a similar face to John but she has changed the . . . nose.

Greta makes up a face.

JOHN: She's chosen a different one from me.

TEACHER: So we need a set of things to make a face.

Teacher expectations about what constitutes a face had structured the expected outcome. Again the children confounded those expectations. The children used the features interchangeably and often embellished the face with extra features such as hair slides, bow-ties and hats. Though the intention had been to explore how many faces could be produced with the features as presented the teaching point was not lost, for the children always used the key features and recognised the idea of a whole comprising a set of features.

Resourcing and mathematics

What is provided for a mathematics task can structure a task and its outcomes. The resources can extend or limit the task. As teachers we have employed a judicious mix of strategies, sometimes setting out all the resources we thought necessary on the table, ready for the children to use, and sometimes relying on them to fetch what they needed. We now feel that teachers should be circumspect about what they provide for children, or even what they label as 'mathematics resources'. Indeed, when working an integrated day in infant classrooms, we have sometimes set up part of the room as the 'mathematics area' and placed what we deemed appropriate resources there. Perhaps a general resource bank for all subjects should be accessible to the children, and enabling children to resource their own work should be seen as an integral part of self-initiated learning.

TEACHER LISTENS

'Teachers don't like pauses – they jump in too quickly and often in a way that doesn't help the conversation. So go to a group and try to listen

before any intervention. 'Talk' before 'listen' can so easily be banal.
Counselling techniques might be worth looking at.'

'To what extent are we looking for evidence of a child's thinking as
against provoking a child's response?'

The teacher placed a Carroll grid card on the table in front of a group of
reception children.

TEACHER: Adele's going to do the first sort. Sort them by colour. Put
           those that are the same colour together.

Adele sorts them by colour and by size.

ADELE: I've got big ones in there and these aren't big.
TEACHER: This is very interesting Adele. Now I've got some pictures
           here that might tell us what Adele has been doing. I'm going
           to put them out and see if you can spot the ones we need.
           Have you seen pictures like this? Can you see any pictures
           here that might fit part of what Adele has been doing? What
           does that tell me? Does it tell me a colour?
ALL: Red.
TEACHER: If I put that there, this is a label to show me these are red
           and these are red.
TEACHER: (shows not red label) What does this mean?
ADELE: Red.
TEACHER: (pointing to the cross that is over the red) What's this bit?
ADELE: No.
TEACHER: No red. Not red. Where do we put this?

Greta assigns the label. The teacher does another sort that is red/not red
and circles/not circles and Greta finds the circle and not circle labels. Sue
and Greta put the labels on.

GRETA: We've got circle and not circles.

Greta is asked to sort and label the shapes.

ADELE: (looking on) I know what she's going to do. She's going to do
           squares and not squares.

The teacher produces labels with 'green 'and 'not green' on them.

TEACHER: Now Greta, what are these?
GRETA: Green.
TEACHER: Have we now got a green label? . . and a not green?

Greta puts labels on diagram.
   A feature of the above episode that we think is particularly striking is the
way in which, with time to read and reread the transcript, one gets a good

sense of Adele thinking. It is as though you can almost see what is happening inside her head! But in the rapid exchange of the classroom this is not always so readily clear to us – an argument, perhaps, for the occasional use of the tape recorder in teaching.

The work that follows is about probability and chance. It was done with top infants (6 and 7 year olds) and highlights where the teacher failed to listen. The children were asked what we use when we play a board game and the children gave their ideas about the shape of the die. The suggestions included some two- and some three-dimensional shapes.

TEACHER: When you are playing a board game what do you use to play?
SULA: Hands.
CLIVE: Dice.
SULA: Counters.
TEACHER: What shape do you think a die is?
JUDY: A pyramid.
RUBY: In a square.
CLIVE: A square with dots on and numbers.
RUBY: You can have them any shape because we've got some round ones.
TEACHER: Can you? How do you play with a round die?
RUBY: It rolls.
TEACHER: Have you got some like that in your classroom?
RUBY: We've got a triangle one. Little triangles that go up to 18.

The teacher then provided an unmarked track game for the children to look at.

TEACHER: If you were playing this game and rolling the die, how many goes do you think you'd need to get along the track?
CLIVE: Six.
JUDY: Thirty.
SULA: Eleven.
RUBY: Thirty-eight.
TEACHER: So the lowest is six and the highest is 38, so maybe it's going to be somewhere between those.
RUBY: (starting to count the spaces on the track) Shall we count?
TEACHER: Well, if you're throwing a die what could you get?
CLIVE: Six, six spaces.
SULA: Three.
CLIVE: A one . . . four.
RUBY: Eight.
CLIVE: You can't get high numbers on a little dice with little numbers on.
TEACHER: What has a die with little numbers got on it?
CLIVE: 1, 2, 3, 4, 5, 6.

TEACHER: If you could go any of those numbers of spaces how many turns do you think it would take?

JUDY: Why don't we find out and play it?

TEACHER: Let's do that.

The children completed the track game by rolling the die and making a tally of the number of goes they took.

TEACHER: Sula is the first to finish. How many goes did Sula take?

ALL: Nine.

Ruby then has a go and finishes in nine goes, then Judy ten, Clive 11 and teacher 13.

At the next session the children played the track game again. The teacher was concerned to see whether the children could start to firm up their predictions about such games.

TEACHER: If we look at that game again and I ask you how many goes do you think you'll need to finish that track?

SULA: If different people play it or we play it again they roll the dice, they might not get all the numbers they need.

CLIVE: If first you throw a six, you might get a two next time.

TEACHER: So how many goes to complete this track?

RUBY: If you kept on having ones . . .

SULA: Eight or nine goes.

CLIVE: No, thirteen.

TEACHER: So it could take us only eight goes. Might it take more goes than that?

JUDY
AND CLIVE: Thirteen.

TEACHER: Might it take even more goes than that?

RUBY: Forty-two . . . I've counted them.

TEACHER: Could it take fewer than eight goes . . . less than eight?

CLIVE: You could go 1, 2, 3, 4, 5, 6 and then 1, 2, 3, 4, 5, 6 . . .

TEACHER: Why are you counting in sixes? . . . (no reply) How can you get along that track the quickest way?

SULA: Cheating!

TEACHER: Yes, apart from cheating?

JUDY: By getting a six, dropping it so that you get a six again and again. (Meanwhile, Clive is counting along the track . . . 1, 2, 3, 4, 5, 6 . . . 1, 2, 3, 4, 5, 6 . . . 1, 2, and so on)

TEACHER: How many sixes?

RUBY: Seven.

TEACHER: So, if you threw a six each time it would take seven goes to get along the track.

The children were then shown a game board with numerals up to 60 on it.

TEACHER: Now that we've played that track game and worked out how many goes we might need to play the game, have you any ideas about how many goes you need to do this game?

SULA: Sixty.

TEACHER: Suppose you were playing with this die though.

CLIVE: Ten.

SULA: If you kept on getting ones . . . 60.

TEACHER: It might take 60 goes, is that the most number of goes it would take?

SULA: Yes.

TEACHER: Now what about the least number of goes?

JUDY: One.

TEACHER: Could you do that in one go with a die like that?

SULA: No.

Judy, Sula and Ruby then go on to hazard wild guesses about the number of goes required, including 21 and 38, despite the teacher's continued reminders that you might throw a six every time and you have 60 squares to cover. Notice Clive, who had responded successfully to the teacher's questions, had been ignored.

Teacher listens

There is currently much discussion in the literature of mathematics education about the importance of mathematics talk among children. Indeed, for teachers in England and Wales there is a mandatory need within the National Curriculum (see Attainment Target 1) for children to talk about their work. However, the culture of many classrooms does not make it easy for teachers to be good listeners. We think this may be for two reasons. First, it sometimes seems that what the teacher says is valued above what children say. Indeed, we ourselves know that we have asked children not to interrupt when we are talking, but we have felt no compunction about interrupting when children are speaking. Secondly, the more informal the class working groups, the more likely it seems that there are many children talking, and then it is often difficult for the teacher to listen to what is important while monitoring all the other things that are going on. Perhaps teachers can find ways of making talk an important part of mathematics learning, and sometimes shift the balance of their own contribution in class towards listening rather than speaking.

LANGUAGE AND MATHEMATICS

'Probability is difficult for children to grasp. It might lead to us teaching them how to bet on the horses.'

'I don't think that children think much about probability.'

A range of situations was offered to the children in order to explore their ideas about chance and predictability, starting with the tossing of a coin.

TEACHER: (showing a 10 pence piece) What happens if I toss this?
RUBY: Heads or tails.
TEACHER: It could be the Queen's head or it could be the other side which we call tails.
RUBY: The lion's tail!
TEACHER: Have all coins got tails on them?
ALL: No.
TEACHER: We always call them tails, whether there's a tail on it or not, don't we?

There are a number of possibilities here which seem to be to do with language. Ruby gives us a clue in the use of 'lion's tail'. The idea of calling the reverse of a coin 'tails' is not yet a part of Ruby's vocabulary. The teacher turned the conversation to other everyday experiences.

TEACHER: What about if somebody's mum has a baby?
RUBY: A girl or a boy.
TEACHER: What about if a mummy cat had kittens?
SULA: Ten.
RUBY: Eight.
TEACHER: Do you know of eight?
SULA: My cats have eight. I've got two cats.
TEACHER: So how many kittens might they have?
JUDY: 1, 2, 3, 4, 5, 6, 7 and 8.

Again the teacher attempted to move the conversation, this time into the children's direct experience.

TEACHER: Let's talk about your day. Tell me some of the things you do.
CLIVE: Most days we do numbers and nearly always writing.
TEACHER: What things can you think of that you think are absolutely certain to happen?
JUDY: We are going to get better at writing.
RUBY: We'll grow taller and older.
TEACHER: What things can you think of that are not absolutely certain but they might happen?
RUBY: We might play out.
CLIVE: We might get run over.
TEACHER: Can you tell me Sula, what you think is impossible?
SULA: What does impossible mean?
TEACHER: Who thinks they know what impossible means? (no response from children) When I say something is impossible it simply can't happen, not ever, anywhere.

JUDY: You'll never stop growing till you're growed.
TEACHER: How about. . . . It's impossible that cats can speak English?
RUBY: My cat can. They can speak English but in cat language!
CLIVE: A cat can't ride a bike.
SULA: A budgie can't eat with a spoon.

There followed a conversation which hinged on the agreement that it is impossible that the moon is made of cheese (hardly a 'happening!'). It was daunting for the teacher to be trying to deal in 'fact' and logic in the face of the children's personal and intuitive explanations.

TEACHER: Do you think it is possible that the moon is made of cheese?
ALL: No . . . ooo.
CLIVE: It hasn't got holes in.
TEACHER: If it had holes in do you think it is possibly made of cheese?
CLIVE: Only if it was yellow.
RUBY: I tried to find out if there were aliens on the moon, so I shouted as loud as I possibly could, but I couldn't hear anything . . . then I shouted hello man in the moon.

The children were then given a number of situations[1] to which they were invited to respond in respect of their probability. One of these presented Clive with problems.

TEACHER: Is it certain that the school holidays will end?
CLIVE: Sometimes.

Only with hindsight can we reflect on the use of language here. Perhaps Clive, aged 6, was saying that they end when we leave school, or by government decree.

Problems with signs and mathematics occurred in work carried out with groups of middle infants (5 and 6 years old). It was not possible to record conversations but notes were made after each group session.

The intention was to introduce the children to the use of a programmable robot.[2] The robot is programmable through the use of a key pad. It has no trailing cables and is fully self-programmable. For the purposes of this exercise the children needed to be introduced to controls for forward, backward and distance and rotation left and right. All of the children were happy to accept the teacher giving a rule about rotation by saying that the 'magic' number was 90 for turning a corner.

The first challenge offered, after introduction to the 'forward' key and the necessarily associated 'distance', was to make the robot travel to a table at the end of the room. The children did this by estimating the distance and pressing the forward and distance keys and then 'GO'. To do this the teacher first gave them some experience of the distance travelled if Forward 2 'GO' and then Forward 3 'GO' were pressed.[3] Having witnessed this the children decided on the distance needed – the responses ranged from four to 30. However, the children did agree that it must be somewhere between these two extremes and settled, in one case, on eight. This took the robot just over half way to the table. After much discussion Forward 13 was agreed and this did cause the robot to reach the table. Whilst there were variations between groups, most arrived at a range of 12–15 and these all gave results which satisfied the children. The use of rotation, though, caused some interesting responses.

The keys on the robot indicate left and right by the use of curved arrows. These are clear to adults but this was the first time these children had seen such a representation. Despite having lots of trials with the teacher, when it came to navigating the robot half way down the room to a cone, turning right to pass the cone and travelling to their real teacher, many of the children elected the 'left' key rather than the 'right' key. Trial and error caused them to re-programme the robot. The 'problem' seemed to be that the children moved their heads to follow the curved arrow and orientated their bodies at right-angles to the head movement. In other words they turned their bodies to the right whilst moving their heads to the left. This raises lots of interesting ideas with regard to orientation of body movements and the co-ordination of such movements with the cognitive ideas signified by head movement. Certainly important questions are raised about 'left and right' and 'clockwise and anti-clockwise'.

Language and mathematics

Our own discussions, which centre on this theme, have been about meanings, and how teachers and children can negotiate and arrive at shared meanings for what they are saying. This is problematic for the teacher who, at least for some of the time, wishes children to 'arrive at' or develop and use their own meanings, but be able to communicate them to others in ways all can understand. Problems in using language in mathematics are addressed at length in Chapter 5. For evaluative purposes teachers need to be aware of their own language usage and alert to possible sources of confusion when working with children and mathematics.

STIMULI FOR MATHEMATICS

The first task was carried out with a number of children in the 5–7 year old age range by teachers with whom we had been working on a course. It had an unpromising starting point from the perspective of some of the teachers in that it looked to be rather limited and limiting: finding out the number of windows in the school. In some cases this was enhanced by an invitation to consider the cost of window cleaning. This led, in one school, to an extended activity which drew in the head teacher with the real figures for the previous year's window cleaning bill.

In this school the children (top infants) having been invited to work out how many windows there were asked a number of questions including:

— do you mean panes or windows?
— are you going to clean them?
— do we include glass doors?

Having established the ground rules – basically that the children should decide for themselves what counted as a window and suggesting that the teacher would clean them for the equivalent of 50 pence per pane, the children set about the task. They used a range of strategies, having decided to count panes of glass. These included not bothering to count panes when they had an identical whole window, and multiplying by two having totalled the panes on one side of a corridor. As the school was in two halves which were mirror images of each other the children only carried out a detailed survey in one half. Having consulted the head teacher about the real cost of window cleaning they eventually determined that their teacher would have to lower her price from 50 pence in order to obtain the contract! From the 'doubtful' stimulus, work emerged which included counts, multiplication, money, bills, fractions, symmetry, 'tendering' and 'competitive rates'.

Calculators proved a powerful stimulus to children's work. A group of children were given the problem; make sums to come to one using just the digits three and four and your calculator. For example one six year old produced:

$$4433 - 3344 - 343 - 334 - 34 - 43 - 334 = 1$$

Groups of 6 and 7 year old children were offered this challenge: start with a pile of counters and put how many you wish into the centre of a square. Then write numbers at the corners of the square which will add up to the number in the centre. Two 7 year old children did this by putting numbers in the range 10 to 20 in the centre. Two 6 year old children put one counter in the centre and then proceeded to use decimals in the corners to total to one.

Mathematics starting points

The examples we have given above show the use of the physical environment and electronic devices as sources for mathematical work. We can extend this point by saying that teachers can draw mathematical projects out of any aspect of children's experience. The challenge is not in *finding* projects that form good starting points for learning, but in *choosing* those which will prove exciting and fruitful to the children in the current class.

REVIEW

When we read what children and teachers have said, we are struck by the ways in which the written words prompt new interpretations of what went on. Of course, the written word is not transitory and can therefore be 'gone over' again and again, but even the first time we read them, transcripts constantly make us say to ourselves things like 'I never realised that' and 'That child understood all along' and 'The teacher changed the whole direction of the learning there'.

There will always be ways we could have improved on the conversations we have had with children. Pleasure, knowing that a child has spoken out for the first time, satisfaction when a child says 'I seeeeeee-eee!' and disappointment when we hear ourselves saying 'Gary!' for the sixth time in half an hour, are the kinds of feelings that can help us to modify our classroom behaviour and management. Listening to or reading what was said in class is one of the most powerful evaluative tools we have. Ruby, Clive, John, Morris and Nadine and all the other children in schools demand more of us than that we should just be their teacher of mathematics.

NOTES

1 Taken from Clemson and Clemson (1992).
2 The robot used was that produced by Valiant Technology (UK) Ltd and known as the Roamer.
3 The robot travels in units of its own length, so Forward 1 will cause it to travel its own length and then stop.

Part V

Assessment, record keeping and evaluation

GENERAL INTRODUCTION

Assessment and record keeping are the life-blood of schools and schooling. They serve two very important purposes. These are, most importantly, to assist teachers in determining the course of children's learning and the directions this should next take. Records of teacher assessments within a class are a reminder to the teacher, and between classes are communications enabling teachers to work as a team. Second, assessment and record keeping provide tangible evidence of what has happened in school. It is 'proof' to outsiders of what has gone on. It is perhaps not surprising that when young children play school, they very often begin by compiling a register. 'Marking work' and 'assessing behaviour in class' also often feature as central to the game. Nor is it unexpected that, in our own memories of our schooldays, marks, grades, results and reports assume importance over much else that happened at school.

In setting about assessment and record keeping teachers hone expertise that is common to everyone. We all make everyday judgements about our own learning and that of others. 'We may tell a neighbour how pretty . . . [their] garden is looking, comment on new recipes tried at home, and we may ask our friends how their evening classes are coming along' (Clemson and Clemson 1991: 1). Most of us also use a calendar, keep a diary and make shopping lists; that is, we make and use records of what we, and other members of the family have done or failed to do. Thus becoming an assessment and record keeping expert involves harnessing something that virtually everyone does.

All teachers use their own assessments at every point in the school day. When Jessie's teacher decides she should stop her work with sand and begin another activity, when the teacher approaches Dudley and Walt and decides to ask the children questions in order to change the course of their enquiry using cubes and squared paper, when the whole class is called together to look at Tamar and Ken's work with construction toys; in all of these and many other moments in the day the teacher has made a series of judgements about how the children's learning is progressing. We feel that teachers regard these judgements as a crucial part of their professional expertise.

In contrast, assessment and record keeping which has to be undertaken for purposes external to the school is, in our experience, thought by teachers to be one of the most arduous parts of their job. Certainly we ourselves have found classroom time spent with children a joy, contrasting starkly with the task of writing end of year reports. The increased accountability that national curricula and the current political climate have brought means that the view of teachers and schooling from outside are impinging powerfully on how teachers approach their work in school. This is where evaluation becomes a significant tool. The 'evaluating' teacher is one whose role has become teacher and researcher. Evaluation enables us to refine not only our assessment and record keeping, but every other part of our work.

All we have said applies to mathematics as to other subjects. What is of concern to us about mathematics in particular is that we should endeavour to broaden what is done and viewed as mathematical. Resulting assessments, records and evaluations will then begin to be a more profound index of what is really happening when children learn mathematics.

Chapter 9

Monitoring progress

INTRODUCTION

Assessment is linked, inextricably, to teaching and learning. Without assessment of children's progress in their learning, purposeful teaching is replaced by serendipity. We have to know what children have learned, where they are finding diffficulties in learning, and by implication, what new learning opportunities should be offered, in order to structure teaching and the content of lessons. Gaining agreement about the indispensability of assessment in principle is easier than identifying what assessment assumptions and strategies are 'best'; for the outcomes of assessment may be required to meet a variety of expectations. The context in which teachers are using their expertise is one in which there are two distinct and sometimes conflicting sets of pressures.

The first of these has to do with the opportunities offered youngsters in order that they may take their place in society. This involves the consideration of a range of issues which education systems are meant to deliver. These national issues include education for leadership, training for work, the development of law-abiding citizens, the promotion of health education, the acquisition of communication skills and many more. Information about the effectiveness of schools in the delivery of these through inspection and formal assessment is seen as a way of securing government feedback. The assessment decisions, requirements and suggestions come, in this case, from sources distant from individual schools and children. The second set of pressures on teachers are local, related to the school they work in, the children they teach, and their own children. This chapter therefore has two parts. The first is about the dilemmas posed at a national level, for teachers assessing children's performance and potential in mathematics. These have to do with things like 'standards', tests and published 'results'. The second part is about assessment of mathematics and the children we know. Teachers' dilemmas here relate to their expectations, how they go about doing assessment, and how to communicate assessment information.

ASSESSING THE NATION'S CHILDREN

In assessing the nation's children there is a necessary concern with the outcomes of educational opportunity. These outcomes are considered for the population of children rather than individuals at different ages or stages. When all children are placed together in this way it is necessary to employ some important basic assumptions in drawing up assessment schedules, and interpreting their outcomes. The essentials for any national system of assessment are thus concerned with:

— the idea of there being standards against which children can be measured;
— the possibility of determining the achievements of the 'average' child;
— criteria against which children will be assessed;
— the use of outcomes for a range of demands.

We shall attend to aspects of these in turn, as all present dilemmas for the teacher.

National standards

Concern about 'standards' has increased pressure on teachers of young children to produce 'results'. It has been the tradition in education that examination and test results have been taken as an index of older children's achievements. There is an assumption that test results can also offer an indication of the efficacy of the education of young children and thereby raise 'standards' in schools. The consequence of this is that some people may devalue the importance of teachers' assessments. However, formal objective tests are often quite inappropriate for assessing the achievements of young children. Teachers are therefore empowered to be extremely influential in assessing young children's performance and potential.

This responsibility is double-edged. Positively, it gives teachers of young children an important platform from which to press their demands for equal status with those colleagues in other sectors (who sometimes view their work as more intellectually demanding than that of teachers of young children). However, it also places on teachers of infants the enormously complex and time consuming task of making constant assessments. This they have done for many years. Only now are they publicly accountable for them.

Meeting the 'national average'

Concern about 'standards' has provoked the proliferation of the idea that goals can be set in mathematics, which should be reached by all children.

For example, the assessment arrangements that have accompanied the National Curriculum (England and Wales) imply that 'Level 2' is what to aim for in mathematics for all children completing their infant education. Teachers know that this takes little account of children as people or the processes of learning, and that a notional level is arbitrary. The 'level' quickly acquires an importance well beyond that of a crude 'marker post'. As Hegarty states, in a discussion of the use of IQ scores, 'The difficulties arise when measures such as this are taken out of context and used on their own. They are then likely to acquire an absolute significance that can be very misleading' (1987: 41).

Nevertheless, the allocation of a minimum threshold of achievement such as that indicated by 'Level 2' does encourage teachers to put effort into work with less able children in order to bring them up to the elected level. However, this would seem to be at the cost of giving sufficient challenge to the abler ones. In the HMI survey of primary education in 1978 the point was made that average and less able children were quite well supported in their mathematics work in terms of matching of appropriate tasks, but that the more able children were not appropriately challenged. Returning to this theme in 1989, HMI report that 'children of high mathematical ability [are] insufficiently challenged' (DES 1989: 14). Whilst it is the case that many able children will achieve minumum thresholds, for they will reach Level 2 or even 3 anyway, there is little incentive for teachers to help them work at Level 4. Thus, given limited resources, there is an understandable concern for many teachers to raise most children to the minimum threshold at the expense of challenging individual children at the appropriate level.

Norm-referencing and the 'average' child

Children's mathematical performances are compared across classes, schools and the nation. It is this kind of assessment that contributes to the 'results' that schools in England and Wales are being obliged to publish. There is a current notion that a school where children do not reach a certain 'standard', for example in mathematics, is a poor school. Clearly this does not take account of the educational opportunity available to children outside school. Teachers have pointed out that such comparisons are invidious. They mask the amount of progress made by individual children.

The thinking behind these ideas is that mathematical ability is distributed through the population so that a few children are very able, a few lack genuine mathematical ability or aptitude and most fall somewhere in between, with many clustered around the half-way point between able and not able. These children typify the 'average' child and their achievements in mathematics are seen to exemplify what most children should achieve. A typical normal distribution curve appears in Figure 9.1.

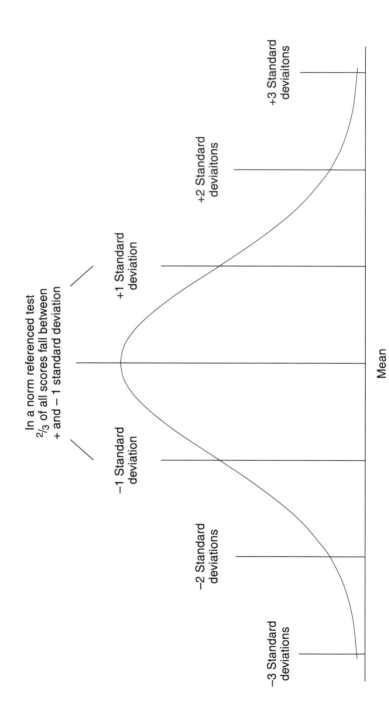

In a norm referenced test
$2/3$ of all scores fall between
$+$ and -1 standard deviation

-3 Standard
deviations

-2 Standard
deviations

-1 Standard
deviation

$+1$ Standard
deviation

$+2$ Standard
deviaitons

$+3$ Standard
deviaitons

Mean

Figure 9.1 Normal distribution curve

Indeed, it is not surprising that test results confirm this sort of spread, as tests are actually constructed so that the results will demonstrate this configuration. In order to raise standards in a normally distributed[1] population it is necessary to raise the mean average for the population. This would not, however, change the fact that the population would still be distributed around the new mean and that we would still have less and more able groups. Because its purpose is to allow comparisons between individual children's attainment and that of the population, norm-referencing is of 'little use in improving teaching' (Shipman 1983: 10).

Assessing using given criteria

In order to have a national perspective on the achievements of schools and children at particular ages or stages, it is necessary to provide criteria against which the measurements are to be made. Criterion-referenced assessment is assessment against predetermined content. Examples that are familiar to many people are grade examinations for music, and the driving test – you pass if your performance matches the appropriate content at the required standard. In the case of national curricula which specify the knowledge and skills that children need to aspire to, the syllabus must contain clear statements of learning outcomes which are expected at the given stage. The use of this criterion-referenced assessment in mathematics is problematic in practice for two reasons. The first is the common use of such assessments to make general, normative statements at a national level (actually talking of a particular 'level' of achievement as 'average' is a normative statement, dependent on mastery of content). The second has to do with common views of the nature of mathematics. For example, it is widely assumed that it is easier to 'tell' whether children have learned a particular part of the mathematics curriculum than whether they have learned a comparable part in English or history. The idea is harboured that mathematics can all be judged 'right' or 'wrong' and 'getting *answers*' (and 'right' ones at that) is all that matters. In other words the determination of criteria for assessment in mathematics carries problems that are specific to the subject.

There are also issues for the teacher in respect of confidence. For example, how many times do we need to see a child meet the criteria before we can safely assume that understanding is complete and that we can leave that area of mathematics? The chosen criteria themselves pose difficulties in how they are phrased, and how they are seen to link to other criteria. If we set out some examples they will serve to highlight some of these problems:

— If a child can write the numerals 1–10 and match them to appropriate groups of items, can we assume they 'know' about counts to ten? How many times should they match and record the numeral '2', for example, before we can say they have a concept for '2'? Or perhaps a concept for '2' implies an understanding which needs to be demonstrated by more than numeral-group matches.

— If a child can draw a block graph and talk about what it shows, does this mean mastery of the principle of block graphs? How many block graphs should they draw or interpret? Does interpretation come before the ability to draw them? Does the number of items of information make a difference to our judgement? What is the next step after block graphs? Is it, for example, work about pictograms, or should these go alongside or before block graphs?

Summative assessment

From the national perspective it is important that we should have snapshots of the outcomes of different phases of the particular education system, and that these snapshots should be relatively easy to use and understand. This leads to the use of *summative* procedures which, by their very nature do not lend themselves to the support of improvements for the cohort of children who have been measured, though they may support changes for subsequent cohorts. Typically summative assessment at the end of phases of education involves testing through external agencies as this is seen as offering objective, and clearly accountable, measurement.

In England and Wales the law relating to the curriculum carries specific summative assessment requirements at particular points in a child's school career. The first of these is of importance to teachers of young children – those at age 7. The current prescriptions are that towards the end of the school year in which children are 7 they are given a series of short tasks called 'standard assessment tasks' (SATs) to complete individually. There are tasks to be presented at each 'level'. The teacher is expected to use discretion in starting at the appropriate 'level' for each child and children can continue to be offered tasks until they get fewer than a given number of the tasks correct. That then signifies the level at or towards which they are working. It is these summative test results that, on publication, are used to compare schools, cities and counties one with another.

Tasks, like those presented as SATs, in common with all partial one-off tests, offer little more than a glimpse at children's performance, and no indication of their potential. Test results are considered to be more significant than teacher assessments where the two differ. This is despite the fact that (in our view) teacher assessments can be more insightful. Without entering a lengthy debate about all the shortcomings of tests, it seems to us that there are only two reasons for overriding the assessments of a professional teacher who has worked with a child every day. They are to try to avoid bias, or better, assess potential. The kind of bias we mean here is referred to as a 'personality clash' when it is negative, and 'favouritism' when positive. Predicting future success is not necessarily something teachers are good at, as we know when we reflect on what our own schoolfriends are doing now. But then there is no indication that tests can assess potential either. Despite their doubtful value head teachers do use external tests even when they are not obliged by law to do so. Thus summative assessment at the end of each school year is generally provided by the school and may be based on teacher assessment and, in some cases, on the use of brought-in tests.

ASSESSING THE CHILDREN WE KNOW

Aside from all the national imperatives which we have just discussed, teachers also, importantly, do assessment because of their professional purposes and principles. The two most important areas of expertise in the profession of a teacher are the handling of interactions with children and the assessment of children's progress. The style and content of the interactions is dependent on the teacher's assessments, from one moment to the next, about how well the teaching and learning is going. Assessment informs every other part of a teacher's work. Knowing where children have got to, what they have achieved, is the starting point for planning. Making judgements about how well children are actually doing a task aids teachers in gauging how they teach and how to allocate and modify what comes next. Telling children how they are getting on can fuel their confidence and enthusiasm. Assessment is as important to children as it is to teachers. Even without national concerns assessment would still be pivotal in education. Without it we would flounder.

In assessing, teachers use their own judgements and test results. While acknowledging that these can never be completely objective, they do try to avoid bias, ensure they actually assess what they mean to (that the assessment is valid) and that their assessment mechanisms are consistent over time (that is that they are reliable). Before we examine the extent of the information available to teachers for assessment purposes, and the management of this information, there is one important source of bias which demands constant vigilance. It has to do with expectations about children's achievement.

Expectations and self-fulfilling prophecies

The views of parents, teachers and children themselves are significant to teachers when they are looking at expected against actual achievement. We are sure that teachers of young children wish them to do as well as they can in mathematics. It is an unpalatable thought to consider that children may not do this, and that one of the reasons may be that they themselves or adults who know them have inappropriate expectations.

Parents' expectations

Most parents want their child be be successful in mathematics and there are many who wish for an 'above average' performance. Indeed, teachers who are parents themselves may well be in accord with these views when they think about the provisions for their own children. There is therefore a tension in the pressures placed on teachers to get every child to a 'national standard' whilst getting individual children to excel in the eyes of their parents and themselves. This tension is to do with teachers deploying available resources to balance the demands of general, public account-ability and personal, private accountability. A further consideration re-garding the views of parents is to what extent they too should be involved in assessment. Holden *et al.* asked a sample of parents of 7 year olds about this. 'Nearly a third of the parents said they would like to be involved in the assessment process' (1993: 3). Other parents who did not want a part in the formal assessments (SATs) said:

> 'That they did want the opportunity to discuss their child's strengths and weaknesses with the teacher as part of the assessment process.'

> 'The teacher ought to know what the children do at home.'

> 'If a child is shy and not forthcoming it could be wrongly assessed . . . so asking parents is a good idea.'
>
> (Holden *et al.* 1993: 4)

Of course, this kind of contribution can not only assist the teacher in assessing, but can also serve to modify parental expectations, forge links between home and school and perhaps change children's ideas about what assessment and tests are for.

Teachers' expectations

Teachers have feelings about their own capacity both to assess and to establish confident statements regarding the outcomes of an assessment exercise. The teacher's attitudes and behaviour toward individual chil-dren can profoundly affect the child's performance and behaviour. As Rowntree indicates:

> In the self-fulfilling prophecy we have a new label for the phenomenon long-recognised in folk-wisdom: 'Give a dog a bad name and you may as well hang him' or 'Trust a man and he will prove true'. That is if we constantly and powerfully express to a person our image of what he is

(lazy, stupid, brave or dependable) he will often gradually adjust his behaviour so as to become more like our image than he was before.

(1977: 42)

The factors that may influence teachers regarding their expectation of a child's ability in mathematics include class, gender, and culture. However, it is the teacher's reaction to perceived differences that is paramount. Screening is not an answer to the question of how to minimise teacher expectations holding sway, for several reasons. First, its introduction implies that there are already difficulties in school. Second, there is the problem of determining screening tests that are class, gender and culture free. Additionally, if applied to new entrants to school, there are problems in making assumptions about whether the children are all equally pre-pared for a 'test' situation.

Children and expectations

The way in which children perceive their own ability to cope with the challenges can seriously affect the outcomes of any assessment. In our own experience, young children are quite capable of responding to support in evaluating their own performance. When Ronny says 'I can't do this', do we not try to give him strategies for going about the task that he may not yet have tried? The aim, for Ronny, is to be able to say 'I've done it! and 'I can do these!' We try to extend 'attack' skills, build on competences, and widen the range of situations in which mathematical concepts can be applied. In all this Ronny can be a willing participant and arbiter. When assessing Ronny's mathematics work we can examine the whole gamut of activities which we regard as mathematical. We shall examine now what it is that all teachers have available to them in gathering data on which to base assessments.

The pool of mathematics information

Teachers have access to 'all the kinds of things that children do when they are working in school' (Clemson and Clemson 1991). If we focus on what children actually do in mathematics, the following list of work categories emerges:

— Oral/aural
— Reading
— Practical
— Written
— Research
— Co-ordination and control
— Aesthetic

If we look at some examples of these kinds of work they can offer pointers to the ways teachers can collect information about them.

Oral/aural work

Speaking and listening involves the whole gamut of things children do under the heading 'mathematics'. Here are a few suggestions that can give the feel of 'real' situations:

— when children think aloud while working with a variety of containers in the sand tray;
— when a child talks to the teacher about the work in their book;
— when they do practical work with counting apparatus while the teacher and the rest of a group of children look on;
— when they respond to the challenge of doing a 'sum' in their head;
— when they play a mathematical game with a friend (even discussion about whose go it is and whether what is happening is 'fair' is mathematical);
— when they answer up to a challenge the teacher places before the whole class.

Reading

Examples of mathematical activities in this area include:

— reading stories and rhymes with numbers in them;
— referring to page numbers and using an index (there is much order and sequence work here);
— looking up mathematical information such as which is the nearest star, the fastest land animal and the date of Pancake Day;
— interpreting road signs;
— following a recipe.

Practical work

The children get plenty of opportunity to produce this kind of evidence for assessment:

— making a tower of nine blocks or a group of six pencils;
— giving coins in exchange for a play book in a class shop;
— setting the calendar to the right day and date;
— threading a bead pattern or continuing a pattern of plasticine blobs;
— drawing a four-sided shape with a finger in the air or in paint;
— measuring the length of the toy-box in hand spans;
— making a collection of things that match a given shape from around the room;

— marking down how many boys and how many girls go through the doorway before a timer runs out.

Written work

This is the area of work which many of us regard as 'safest' for conducting assessment. It may have to do with our memories of mathematics in childhood, or that written evidence is sought in conventional tests. One additional advantage is that it is permanent and can be perused, unlike the remarks Ishmail made or Erich's drawing in sand that Jill poured more sand on moments later. Examples here include:

— counts and calculations on worksheets or in workbooks;
— number stories;
— drawings of patterns and shapes;
— a tally of the number of children who remembered to bring their reading book to school each day or a block graph of favourite colours.

Research

This heading is a word used across all subjects in the curriculum. In mathematics it is sometimes subsumed under 'problem solving'. Examples include the following:

— finding the operation going on in a function machine;
— answering the question, 'Are there more children aged 6 than 5 in the class?'
— explaining what happens to a picture when we place a mirror at its edge;
— finding out how many different shapes can be made by cutting squares into two pieces.

When we do research we use study skills. Examples will indicate what we mean when we apply these terms to young children's mathematics.

— posing questions like 'I would like to try to estimate how many conkers are in the box' or 'I wonder if the balance will go down this side when I put another toy car on it?'
— choosing the equipment they need to play a shop game or build a construction straw house;
— repeating experiments as in filling a beaker with egg-cups of water to test a previous result;
— reporting to classmates about the experiments to see what could be done before a minute timer ran out;
— deciding to modify a task to achieve success; for example, when

marbles roll off the balance pan deciding to put them in a bag and add a bag to the other side of the balance;
— writing down results so that other children can understand them;
— forming general ideas based on the work done in a variety of sessions.

Co-ordination and control

These skills are demonstrable in mathematics sessions when children do things like the following:

— hold and use scissors and pencils appropriately and accurately;
— draw straight lines;
— make shapes and models from construction apparatus and modelling material like plasticine;
— pour, hold steady and measure fixed volumes of water.

Aesthetic

In mathematics this aspect of work has to do with pattern recognition, replication and invention. For example:

— inventing a pattern of beats on a drum for a friend to replicate on another instrument;
— printing a repeat pattern with potato cuts;
— exploring pattern in wallpaper and fabric, photographs, drawings and paintings.

Mathematical work throughout the day

The examples of work above have been drawn from activities which might occur in mathematics sessions in infant classrooms. However, work does not have to occur in such sessions to be mathematical. Thus evidence from right across the school day can be used for assessments. Here are some examples of the kinds of things we mean:

— when children are taking a message to another teacher, this may involve directions;
— estimating how many crayons their group will need;
— cutting paper shapes to make a collage;
— following instructions at an interactive display table;
— when reporting what happened at a birthday party, there may be evidence of sequencing;
— the growth of a plant or a discussion of bedtimes involve elements of time;

— baking in school can mean using standard measures;
— paying for a school dinner means counting out the value of the coins.

Collecting information

Teachers have at their disposal five methods of assessment information collection. These are observing, listening, participating, scrutinising written outcomes and giving tests.[2] If we match the categories of work children do in mathematics with the appropriate ways teachers have of collecting information the outcome is as shown in Table 9.1.

Table 9.1 Assessment information collection

What children do in mathematics	How teachers can collect information
Oral/aural work	Observe, listen, participate
Reading	Observe, listen, participate, give a test
Practical work	Observe, listen, participate, scrutinise written outcomes, give a 'multi-task' test
Written work	Scrutinise outcomes, give a test
Research	As for practical work
Work involving co-ordination and control	Observe, scrutinise outcomes (e.g. layout of data in book, model making)
Work involving aesthetic considerations	Observe, listen, scrutinise outcomes (e.g. patterns, models)

Source: Adapted from Clemson and Clemson 1991

Using information

All the assessment information teachers collect can be used in one of two ways. It can be used immediately to alter the course of classroom events. Thus if Marcus is repeatedly having trouble working out how many cardboard ducks are left when some 'fly away' the teacher will make a snap assessment that more preparation for subtraction activities has to be done. It may be that Marcus can do this work right away with the teacher's help, or that it has to be timetabled for another day. If that is the case Marcus will probably get on with some other activity until the end of the session. Assessment information can also be set aside for later use. It may then be used to fuel planning, to provide evidence for classroom records, or to contribute to 'hand-on' records for the next teacher. Assessments are either stored as records which 'track' the class or groups within it or they focus on individual children.

Assessments and groupings

Ability grouping within a class makes use of judgements about children's work in relation to others. There is a danger of setting up classroom 'systems' which enforce a normative distribution of performance. We can well recall the problems that we had as teachers when an 'atypical' class arrived. A class of top infants (6 and 7 year olds) provoked comments like these:

— half the children seem to be able to do everything I ask of them and the other half can do nothing I ask of them;
— having such a large part of the class weak in mathematics poses problems for resourcing – I simply have not enough to go around;
— the weak mathematicians need so much support I cannot give enough time to stimulating the able children.

The teacher was commenting on the fact that past experience and current classroom management was geared to normative ideas about performance in mathematics. We do perhaps need to view ourselves as 'ever ready' to meet the needs of children, not classes or populations of children. The key to managing this effectively is to apply constant assessment to the children so grouped. None of us would wish to feel that we could assess children's learning before they have undertaken it. Thus groupings must be flexible and subject to change to avoid the chance that children will confirm our expectations rather than do their best.

Assessments and individual children

The summative assessments we have described as being of national interest represent a retrospective view of a child's progress and achievements. In contrast formative assessment is about prospect and potential. It can help us in teaching children we are working with now. The intention of formative assessment is to promote the learning opportunities and progress of the children in our class this year. Frith and Macintosh see formative assessment as ' the teacher ... getting to know the students in order to teach them better' (1984: 17). In undertaking formative assessment of children's mathematical work we are continuously alert for instances when we can get more insight into a child's mathematical thinking and understanding. As part of a formative approach (and of the diagnostic one described below) it is useful to consider the 'mistakes' that children make in their mathematics. Children should be encouraged to talk about their work whether it is right or wrong. The ways children describe what they have done and the mistakes they make are often our best view of their mathematical thinking.

Formative assessment should not be confused with *continuous assess-*

ment which is a term employed to describe pieces of work which are done over a set period for the purposes of a formal assessment. In formative assessment we are concerned with the piecing together of formal and informal assessments to further the successful learning of each child. Embraced within the wide-ranging formative assessment work that teachers undertake is the specially focused diagnostic assessment.

'Diagnosis' is a medical term and as such is commonly associated with problems. Whilst the prognosis from a diagnostic test may pronounce good health, there is an assumption that there may be a problem in the first instance. This is regrettable, for 'sickness' and 'cure' are inappropriate concepts to transfer to education. Along with diagnosis comes the idea that 'everything will be alright again'. In education there is no point of stasis. We expect constant change. Thus diagnostic assessment can be said to be a 'deficit' model. This is a contentious thing to say as some would argue that strength as well as weakness can be diagnosed. However, it is our experience that most diagnostic assessment is triggered with a view to action through remediation. Perversely, herein also lies the strength of a diagnostic approach. Used appropriately it supports a thorough appraisal of a child's mathematics work in order to help the teacher identify the learning opportunities that are needed to further the understanding of that child in relation to mathematics.

In undertaking a diagnostic approach to assessment there are a number of necessary conditions:

— the teacher must take time to inspect a range of work from the child;
— this range of work should include a variety of forms;
— the diagnosis should take account of context but not be formed as a result of expectations about that context;
— a second opinion should be available.

There are a number of steps in a diagnostic procedure:

— establish what the child can do as a baseline;
— contrast this against what is desired in respect of both predetermined criteria and one's experience;
— involve the child in a discussion of their needs;
— take action on completion.

These will also feed the wider formative responsibilities that we have.

Communicating information

In order to pass on information about assessments, both to ourselves at a later date and to colleagues, fellow professionals (for example, the educational psychologist) and parents, we have to 'put it on record'.[3] Tick lists serve little purpose in communicating information to others, though they can serve as a 'summary indicator' to a class teacher about the teaching areas covered. The creation of vehicles for recording assessments of learning requires a consideration of the following:

— how children's individual strengths and weaknesses can be indicated;
— how the record can go beyond recording progress through a published scheme;
— how systems of recording within school can link with those that pass on with each child to the next phase of education;
— how recording links with reporting to parents.

There follow some suggestions about the possible ways in which mathematics assessments might be put on record, the form such records might take, and the link between records and reports.

Mathematics assessments on record

To ensure continuity, record systems need to be consistent through the school. The need for similar records over children's entire infant career offers teachers a number of possible ways of 'tracking' mastery of mathematics. For example, for each child they could conform to one of the following patterns:

— a year record which summarises all that a child works on or achieves in a school year;
— an 'area of mathematics' record which records how a child is working in, for example, 'number' or 'algebra', regardless of the year or class they are in; thus one record for each part of mathematics will go with the child through the school;
— a 'level' record which sets down all those concepts and activities which the staff feel are comparable in terms of mathematical demand; thus a single child may have a 'Level 1' record, and then a 'Level 2' record, and so on.

Types of record

However the record is constructed, it can then be offered in a variety of ways which include an annotated tick list, in written form by the teacher, or as part of a portfolio or profile. The first two of these are self-explanatory. A portfolio could contain things like work samples, photographs and drawings. A sample portfolio is shown in Figure 9.2.

A profile[4] maps on to what has happened in many infant schools for a long while. It comprises recorded information which is used formatively and summative statements made for the purposes of reporting.

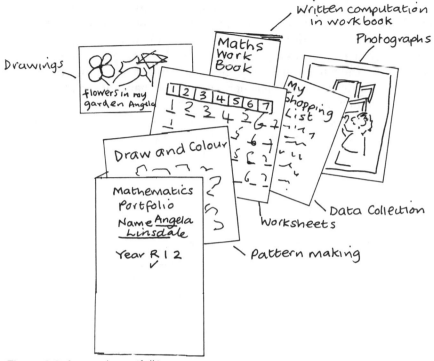

Figure 9.2 A sample portfolio

Records and reports

Whether through externally driven phase assessments or internally driven class assessments, there is the tradition of the annual report to parents. The National Curriculum (England and Wales) legislates for annual reports to be given to parents regarding children's attainment in all subjects. At the end of the final year in the infant school or department parents are also informed of children's SATs performance in the core subjects including mathematics. This requirement should not preclude teachers from compiling comprehensive records and reports, related to all that children have learned, even if it is additional to what is in a prescribed curriculum. As Johnson *et al.* suggest, 'Good management of report writing ... involves a programme of work which is spread out over the year, then drawn together and focused during the summer term' (1992: 51).

REVIEW

It may seem a straightforward matter to make mathematics assessments according to criteria related to the subject matter of the task.

Even so, our assessments need to take in the manner of doing this. When we think 'mathematics' many of us (even though we know better) still think of pages of computations with ticks and crosses against them. Because teachers know that mathematics involves more than computation, and that children spend much mathematics time doing things other than writing out computations, teachers are aware that mathematics assessment is infinitely more complex than merely marking a workbook.

The idea that assessment is marking has consequences for the mathematics assessment we do with young children. If we express these consequences in a rather extreme form, this will serve to emphasise the points:

— 'mastery' in mathematics is easily demonstrable;
— the products of mathematical thinking are enough to measure attainment;
— 'successful performance' is what should be stressed.

If indeed mathematics were pages of computations then the above would form the principles of assessment in mathematics, and it would be an easy business. That is not to say that children's written mathematics should not serve as one of the performances we assess, but it is only one of them.

NOTES

1 The Normal or Standard Distribution Curve underpins much statistical work. There are a number of texts which deal with this sort of distribution and its implications; for example, Rowntree (1981).
2 For more information about the skills involved in collecting information see Clemson and Clemson (1991).
3 For more details about records see Clemson and Clemson (1991).
4 There are many texts describing profiling in great detail; for example Clift et al. (1981) and Garforth and Macintosh (1986).

Chapter 10

Modifying practice

INTRODUCTION

Our intention throughout this book has been to raise questions about the nature of mathematics education in the early years of schooling. In that respect the whole of the book is intended to promote evaluative ideas and principles. However, it is also necessary to focus on the field of evaluation itself so that we can review the major elements for evaluative judgements.

Assessment and evaluation are not the same thing; evaluation is about making judgements and taking actions on the basis of those judgements. Assessment data can, and does, provide information for evaluative purposes but there are many other sources of data that should be used. These data come from the teacher's self-evaluation, observation, discussion, reading and reflection, and the perspectives of others and what they say about schools and schooling experiences. In this chapter we explore some of these areas and identify where some have appeared in discussion earlier in the book. But first we briefly outline the origins of modern curriculum evaluation so that the processes and jargon can be set in context. Then we can better judge the statements of those who proclaim about the efficacy, or otherwise, of our schools and curricula.

EVALUATION IDEAS AND ORIGINS

In the USA early formal evaluation approaches and methods grew out of a desire to evaluate the efficacy of curriculum development initiatives. In no small part, the desire to develop new teaching and learning packages was related to the achievements of the USSR in the space race (see, for example, Carr and Kemmis 1986). New curriculum materials were trialed, discussed, modified and disseminated and increasingly these processes were formally evaluated. At the outset the evaluation was linked to the stated purposes, aims and objectives, this approach being based on the work of Tyler (1949) and others. The performance of children exposed to educational material was the index of its success against stated objectives. Measurement, often through formal written tests, was seen as the basis of this approach.

In the UK evaluation had somewhat different beginnings; it is closely associated with the Schools Council, which had responsibility for curriculum and examinations and was founded in the 1960s. This organisation had no statutory powers and there was no requirement that teachers adopt the materials from the Schools Council funded projects. With regard to curriculum development, the remit was to review development proposals that came to it, prioritise them and fund what was affordable and seen as high priority. There was evaluation of such projects both in development and in outcome. The evaluators were not trained, as Simons indicates. She goes on to state:

> Evaluators had to work with what skills they had and develop approaches they thought relevant to the projects they were evaluating, articulating and developing evaluation theory as they went along. That made for an interesting, diverse field of evaluation practice and partly explains its amateur status and its interest in alternating to classic research models.
>
> (1984: 47)

From this multiplicity of approaches there arose a plethora of evaluation styles and models[1] across a broad spectrum of belief and opinion. Some important current terms emerged, notably the use of participant observation, formative evaluation and illuminative evaluation, as well as the development of techniques of observation and the idea of the reflective practitioner. It is important to remember, though, that all these evaluation stances and approaches are rooted in the evaluation of curriculum and curriculum development. Recently the term 'evaluation' has been adopted for other purposes which are focused, essentially, on the management of systems rather than ideas and learning.

Evaluation and management

In the UK there has, over the last decade, been a growth in discussion of the idea of 'quality'. Much of the driving force for this discussion has come from the industrial and commercial sector. The establishment, for example, of a British Standard (BS5750) which is concerned with consistent quality control has been considered by some educational establishmments as a target for their own operations. Other initiatives include the development of Total Quality Management (TQM) approaches which is used by a number of international companies in, for example, car manufacture and again is under consideration by a number of educational establishments.[2] With this growth in concern for 'quality' of a particular kind there has been the promotion of a new language of evaluation closer to the objectives approaches that emerged in the USA. Words that are now commonplace in educational discourse include 'performance indicators' and 'value added'. These terms have been generated in settings like that of the factory, where 'production' is the goal. Whilst it is possible to be cynical about these ideas in educational contexts, we must address the concerns of those who *do* see them as appropriate. Meeting such challenges can be turned to advantage. We can modify them and use them, and thereby gain additional credibility. Evaluation, today, has moved on from its curriculum development roots.

TIIE EVALUATIVE PROCESS

The evaluation process is continuous in the school setting. It is not summative in the way that it is when an outside agency develops curriculum materials. Teachers in school need to be continuously monitoring activities at all levels with a view to the continuous enhancement of the institution's main mission – the education of young children. In order to do this the staff within schools must have a corporate, clear and resourced self-evaluation responsibility. This means, of course, that each teacher has to see their classroom role as embracing self-evaluation of their teaching. In order to do this it is necessary to be cognisant of what constitutes an evaluative approach, and by what means data can be generated upon which evaluative judgements can be made. These are the things to which we now turn.

Phases of evaluation

There are many models of the evaluation process[3] but all have the same basic facets. In order to carry out evaluation, whether of the curriculum or the systems and structures which support children's learning and teachers' teaching, it is necessary to follow an agreed set of processes in a particular order. This might be as follows:

— identifying priorities and issues
— collecting and analysing data
— reflecting on the analysis
— making and monitoring changes
— reflecting on the whole including the changes
— identifying new priorities and issues.

Small scale 'local' change in its turn becomes part of the whole school and class evaluation. These elements of the evaluation process are not discrete, each affects the other and all need to be kept in view. They can be seen as a cycle of events, or more accurately a spiral, for you do not return to where you were in carrying through evaluation. There follows some indication of what the evaluative process might look like in a series of example situations.

Issue: timing/task match

Children finish their mathematics tasks too soon, or fail to finish in a session.

— collecting and analysing data: list, over a number of sessions, the names of the children, the tasks the children do, the time they take and their performance of that task;
— reflecting on the analysis: if the children are successfully completing tasks quicker than anticipated, could it be that they are rehearsing what they already know? Task–child match needs review. If the task is challenging enough but children still finish too quickly, can session times be reorganised, or can sessions be broken down into shorter periods, after which there is a change of activity? If the children fail to finish, do they understand what has to be done? If not, then task–child match needs to be reviewed, or perhaps the task is simply too long to do in the time, and needs breaking up into small pieces of work;
— making and monitoring changes: implement a single change in the likely direction, reviewing timing as before;
— reflecting on the whole including the changes: note change, and the time taken for tasks by all the children.

Issue: balance of activities

Children are not doing enough practical work in mathematics.

— collecting and analysing data: read and research ways of covering the next steps in mathematics using practical approaches; also invent some to try;
— reflecting on the analysis: choose some strategies and ways of organising the school day, so that children can do a set of activities practically;
— making and monitoring changes: set up resources and put the planned activities into the classroom timetable;
— reflecting on the whole including the changes: review how the activities and all other classroom events have gone.

Issue: pacing

The start to mathematics sessions is 'ragged' with much time 'wasted' before children settle to their tasks.

— collecting and analysing data: during a week or so, review exactly what the children do for the first ten minutes of each mathematics session, choosing different children to observe in each session; list and group the kinds of things they do. For example, they may spend the time searching for resources, 'messing about', or finding out what it is they are supposed to be doing;

— reflecting on the analysis: rank what the children do, putting the most frequent way of spending time at the top of the list. Decide how this item can be tackled. Thus if the children are 'messing about' list some strategies which can be tried to instil higher standards of behaviour in class, and to alter the tasks so that children are better motivated to get on with them;
— making and monitoring changes: implement the changes decided upon for a period of time;
— reflecting on the whole including the changes: try observing what the children do at the beginning of mathematics sessions; include those who did and those who did not 'mess about'. Embark on the next evaluation using the next item on the ranked list of ways children spent their time.

Issue: resource use

Some mathematics scheme resources seem to be used by no class in school.

— collecting and analysing data: ask every member of staff to list the scheme resources they do use, and in which contexts, and those they have no use of and why; review from the teachers' guide to the scheme the predicted use for the resources; examine the match or lack of it between resources and their predicted as against actual use;
— reflecting on the analysis: make judgements about whether resources are defective for the purpose they are intended, whether staff do not understand their use, or whether there are other resources in use which do the job better;
— making and monitoring changes: if the resources are defective and cannot be modified or used in other ways, give them away, throw them out or return them to the supplier; if the problem lies in staff misunderstanding, plan an in-school training course in their use; if other resources are better, write them into the school programme of work;
— reflecting on the whole including the changes: review the whole of the mathematics resource bank and isolate other areas for evaluation.

We now turn our attention to the ways in which data can be collected.

Sources and collection of data

The techniques discussed here are dealt with separately in order to offer the main features of each. In practice a number of techniques may be used in parallel.

Observation

There are two common sorts of observation possibility; observation by the teacher of children in the class, and observation of a teaching episode by a colleague. Both offer a range of evaluation data. In observing the children in your class it is necessary either to accept that the observations will be partial, swift and intermittent or to set up a specific opportunity to observe which enables you to give a period of time for the observation to take place and for notes to be made at that time. Whichever observational approach is being used, the sorts of data about mathematics that can be most easily focused on are:

— children's time on task
— resourcing needs and demands
— co-operative activity in practical and investigative mathematics
— the nature and quality of speaking and listening
— children's responses to the mathematics.

Similar data can come from the observations of another teacher. In this case it is necessary to identify the purposes of an observation session prior to that session and there must be agreement about those purposes and the way in which feedback will be given. In addition to information to fill the categories above, an observer colleague can offer information about the teacher–child interactions, how the teachers spend their time, and the clarity of exposition about the given mathematics topic.

Content analysis

This can be carried out away from the classroom by individual teachers or as part of a whole staff team exercise. The essential ingredients are to do with the match between chosen materials and the mathematics curriculum. This will include looking not only at the level of the topic title but also sampling specific content. There is also a need to look at appropriateness in terms of, for example, reading demand, level of independence demanded of the child, and the teaching styles necessary to fully employ the materials.

Discussion

In Chapter 11 we have identified a number of approaches to structuring group discussions. The important point here is that from such discussions can arise valuable data as well as the identification of issues. Furthermore it is important to see the strength of varied discussion techniques in use with the children as well as with colleagues.

Diaries and logs

In order to capture data for future reflection and use we cannot rely solely on our memories – although this is a part of our experience of classroom life. We need to make notes which, over time, may be helpful in determining trends and issues that are not so readily detected on a day-to-day basis. Such diaries need not be lengthy but should be kept regularly. Again, as children get older, it is worth getting them to write regularly about the mathematics they are doing including a review of the 'hard' bits and how they managed to get over the problems. As children are invited to review books in English, so too they can review their mathematics.

Logs can be kept of particular aspects of classroom life. Here are some examples:

— time spent in introducing different mathematics sessions and topics;
— typical requests for help from the children;
— time spent on different topics against the time planned for that topic.

Assessment

Assessment of children's mathematics work, described in Chapter 9, provides data which can be added to more general evaluative data. Particular value can be obtained from the sharing of children's mathematics work with other colleagues as can the use of diagnostic assessment which should also be shared. Some examples of this kind of exercise are set out in Chapter 11. From these sorts of initiatives can come ideas for action to improve the quality of mathematics learning for children through the school.

Recording

Observation of children and teachers can usefully be supplemented by periodic use of the tape recorder (or indeed the video recorder, though this tends to be more labour intensive). We sometimes find that because of the particular use of language and symbolism we can lose sight of important aspects of learning as we 'drive' to the 'right answer'. As indicated in Chapter 8, the opportunity to re-examine a teaching episode can help with a reflection on children's thinking in mathematics. Tape recordings do not have to be transcribed; listening to them a few times and making notes can be effective and less time consuming.

Another form of recording is photography. Photographs of mathematics displays, children's constructions and groups of children at work can all aid a consideration of positive aspects of your mathematics as well as help identify areas for improvement and change. Such recordings can also feed useful whole staff discussion. Again, as with most of these data sources and techniques the use of photography and audio recording can be a useful addition to the children's repertoire in their mathematics work.

Reading

It is not the case that all of our evaluation need use firsthand data. The reading of articles and books, as well as official documents and the minutes of meetings can all feed our considered reflection of our current practices. Indeed, this professional reading is a traditional and important means of promoting the analysis and sharing of good practice as well as being an agenda-creating exercise.

Staff development

In the past staff development opportunities have been seen as being personal and geared towards change for the individual. With the advent of increased local management of schools and a National Curriculum in the UK, it is now the case that such development has to be seen as contributing to whole school needs and developments whilst being motivating to individual teachers. Increasingly teachers are attending courses on behalf of staff teams, and whole school development initiatives are planned by the staff team. In these circumstances full use of the latter can further the evaluation of school practices and class activities. Recent initiatives by the Department for Education (England and Wales) in the provision of specially funded courses in mathematics have been concerned not only with the enhancement of individual teacher knowledge but also, in practice, with the ways in which this experience can be capitalised upon by schools.

Interviews and questionnaires

The use of interviews and questionnaires have a wide range of applications. In the former, detailed, in-depth information on an individual basis can be obtained. Questionnaires provide more superficial data. Both interviews and questionnaires can include closed and open questions of, in the first instance answers of the yes–no variety, and, in the second, open questions of the 'What if?' type. In our experience we find that interviews are most useful if carried out within a brief which is not too rigid and which allows for the following up of responses at the time. Questionnaires need to be carefully constructed and unambiguous with a clear framework for the recording of responses.

EVALUATING MATHEMATICS EDUCATION

We have set out the factors in mathematics evaluation, and the links between them, in terms of two 'triangles'. They can be linked, but for the current discussion they will be treated separately. In any event readers will be able to forge satisfactory connections for themselves.

The first triangle is built around the classroom, the second the school. They are shown in Figures 10.1 and 10.2. Each offers entry points for evaluation at the corners and the sides of the triangle. Using these six entry points we will illustrate each in turn. This is not to suggest that the entry points are in reality discrete and separate. There is a 'dynamic balance' between them.

Classroom factors

Figure 10.1 uses the teacher, the child (and/or groups of children) and mathematics as the three factors at the points of our first triangle. This gives us the six entry points:

— teacher
— children
— mathematics
— teacher–child
— teacher–mathematics, and
— children–mathematics

We can take each of these and illustrate the issues and ideas that they can help us to concentrate upon. In so doing it is important to bear in mind that the triangle must be viewed from the teacher perspective. It is the teacher who has the responsibility to evaluate their classroom and it is the teacher who is best placed to do so.

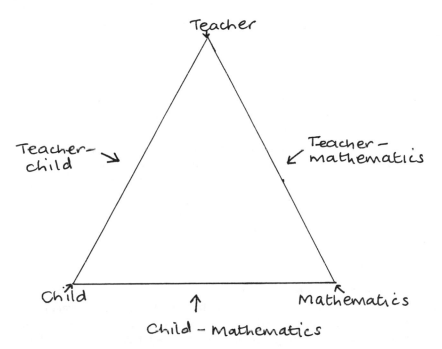

Figure 10.1 The first triangle

Teacher

Here we are concerned, essentially, with teacher self-evaluation. This, as indicated earlier in the chapter means that the teacher is concerned with planning, intentions, delivery, assessment, and the unexpected or un-anticipated outcomes of their teaching with a view to optimising children's learning opportunities. The range of teaching approaches and personal time-management are also integral to a consideration of self as a teacher (see Chapter 7). Action points may arise which will lead to staff development opportunities being taken. The means for establishing evidence for evaluative judgement might include the use of a reflective diary, observation by a colleague, tape recording and reading and reflection.

Children

Here we are concerned with what we know about how a single child or children learn and how they can be supported in developing positive images of themselves and others. The importance of interaction within groups and between individuals and the concerns of the child are of central importance. Data can be collected through the use of observation, diagnostic assessment and examining children's work which helps in the understanding of how they view themselves in mathematical settings. Children should also be encouraged to discuss their needs and expectations and not be hampered by having mathematical feedback which inhibits their honest appraisal of need, and achievement.

Mathematics

Mathematics, as indicated in Part II of this book, brings its own imperatives and these need to be understood in relation to that mathematics which is offered at school. Here, then, we are primarily concerned with evaluation of the formal mathematics materials and ideas presented to children. This evaluation includes looking at the mathematics scheme, other materials presented to the children, mathematical resources, and the sequencing of content and ideas. Data collection techniques will include readability measures, and the degree of match between scheme (and other materials) and the school mathematics plan.

Teacher–children

The interaction between child and teacher is clearly at the heart of the educational process. In looking at the quality of this interaction in mathematics, we are concerned with attitudes to mathematics and the behaviours which may transmit positive (or negative) ideas about the nature of mathematics – for example, giving a child 'a page of sums' as a punishment will surely reinforce negative reactions to mathematics. Data collection can come through observation of children and the teacher by a colleague. This is also the area in which to reflect upon the use of language including the use and style of questioning and answering, and the opportunities for speaking and listening in a mathematical context.

Teacher–mathematics

The major dimension to this interaction is the management of the mathematics provision. Here we are concerned with those organisational necessities which will support the effective and efficient offering of learning opportunities to the children. Facets include the appropriate use of the scheme, the co-ordination of resource provision, the allocation of time for mathematics work, the keeping of records of coverage, and the place of mathematics in the whole curriculum. Data can be collected through checks of children's time on a task, reflection on records, and discussion with colleagues.

Children–mathematics

Whilst all the elements of the triangle are important this dimension is the one which all the others are intended to support. The ways in which the children interact with their mathematics tasks and activities are the concern here. Progression, matching and achievement are key ideas as are concerns with motivation and challenge. Aspects of these are discussed in Chapters 6 to 9. A major issue is the extent to which children are having to respond to relatively fixed mathematics content. Teacher intervention is essential to avoid the curriculum being entirely fixed and knowledge-driven. Children will vary in their approaches and needs in relation to what it is necessary for them to learn; it is important, therefore, that the teacher considers a variety of ways in which the content can be structured and offered. Data collection opportunities are many and include discussion with colleagues, observation, diagnostic and formative assessments of the child's work, and content analysis.

School factors

In Figure 10.2 the features of the second triangle are depicted. These are concerned with the school and its main interested parties. Again this gives us six entry points for evaluation discussion. These are:

— School
— Parents
— Community
— School–parents

— School–community
— Parents–community

We can take each of these and illustrate the issues and ideas that they can help us to concentrate upon. As with the classroom milieu it is the duty of the staff in a school to hold the given points of the triangle, and the interactions, in view.

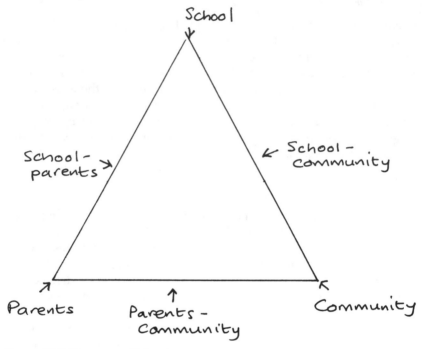

Figure 10.2 The second triangle

School

The role and function of the school is pivotal in this triangle. The emphases here must be on school plans, communication – both internal and external – clear structures of responsibility, meeting any statutory requirements, and the promotion of mathematics in the whole school curriculum. Data collection opportunities include staff discussions, logs of meetings with parents and others, reports and minutes of meetings, analysis of time use, and the use of official documentation.

Parents

As has been indicated in, for example, Chapter 2, there is a need to be cautious about the stereotyping of parental expectation, life-style and attitudes. But it is necessary to understand the rights, and responsibilities, of parents in relation to the legal requirements for children's schooling, and the expectations that a school may place upon parents. Data collection opportunities are parents' evenings, interviews with parents, and surveys of literature which is available to parents.

Community

By community is meant all those agencies and groups that have a legitimate concern with the efficacy of the school and the opportunites and demands offered to the children. These include governors, local education authorities, quasi-governmental organisations and government bodies. In many cases these groups hold a responsibility in relation to the statutory duties imposed upon schools. In this case it is clear that evaluation must serve the demands of accountability. Data collection will come mainly from reading official documentation and scholarly works.

School–parents

The ways in which parents may be supported in understanding the life of their child at school, the sharing of the assessment requirements and demands on their children, and the engagement of parents in the daily life of the school also offer opportunities for a school to reflect upon its mission. Home–school links, as indicated in Chapter 2, are of central importance here. As with 'Parents' above, data collection opportunities lie in interviews with parents, but questionnaires may also have a place. Additional opportunities lie in a review of communication links and reports to parents.

School–community

Data collection to prepare for responses to community requests will embrace the points and interactions of both of the triangles. The differences will lie in the form of presentation as different audiences will require different levels and styles of analysis and reporting. Some of the available information held within a school will, of course, be confidential and not available to all outside groups – for example, that concerning individual children.

Parents–community

Here we are concerned with three particular aspects of the experiences of parents and how these can impact on schools; school policies which reflect the beliefs of society, the concerns that parents may have about schooling through the media, and the official information aimed directly at parents. School plans and policies need to be evaluated in the light of general expectations to do with, for example, equal opportunities. Reporting in the media of partial research findings and mathematical achievement need to be evaluated by the school in relation to the school provision and beliefs in mathematics education. In the UK there are now many leaflets prepared for parents. These need to be kept in the staff library and used in conjunction with the information that has to be prepared by the school.

REVIEW

Evaluation is an imperative for any organisation and particularly so for schools where the outcomes of work are so much wrapped up in promise and potential. It is important to use all that we know about teaching and learning, education management and communication to create the optimum climate for positive learning for children. Because of the dynamic nature of education evaluation can never be a once and for all activity. Continuous monitoring and the management of change are essential ingredients. However, there is a limit to what can be reasonably achieved by a teacher and a staff team – collecting data must not take over from the teaching. In order, therefore, to keep abreast of the curriculum provision and associated systems and links with partners it is necessary to plan evaluation initiatives and to prioritise the evaluation agenda. This can be helped by ensuring that all colleagues both understand the needs of and for evaluation, and have the means to carry out evaluative work. We have to avoid jumping to conclusions however, and it is essential that we are proactive in evaluation and not merely reactive to external demands. Evaluation of the mathematics curriculum, its teaching, the effects of that teaching, and the systems and resources needed to support mathematics should be part of all schools plans and initiatives.

In Part VI of this book we offer a number of ideas and activities that can support teachers in schools in evaluation and development responsibilities. Chapter 11 should be read in close conjunction with the ideas, descriptions and techniques set out in this chapter.

NOTES

1 For those wishing to pursue this area further see, for example, Hamilton (1976) and Simons (1987).
2 The early initiatives in this area and the British Standard has been mainly in the further and higher education sectors but, especially in the context of the Parent's Charter (one of a series of charters developed by the British government) we anticipate schools becoming more involved in a discussion of such matters.
3 Stenhouse (1975) remains a must for those wishing to get insights into process in development. There are many reprints.

Part VI

In-service education

GENERAL INTRODUCTION

Among the general principles that, in our view, are commonly adhered to by teachers of infant mathematics are things like the importance of variety in experience, the need sometimes for practice to achieve mastery and confidence, the need to offer increasingly more complex challenges, and the importance of encouraging personal management and study skills. If we look at the support and development opportunities for teachers in their own learning about mathematics education, the same principles seem to be applicable. When set down with teachers in mind they produce the following suggestions:

— Variety in experience: we embrace this when changing posts or taking a different class within the same school; we can also visit colleagues in other schools to look at a range of ways of teaching mathematics.
— 'Practice' for mastery and confidence: we 'practise' teaching strategies for mathematics in the classroom and continually modify what we do in the light of our evaluations, and we can share in this process with colleagues in the same school.
— Increasingly more complex challenges: we take these on when we seek a more senior post, but also when we increase our knowledge by reading up about mathematics teaching or research.
— Personal management and study skills: we acquired these when we were at school and in initial training, but we refresh these by going on local courses or seeking further qualifications.

While in a post we can take up a range of possible opportunities to invest in our own learning. Aside from courses run by authorities outside school, much in-service work can be accomplished in school.[1] It has definite advantages, for it can focus on the precise needs of individual teachers and it serves to support co-operation by increasing contact between immediate colleagues. In Chapter 11 we have therefore focused our thinking on the kinds of in-service education that can be taken on in school, mostly at low cost to teachers' time or the school budget.

NOTE

1   For a discussion of types of in-service support see Cockcroft (1982).

Chapter 11

Workshop ideas

INTRODUCTION

We have compiled here a series of ideas related to some of the issues raised throughout the book. The issues have been treated in a variety of fashions to offer a range of approaches. Some possible strategies to use in a discussion session when using the in-service ideas we present include the following:

— Maps: drawing a net like a topic web to connect related items or ideas.
— 'Brainstorming': amassing as many ideas as possible, from everyone, without any limits to the range of the contributions.
— Snowball: ideas each individual has written down are shared with another person and an outcome is agreed; the pair then merge with another pair of people to make a bigger group and another collective contribution is arrived at, and so on.
— Nominal group technique: for a polarised issue like, for example, 'the strengths and weaknesses of our internal mathematics records' each member of staff is asked in turn to contribute first to a list of strengths, then to a list of weaknesses. The idea is that people should each give a point in turn, until no one can think of any more. There are no 'right' or 'wrong' contributions and two lists, the positives and the negatives are compiled. These form the agenda for subsequent discussion and action.

(Clemson and Clemson 1989)

These techniques may, of course, be put to use in discussions of issues you have identified as requiring work in your particular school. For example, you may wish to employ the 'snowball' technique to produce a topic web for use across the school, or ways of teaching place value. Before we turn to the examples for in-school workshops it is important to consider those features which we feel contribute to the success of such ventures.

Features of successful workshops

We think it important, when planning workshops, to consider a number of factors which may add to their chances of success. We have set down some of the features which we think important. This list could be the basis for planning or evaluation of such events.

— Take note of the differences between meeting the need for personal development and staff team development in school.
— Plan ahead and in good time.
— Have a clear focus and well-articulated aims (spend time working out exactly what is the theme and the intended outcomes).
— Make sure the resources required are accessible.
— Make sure that there are people within the group who are confident about the mathematics content and processes to be addressed. (If there are none, the first stage in the INSET is either to give people within the school the time and support to study and master what is relevant and/or to enlist the help of someone outside the school).
— Do not attempt too much at one time. (If the 'problem' is extensive break it down into two or three parts and devote a separate session or series of sessions to each).
— Give a clear brief to guest contributors or consultants and planners and organisers (for example, enlisting the help of local 'mathematics expert' may not serve the purposes of the workshop unless the speaker can address the exact issue identified).
— Build on what is known and already achieved (look for current strengths and try to maintain them).
— Devise and secure an agreement which is a form of 'contract' among all the people involved (desultory take-up of changes may jeopardise the whole exercise).
— If possible, pilot the kinds of things the teachers may do in the sessions and following the sessions, before the workshop begins.
— Use techniques (like discussions) which allow everyone to contribute.
— Listen to all that is said.
— Give time for innovation and change to take place, and then review what has happened (do not expect immediate outcomes).
— Make a systematic evaluation with contributions from everyone who took part.

Workshop examples

Now we turn to the themes considered in this chapter. They are as follows:

— Children's learning
— Involving parents

— Increasing mathematics talk in class
— Devising or modifying a school programme of work
— Identifying resource needs
— Sharing teaching difficulties
— Comparing mathematical methods
   Compiling a puzzle or game bank
— Accruing mathematical data
— Creating mathematical displays
— Internal moderation
— Developing internal records
— Using calculators
— Teachers doing mathematics
— Becoming a centre of excellence

Each example given here may be used directly or as a template for other issues which fit real schools and classrooms.[1] Most ideas can be used in a whole staff setting, or just involve some of the staff. We have pointed out those activities that are particularly suitable for teachers in their own classrooms.

CHILDREN'S LEARNING

Aims

To compare samples of children's work and discuss how children learn.

Procedure

Ask each teacher to assemble a collection of pieces of work done by some of the children in the class. They may include written work from one child over a period of time, written work from a group of children or notes about what children have said while doing an activity. At a meeting each teacher can talk about the samples of work assembled. Teachers can share their analysis of the learning steps, and any difficulties encountered.

INVOLVING PARENTS

Aims

To compile a list of ideas about how parents can be involved more in their children's mathematics education, with a view to implementing some of these ideas.

Procedure

At an initial meeting, decide who will try to find out more about 'parents into mathematics' by carrying out the following:

— A literature search
— Contact colleagues in other schools
— Contact mathematics adviser
— Talk to parents who already help in school

Convene a second meeting and share all the information accrued. For example, you may then have a book list, details of important research projects,[2] details of parent–teacher mathematics ventures in schools in your area, advice from the adviser as to which schools have projects working, ideas from parent helpers about what they would like to know about school mathematics, and so on.

Using this information as a starting point brainstorm a list of the possible ways of getting parents of the children you teach involved in mathematics.[3] Rank them in order of feasibility. Carry the first through. Reconvene a meeting to plan the next step.

INCREASING OPPORTUNITIES FOR MATHEMATICS TALK IN CLASS

Aims

To increase the possibilities for children to talk about mathematics, not only to the teacher but to one another.

Procedure

This is a task to tackle over a period of time, for it involves developing an oral culture in the classroom where children know the value of talking and listening, not only to the teacher but to their classmates. Warden (1981) develops a series of strategies for producing this kind of culture. Her class of 9 and 10 year olds was systematically taught skills of discussion, self-control, thinking for themselves and self-assessment. This may be too much to try to achieve with an infant class, but it should be possible to begin the process, using the whole class group at first. Here are some strategies to try:

— Having a whole class 'showing time' and then letting one or two children move around the room while the children are working, showing and talking again with groups of children in turn.
— Giving children clear strategies about what to do for a period of time (perhaps ten minutes or so) including alternative activities if they

cannot get on without consulting you first. This can free you to be with a group of children while they talk about their mathematics work without interruptions. Make a sign to show that you and the group should not be disturbed unless there is a crisis.

— Using a shell, box or other 'special' item to indicate whose turn it is to speak. Let children talk about their mathematics task and then hand the item on to the next speaker. This is a powerful signal to other children that they should listen and not interrupt.

DEVISING OR MODIFYING A SCHOOL PROGRAMME OF WORK

Aims

As a whole, staff to set down a detailed description of the mathematics to be taught in school.

Procedure

Here are a number of 'sound-bites' related to school issues of planning and schemes.

— Planning is going well in many Infant schools but the implementation of plans is quite a different matter. There is a gap between policy and practice.
— Number work still predominates but the time spent is not necessarily productive.
— Don't try to do it all. Do what you choose as a team and do it better.
— Doing *all* of the scheme is not actually justifiable on 'practice' grounds.
— Teachers could probably produce a scheme of their own, but with all there is to do there is simply not the time.

According to Desforges and Cockburn, 'Schemes are dangerous . . . they absolve you from decisions about appropriate work and sequence' (1987: 42)

Assemble all the written resources used for mathematics, including, for example, National Curriculum documentation, teachers' books attached to published schemes and other books you and colleagues have found useful in your mathematics teaching. Ask colleagues to bring any personal resources to a meeting.

Allow time for everyone to look through the written resources in use. Brainstorm a series of overall aims in mathematics for the school. For example, one of these may be to give children the feeling that mathematics is fun. Give each member of staff a copy of the list of aims so that they may compile a series of suggestions regarding how the aims can be met.

Convene another meeting in which everyone discusses their entries under each aim. Use the 'snowball' technique to arrive at a definitive list of aims and steps to reach these. Get this typed up so that each member of staff can have one. A précis of this document should serve as a mission statement to show governors and parents.

IDENTIFYING RESOURCE NEEDS

Aims

To identify resource needs, resources currently in use and to consider resource access.

Procedure

Ask each member of staff to compile an inventory of all the resources they hold. They should indicate which ones they use, those that are redundant, and then add in resources they would like but do not have at present. Add to this a school inventory of centrally held resources. Discuss the following:

— how resources in use can be allocated and stored for best access;
— how redundant resources can be disposed of (perhaps by re-allocation to another class, or by passing them on to another school);
— how resource needs that are not yet satisfied can be met.

Here are two lists of resouces which may be used to contribute to the discussion:

Some suggested general resources

— Beads, conkers and other nuts, shells, marbles, sticks, timber offcuts, wooden blocks, cotton reels, pressed and mounted leaves, seeds, feathers, egg cups, spoons, soft toys, model farm animals, 'dolls house' furniture and dolls, model cars, socks, balls of wool, spent matches, elastic bands, pebbles, pieces of string and rope.
— Containers, cartons and boxes of all kinds, including jugs, beakers, jars and plastic bottles, tins, yogurt pots, margarine tubs, matchboxes, food boxes, egg boxes and boxes big enough for children to get into.
— Marbles, beads, dice and spinners.
— Building bricks, modelling clay, paper and plastic straws.
— Pictures from magazines and catalogues, old greeting cards and postcards.
— Number lines, play money, metre sticks, cardboard clock face, rubber stamps with pictures, numbers, coins or shapes on them; number games; calculators.
— Fabrics, metal objects and samples of natural materials.

— A wide variety of art materials, including a range of varieties of paper, cardboard, gummed shapes, scissors, sticky tape, chalks, brushes, paints and inks.
— Blank dice and many sided dice.
— Counting books and story books.
— Mathematics books for the teacher.

Some suggested resources for parts of mathematics

— Plastic money and play paper notes.
— Containers of different shapes and volumes and measuring jugs.
— Balances and scales and standard 'weights'.
— Interval timers, play clock face and a stopwatch.
— Rules and tapes and trundle wheels.
— Constructional materials, from paper straws and card to plasticine and bought in 'building kits'.
— Plasticised mirrors.
— Compasses.
— Set-squares.

(Clemson and Clemson 1992: 5, 69)

There are many possible additions to these basic lists.

SHARING TEACHING DIFFICULTIES

Aims

To share possible strategies for teaching children who are in difficulty with mathematics concepts.

Procedure

This idea is similar to a 'problem page' in a magazine, except that all members of staff can contribute problems and be the 'experts' who give the replies. This can be an ongoing activity throughout every school year. For example, as part of regular staff meetings time can be set aside for sharing teaching difficulties.

As a starter to this development ask each member of staff to come to a staff meeting with an anecdote from the past about a specific difficulty a child in their class experienced in mathematics, and how it was resolved. Ask everyone to write up their case study for a confidential staffroom file.

Ask everyone to come to the next meeting with details of any current difficulties children in their class are having. Discuss each dilemma in turn during the meeting, and arrive at some strategies to try.

At the next meeting get feedback as to which strategies were attempted and which worked.

COMPARING MATHEMATICAL METHODS

Aims

This is a two-step exercise. The first is to find out some of the methods teachers use to solve computation problems and the second is to look at some of the methods the children use. The ultimate aim is that everyone should feel confident about allowing the children to use a variety of methods.

Procedure

This may prove a rather threatening idea for some people. To open up the issue ask everyone to read about the teachers' methods we explored in Chapter 5, then set everybody a few computations to set down or do in their heads. Ask them to write notes about exactly what goes on as they find the answer. Discuss the different strategies that emerge.

To open the discussion of children's methods find some case studies in books that show children's ways of doing mathematics. See, for example, Hughes (1986) and Atkinson (1992). Let everyone have a look at these examples. This anecdote from Desforges and Cockburn (1987) may support initial discussion:

Six-year-old Darren was seen using a standard procedure with Unifix cubes to complete addition sums with a limit of nine whilst in a previous interview had exhibited a wide range of approaches to such problems:

INTERVIEWER: Try this. $5 + \square = 6$.

DARREN: Five to make six (immediately writes '1' in the box).

INTERVIEWER: Okay. $2 + \square = 10$.

DARREN: Two to make ten. (Holds up 10 fingers. Puts down two, counts the rest and puts '8' in the box.)

INTERVIEWER: Okay. $5 - \square = 2$.

DARREN: Five take away to make two (immediately writes '3' in the box).

INTERVIEWER: Now this, $11 - \square = 5$.

DARREN: Oh dear I haven't got enough fingers. (He puts a pencil on the desk and his fingers alongside it.) I've got eleven fingers now. (Puts down five fingers and nods serially at the rest – presumably counting them. Puts '6' in the box.)

INTERVIEWER: Try this, $10 + \square = 16$.

DARREN: (Writes '10' in the box. Then) No! That would make 20. Oh, it's six!

It seemed that Darren was well in advance of the tasks his teacher set him. He appeared to have a number of strategies for doing both addition and subtraction problems including direct answering, using fingers, using props and checking answers. Left to his own devices he used the technique that he felt he needed, resorting to props only when he could not directly answer. Told what to do he did as he was told.

(1987: 92)

Over a period of a few weeks ask everyone to collect three samples of children's own work in the classroom. The children do not need to be 'set' to work specifically for this exercise. Draw on examples which are already in their books or which occur in everyday work, or write down explanations children have given about how they do their mathematics.

In a whole staff meeting let everyone compare notes and decide on how to act on outcomes. For example, you and your colleagues may want to file all the methods children use, keep a portfolio of 'methods for addition', 'pictures of information' and so on. Or you may believe your findings are of value to other teachers, in which case you could compile an article and submit it to the editor of a suitable journal.

CREATING A PUZZLE OR GAME BANK

Aims

To add to school resources by collecting puzzles and making games.

Procedure

With whole staff commitment each teacher can agree that over, say, two months, they will find six mathematical puzzles and invent and make a mathematical game. The puzzles can be of the sort that appear in children's comics. Copied, modified or extended they can be added to classroom resources. Inventing a game may involve a survey of the kinds of games available, and an audit of the games available in school. If you are starting a collection teachers could elect to make one of the following:

— a track game
— a matching game
— a strategy game.

If these work well you can extend the collection by asking each teacher to make another game of a different kind. Volunteer parents are sometimes very willing to make a 'good' copy of a game you have roughed out.

ACCRUING MATHEMATICAL DATA

Aims

To examine ways of creating a school data bank or data base which children can access and use in a variety of ways.

Procedure

In a staff meeting 'brainstorm' all the ideas everyone can offer about data that can be collected from all possible readily accessible sources, including perhaps the following:

— The children themselves in school (for example, eye colour and height).
— The children themselves about their lives outside school (for example, the kind of house they live in, their pets, the names of their brothers and sisters).
— The adults in school (from lunchtime assistants, secretary, caretaker, cleaner, teachers, visitors – things like views on conservation, news-papers read).
— The school buildings and environment (for example, brick patterns in school walls, colours of flowers in the school garden).
— School records (birthdays and addresses – noting the need for anonymity here).

Devise a series of strategies for collecting and storing the information so that the children can access it. For example, the school may wish to declare a 'data fortnight' in which all the children in all the classes work on collecting information about some aspects of themselves, their school, where they live, or some other topic. The results would make an impressive through-school display, and the information could be put in store for subsequent classes of children to use.

As an extension of this activity the staff can inspect a range of computer software packages which have data base facilities, and choose a package which is suitable for teachers and young children to access and use.

CREATING MATHEMATICAL DISPLAYS

Aims

To compile a file of ideas for mathematical displays.

Procedures

At a first meeting share ideas about display principles, standards and what displays are for. Your list may include some ideas like this:

— to make a good impression on visitors;
— to present a positive image of mathematics to children and parents;
— to tempt children into 'doing' mathematics through an interactive presentation;
— as a stimulus to begin work on a mathematics theme;
— as a presentation of work completed, to give teacher and children a sense of achievement.

From the list of reasons you and your colleagues have for creating a display, let each member of staff choose one. Identify the possible locations for displays, and let each member of staff choose one that is appropriate for their display. For example, the display for visitors to the school may be best placed in the entrance hall. Work out a time scale for producing all the displays; perhaps three weeks or so. When the deadline is reached, convene a meeting at which problems in creating the displays can be shared, as well as impressions as to their usefulness and effects on the children.

INTERNAL MODERATION

Aims

To find out whether teachers' judgements about the standard of the children's written work in mathematics have reliability across the school.

Procedure

Ask each member of staff to select two or three pieces of mathematics recording what different children in their class have done. Ask them to block out the children's names on the work and assign them a letter to identify them. Ask each teacher to write their own judgement about the standard of each piece of work. Lay out all the pieces of work (but not the class teachers' judgements) on the table. Let all the teachers identify the standard of work in all the work samples other than those they themselves submitted. Compare and discuss the judgements made.

DEVELOPING INTERNAL RECORDS

Aims

To develop internal records in mathematics which are clear and useful to everyone who is allowed access to them.

Procedures

Begin by asking everyone to examine the current record system carefully. In a staff meeting, using, for example, nominal group technique, share all the strengths and shortcomings of the present system. Work out some strategies to overcome the shortcomings. Elect a member of staff to produce a draft version of a new record. You may find that there is a variety of suggestions about the form a record should take. For example, it may be for one child and cover part of mathematics through the school, or the whole of mathematics through the school, or the whole of mathematics for the year or at a given level. Circulate copies of the draft so that everyone can write their comments on it. In a second meeting discuss possible modifications. Ask a volunteer to redraft the record form. Before it is produced for mass consumption run off some pilot copies which colleagues can try out. When everyone is happy with the form put it into full use. At the end of the school year review the form to see if modifications are necessary. Thereafter, subject it to annual review.

USING CALCULATORS

Aims

To remind teachers that calculators can be used in a variety of mathematics tasks throughout the infant years.

Procedure

Ask each member of staff to write down an example of each of the ways they use calculators in their classroom. For instance, they may let children use them to check work, or 'invent' calculations for others to do. At a meeting, collate these examples and invite everyone to try them all with children. When they have tried them, ask each teacher to write or draw a draft 'calculator fun sheet' suitable for some of the children in their class. Make copies of these and at another meeting talk about the following:

— How they might be adapted for more or less able children.
— How calculators can be used with children with limited reading skills.
— How a school bank of calculator work might be assembled.
— How the teachers' understanding of calculator work might be extended.

For example, under this final item you may decide to subscribe to suitable journals,[4] join professional organisations which may produce publications about using calculators, or view some resources for teacher education.[5]

TEACHERS DOING MATHEMATICS

Aims

To enable teachers to increase their mathematical confidence by taking pleasure in doing mathematics.

Procedure

Ask each member of staff to find some mathematics books, including some written for children from about 10 years old and some for adults. There follow some suggested titles:

ApSimon, H. (1984) *Mathematical Byways in Ayling, Beeling, and Ceiling*, Oxford: Oxford University Press.

Bolt, B. (1982) *Mathematical Activities: A Resource Book for Teachers*, Cambridge: Cambridge University Press.

Clemson, D. and Clemson, W. (1993) *Blueprints: Mathematics Investigations*, Cheltenham: Stanley Thornes.

Gardner, M. (1985) *Mathematical Magic Show*, London: Penguin Books.

Hogben, L. (1936) *Mathematics for the Million*, London: George Allen & Unwin.

Jones, L. (ed.) (1991) *Teaching Mathematics and Art*, Cheltenham: Stanley Thornes.

Mottershead, L. (1985) *Investigations in Mathematics*, Oxford: Basil Blackwell.

Paulos, J.A. (1988) *Innumeracy: Mathematical Illiteracy and its Consequences*, London: Penguin Books.

Stewart, I. (1989) *Game, Set and Math: Enigmas and Conundrums*, London: Penguin Books.

Wells, D. (1991) *The Penguin Dictionary of Curious and Interesting Geometry*, London: Penguin Books.

Woodman, A. and Albany, E. (1988) *Mathematics through Art and Design*, London: Unwin Hyman.

Ask colleagues to explore the books, try out the puzzles or exercises and choose two or three. Make enough copies of these examples for every member of staff to have one. Let all the staff come to a workshop and try out all the puzzles and exercises and discuss which ones they enjoyed. Such meetings can then be held regularly so that the staff can get more involved in mathematics.

BECOMING A CENTRE OF EXCELLENCE

Aims

To create and promote the school as one in which the teaching and learning of mathematics is excellent.

Procedures

This is to take on all the messages within this book. There is a series of initiatives that could be taken. You and your colleagues can assemble additional ones following these suggestions:

— Create a study programme for the staff, by suggesting a series of seminars on various aspects of mathematics in infant schools. Compile a reading list, and let each member of staff prepare a short paper to present at each seminar.
— Do a through-school evaluation exercise about mathematics teaching and learning, resourcing, space and time. Devise a list of actions to improve each of these aspects.
— Involve advisory staff and staff at the local higher education institution if they are available, to make their suggestions about what makes a centre 'excellent'.
— Suggest to local schools that you would like to have a mathematics open day, and could they contribute by bringing along and erecting a display showing some of the work done by children in their school. Invite all the children and their parents to view the display one evening.
— Create an exemplary work display either in the staffroom or for the children to look at. Change the items on display each week.
— Give children mathematical challenges to do in the holidays (*not* '*sums*'). Here are some examples of the kind of project they might enjoy:

> make a junk model cart with wheels that turn;
> do a picture story showing what you do on one Sunday in the holidays;
> make a counting chart for a toddler (no numerals, just groups to count);
> make a little book with all the nursery rhymes that have numbers in them;
> make up a maze puzzle for your friend to do.

REVIEW

We know that teaching is arduous and that teachers are extremely busy. However, we also believe that teachers hold to the idea that everyone is a 'learner for life' and that they themselves are constantly learning. Teachers do not therefore need to be persuaded that their expertise in mathematics education can be enhanced by continuing to learn about it. Teachers would, we are sure, also agree with us that it is they who are at the 'sharp end' of criticism of school mathematics and it is they who are obliged to 'raise standards' and bring about a numerate society.

Cockcroft (1982) puts the need for in-service support very powerfully:

All those who teach mathematics need continuing support throughout their careers in order to be able to develop their professional skills and so maintain and enhance the quality of their work. . . . Any improvement in the standards of mathematics in schools must come largely as a result of the efforts of those who are already in post.

(paras 715, 716)

Cockcroft implies that such support should extend beyond that accorded to other subjects for reasons which have to do with the following:

— the importance of mathematics both in its own right and as an adjunct to other subjects;
— concern about 'standards';
— lack of teacher expertise or training;
— the changing curriculum including increased use of calculators and computers.

Now, more than a decade after that report, the imperatives remain the same.

Judicious take-up of appropriate in-service provision, and evaluation of what is done in other curriculum areas, can set us thinking afresh about sessions of mathematics. As Dawson and Trivett suggest:

In art, for example, do you have an emphasis on correction? Do you have children only copy the art of others?

In science do you enquire, with lots of discussion? Whose authority do you rely on for what each individual sees?

In physical education is there only one way of kicking the soccer ball . . ?

If letters to the Queen are taught in their particular formal way, is there only one form for thanking grandma for a birthday present?

When children talk to us do we stop them every moment to correct their speech, their accents, their intonations. . ?

. . .think of teaching maths in the ways *you* teach other subjects and try to use the same processes in maths. . .

(1981: 132)

By constantly seeking learning opportunities both for themselves and young children teachers can, we are sure, find ever more successful ways of helping to make mathematics as exciting and accessible as anything else done in school. We hope this book will help them to do just that.

NOTES

1 There are more examples of workshop ideas in Clemson and Clemson (1991).
2 For example, the IMPACT Project: Maths with Parents and Children and Teachers (see Merttens and Vass 1990).

3 Ideas compiled by the Mathematical Association (1987) are listed in Chapter 2.
4 For example, *Strategies: Maths and Problem Solving 3–13* (Questions Publishing Company); and *Mathematics Teaching* (the quarterly journal of the Association of Teachers of Mathematics).
5 See, for example, The Calculator-Aware Number Curriculum video referred to in footnote 6 in Chapter 3.

Bibliography

Aldrich, R. (1982) *An Introduction to the History of Education*, London: Hodder & Stoughton.

Alexander, R. (1992a) 'Faith and the fruits of heresy', *Times Educational Supplement, Update* September.

Alexander, R. (1992b) *Policy and Practice in Primary Education*, London: Routledge.

Alexander, R., Rose, J. and Woodhead, C. (1992) *Curriculum Organisation and Classroom Practice in Primary Schools: A Discussion Paper*, London: Department of Education and Science.

Arcana, J. (1983) *Every Mother's Son: The Role of Mothers in the Making of Men*, London: The Women's Press.

Atkinson, S. (ed.) (1992) *Mathematics with Reason: The Emergent Approach to Primary Maths*, London: Hodder & Stoughton.

Ausubel, D.P. (1968) *Educational Psychology: A Cognitive View*, New York: Holt, Rinehart & Winston.

Belotti, E.G. (1975) *Little Girls: Social Conditioning and its Effects on the Stereotyped Role of Women During Infancy*, London: Writers and Readers Publishing Cooperative.

Bennett, S.N. (1976) *Teaching Styles and Pupil Progress*, London: Open Books.

Bennett, S.N. (1978) 'Recent research on teaching: a dream, a belief, and a model', *British Journal of Educational Psychology,* 48: 127–47.

Bennett, S.N. (1992) *ASPE Paper Number 1: Managing Learning in the Primary Classroom*, Stoke-on-Trent: ASPE/ Trentham Books.

Bernstein, B. (1971) *Class, Codes and Control, Vol. 1: Theoretical Studies Towards a Sociology of Language*, London: Routledge & Kegan Paul.

Bird, M. (1991) *Mathematics for Young Children: An Active Thinking Approach*, London: Routledge.

Bird, M. (1992) 'Asking ourselves questions', in Atkinson, S. (ed.) *Mathematics with Reason: The Emergent Approach to Primary Maths*, Sevenoaks: Hodder & Stoughton.

Blenkin, G.M. and Kelly, A V. (1987) *The Primary Curriculum: A Process Approach to Curriculum Planning* (Second edn), London: Harper & Row.

Boydell, D. (1978) *The Primary Teacher in Action*, London: Open Books

Brissenden, T.H.F. (1980) *Mathematics Teaching: Theory in Practice*, London: Harper & Row.

Brissenden, T.H.F. (1988) *Talking about Mathematics: Mathematical Discussion in Primary Classrooms*, Oxford: Basil Blackwell.

Brown, T. (1987) 'Infant classroom practice', *Mathematics Teaching* 118 (March), 2–5.

Bruner, J.S. (1966) *Towards a Theory of Instruction*, Boston: Belknap Press of Harvard University Press.

Buxton, L. (1984) *Mathematics for Everyman*, London: Dent.

Campbell, J. (1992) *ASPE Paper Number 2: Managing Teachers' Time in Primary Schools: Concepts, Evidence and Policy Issues*, Stoke-on-Trent: ASPE/ Trentham Books.

Carr, W. and Kemmis, S. (1986) *Becoming Critical; Education, Knowledge and Action Research*, Lewes: Falmer Press.

Central Advisory Council for Education (CACE) (1967) *Children and their Primary Schools* (The Plowden Report), London: HMSO.

Chazan, M, and Laing, A.F. (1982) *The Early Years*, Milton Keynes: The Open University Press.

Chazan, M., Laing, A.F., Shackleton, Bailey M. and Jones, G. (1980) *Some of our Children: The Early Education of Children with Special Needs*, London: Open Books.

Choat, E. (1980) *Mathematics and the Primary School Curriculum*, Slough: NFER.

Clemson, D. (1992) 'An eight year old Pythagoras?', *Link*, 13, Summer, University of Lancaster: Department of Educational Research.

Clemson, D. and Clemson, W. (1989) *The Really Practical Guide to National Curriculum 5–11*, Cheltenham: Stanley Thornes

Clemson, D. and Clemson, W. (1991) *The Really Practical Guide to Primary Assessment*, Cheltenham: Stanley Thornes.

Clemson, W. and Clemson, D. (1990) *Beyond the School Gate: A Parent's Guide to Primary Schools and the National Curriculum*, Sevenoaks: Hodder & Stoughton.

Clemson, W. and Clemson, D. (1992) *Blueprints Maths Key Stage 1: Teacher's Resource Book*, Cheltenham: Stanley Thornes.

Clift, P., Weiner, G. and Wilson, E. (1981) *Record Keeping in Primary Schools*, Basingstoke: Macmillan.

Cockcroft Report (1982) *Mathematics Counts: Report of the Committee of Inquiry into the Teaching of Mathematics in Schools under the Chairmanship of Dr W. H. Cockcroft*, London: HMSO.

Dahl, R. (1988) *Matilda*, London: Jonathan Cape.

Daintith, J. and Nelson, R.D. (1989) *The Penguin Dictionary of Mathematics*, London: Penguin.

Davies, I.K. (1976) *Objectives in Curriculum Design*, London: McGraw Hill.

Dawson, S. and Trivett, J. (1981) 'And now for something different: Teaching by not teaching', in Floyd, A. (ed.) *Developing Mathematical Thinking*, Wokingham: Addison-Wesley in association with the Open University Press.

Dean, J. (1983) *Organising Learning in the Primary School Classroom*, London: Croom Helm.

Department for Education (DFE) (1992) *Education Observed: The Implementation of the Curricular Requirements of ERA* (An overview by HM Inspectorate on the second year 1990–1), London: HMSO.

Department of Education and Science (DES) (1978a) *Primary Education in England: A Survey by HM Inspectors of Schools*, London: HMSO.

Department of Education and Science (DES) (1978b) *Special Educational Needs: Report of the Committee of Enquiry into the Education of Handicapped Children*, (The Warnock Report), London: HMSO.

Department of Education and Science (DES) (1979) *HMI Series: Matters for Discussion, Mathematics 5–11: A Handbook of Suggestions*, London: HMSO.

Department of Education and Science (DES) (1988) *Attitudes and Gender Differences: Mathematics at Age 11 and 15*, Assessment of Performance Unit, Windsor: NFER Nelson.

Department of Education and Science (DES) (1989) *HMI Aspects of Primary Education: The Teaching and Learning of Mathematics*, London: HMSO.

Department of Education and Science (DES) (1990) *Education Observed: Special Needs Issues: A Survey by HMI*, London: HMSO.

Department of Education and Science (DES) (1991) *Mathematics in the National Curriculum*, London: HMSO.

Desforges, C. and Cockburn, A. (1987) *Understanding the Mathematics Teacher: A Study of Practice in First Schools*, Lewes: Falmer Press.

Dewey, J. (1938) *Experience and Education*, New York: Kappa Delta Pi (London: Collier-Macmillan, 1963).

Dickson, L., Brown, M. and Gibson, O. (1984) *Children Learning Mathematics: A Teacher's Guide to Recent Research*, London: Cassell.

Dienes, Z.P. (1960) *Building up Mathematics*, London: Hutchinson.

Dienes, Z.P. (1966) *Mathematics in the Primary School*, London: Macmillan.

Docking, J. (1990) *Primary Schools and Parents*, Sevenoaks: Hodder & Stoughton.

Donaldson, M. (1978) *Children's Minds*, London: Fontana/Collins.

Duffin, J. (1987) 'The language of primary mathematics', in Preston, M. (ed.) *Mathematics in Primary Education*, Lewes: Falmer Press.

Early Years Curriculum Group (1989) *Early Childhood Education: The Early Years and the National Curriculum*, Stoke-on-Trent: Trentham Books.

Ernest, P. (1991) *The Philosophy of Mathematics Education*, London: Falmer Press.

Evans K. (1985) *The Development and Structure of the English School System*, Sevenoaks: Hodder & Stoughton.

Fauvel, J. and Gray, J. (1987) *The History of Mathematics – A Reader*, London: Macmillan Education in association with the Open University.

Flegg, G. (1984) *Numbers: Their History and Meaning*, Harmondsworth: Penguin Books.

Floyd, A. (ed.) (1981) *Developing Mathematical Thinking*, Wokingham: Addison-Wesley.

Foss, B. (1969) 'Other aspects of child psychology', in Peters, R. (ed.) *Perspectives on Plowden*, London: Routledge & Kegan Paul.

Frith, D. and Macintosh, H. (1984) *A Teacher's Guide to Assessment*, Cheltenham: Stanley Thornes.

Gagné, R.M. (1970) *The Conditions of Learning (second edn)*, New York: Holt, Rinehart & Winston.

Galton, M. and Simon, B. (1980) *Progress and Performance in the Primary Classroom*, London: Routledge & Kegan Paul.

Galton, M., Simon, B. and Croll, P. (1980) *Inside the Primary Classroom*, London: Routledge & Kegan Paul.

Garforth, D. and Macintosh, H. (1986) *Profiling: A User's Manual*, Cheltenham: Stanley Thornes.

Gifford, S. (1990) 'Young children's representations of number operations', *Mathematics Teaching* 132, September.

Goodwin, J. (1987) 'Mathematical resources in the primary school', in Preston, M. (ed.) *Mathematics in Primary Education*, Lewes: Falmer Press.

Hamilton, D. (1976) *Curriculum Evaluation*, London: Open Books.

Hardy, G. (1940, 1992) *A Mathematician's Apology*, Cambridge: Canto, imprint of Cambridge University Press.

Harling, P. and Roberts, T. (1988) *Primary Mathematics Schemes*, London: Hodder & Stoughton.

Haylock, D. and Cockburn, A. (1989) *Understanding Early Years Mathematics*, London: Paul Chapman Publishing.

Hegarty, S. (1987) *Meeting Special Needs in Ordinary Schools: An Overview*, London: Cassell.

Hogben, L. (1936) *Mathematics for the Million*, London: George Allen & Unwin.

Holden, C., Hughes, M. and Desforges, C. (1993) 'What do parents want from assessment?' *Education* 3–13, 21 (1), March.

Hollingdale, S. (1991 second impression) *Makers of Mathematics*, Harmondsworth: Penguin Books.

Hughes, M. (1986) *Children and Number: Difficulties in Learning Mathematics*, Oxford: Basil Blackwell.

Inner London Education Authority Learning Resources Branch (1985) *Everyone Counts: Looking for Bias and Insensitivity in Primary Mathematics Materials*, London: ILEA.

Joffe, L. and Foxman, D. (1984) 'Attitudes and sex differences', *Mathematics in Schools*, September.

Johnson, G., Hill, B. and Tunstall, P. (1992) *Primary Records of Achievement*, London: Hodder & Stoughton.

Killworth, S., Neilson, L. and Atkinson, S. (1992) 'Nursery children explore maths', in Atkinson, S. (ed.) *Mathematics With Reason: The Emergent Approach to Primary Maths*, London: Hodder & Stoughton.

Kline, M. (1972) *Mathematics in Western Culture*, Harmondsworth: Penguin (Pelican) Books. (First published in the USA 1953.)

Lawton, D. (1981) *An Introduction to Teaching and Learning*, London: Hodder & Stoughton.

Lawton, D. (1983) *Curriculum Studies and Educational Planning*, London: Hodder & Stoughton.

Mathematical Association (1987a) *Maths Talk*, Cheltenham: Stanley Thornes.

Mathematical Association (1987b) *Sharing Mathematics with Parents*, Cheltenham: Stanley Thornes.

McIntosh, A. (1977) 'When will they ever learn?' *Forum for the Discussion of New Trends in Education*, 19 (3), Summer.

McLeod, W. (ed.) (1987) *Collins Dictionary and Thesaurus in One Volume*, Glasgow: Collins.

McPherson, T. and Payne, G. (1987) '"Is it an add, Miss?": Mathematics in the early primary years', in Preston, M. (ed.) *Mathematics in Primary Education*, Lewes: Falmer Press.

Merttens, R. and Vass, J. (1990) *Sharing Maths Cultures*, Lewes: Falmer Press.

Mortimore, P., Sammons, P., Stoll, L., Lewis, D. and Ecob, R. (1988) *School Matters: The Junior Years*, London: Open Books.

National Curriculum Council (NCC) (1989) *Curriculum Guidance Two: A Curriculum for All: Special Educational Needs in the National Curriculum*, York: NCC.

Northam, J. (1982) 'Girls and boys in primary maths books', *Education* 10(1), Spring.

OFSTED (1993) *Curriculum Organisation and Classroom Practice in Primary Schools: A Follow-up Report*.

Orton, A. (1987) *Learning Mathematics: Issues, Theory and Classroom Practice*, London: Cassell.

Papert, S. (1980) *Mindstorms: Children, Computers, and Powerful Ideas*, Brighton: Harvester Press.

Piaget, J. (1952) *The Child's Conception of Number*, London: Routledge & Kegan Paul.

Piaget, J. and Inhelder, B. (1956) *The Child's Conception of Space*, London: Routledge & Kegan Paul.

Pimm, D. (1981) *Mathematics? I Speak it Fluently*, in Floyd, A. (ed.) *Developing Mathematical Thinking*, Wokingham: Addison–Wesley.

Plowden Report (1967) *Children and their Primary Schools: Report of the Central Advisory Council for Education in England*, London: HMSO.

Plunkett, S. (1979) 'Decomposition and all that rot', *Mathematics in Schools* 8 (3), 2–7, May.

Pollard, A. and Tann, S. (1987) *Reflective Teaching in the Primary School: A Handbook for the Classroom*, London: Cassell.

Polya, G. (1957 second edn) *How to Solve It*, Harmondsworth: Penguin Books (published in 1990 with permission of Princeton University Press).

Pound, L., Cook, L. Court, J., Stevenson, J. and Wadsworth, J. (1992) *The Early Years: A Curriculum for Young Children: Mathematics*, London: Harcourt Brace Jovanovich.

Preston, M. (1987) *Mathematics in Primary Education*, Lewes: Falmer Press.

Proudfoot, M. (1992) 'Teaching maths without relying on a scheme', in Atkinson, S. (ed.) *Mathematics with Reason: The Emergent Approach to Primary Maths*, London: Hodder & Stoughton.

Reynolds, J. and Skilbeck, M. (1976) *Culture and the Classroom*, London: Open Books.

Reynolds, P. (1982) 'Teaching mathematics in primary and middle schools', in Cornelius, M. (ed.) *Teaching Mathematics* London: Croom Helm.

Richards, P. (1982) 'Difficulties in learning mathematics', in Cornelius, M. (ed.) *Teaching Mathematics*, London: Croom Helm.

Rowntree, D. (1977) *Assessing Students: How Shall We Know Them?*, London: Harper & Row.

Rowntree, D. (1981) *Statistics Without Tears: A Primer for Non-mathematicians*, Harmondsworth: Penguin.

Rowntree, D. (1982) *Educational Technology in Curriculum Development* (second edn), London: Harper & Row.

Rutter, M., Maughan, B., Mortimore, P. and Ouston, J. (1979) *Fifteen Thousand Hours: Secondary Schools and their Effects on Children*, London: Open Books.

Shipman, M. (1983) *Assessment in Primary and Middle Schools*, London: Croom Helm.

Shuard, H. (1986) 'The relative attainment of girls and boys in mathematics in the primary years', in Burton, L. (ed.) *Girls in to Maths Can Go*, London: Holt, Rinehart & Winston.

Shuard, H. and Rothery, A. (eds) (1984) *Children Reading Mathematics*, London: John Murray.

Simons, H. (1984) 'Issues in curriculum evaluation at the local level', in Skilbeck, M. (ed.) *Evaluating the Curriculum in the Eighties*, London: Hodder & Stoughton.

Simons, H. (1987) *Getting to Know Schools in a Democracy; The Politics and Process of Evaluation*, Lewes: Falmer Press.

Skemp, R.R. (1971) *The Psychology of Learning Mathematics*, Harmondsworth: Penguin Books.

Skemp, R.R. (1989) *Mathematics in the Primary School*, London: Routledge.

Skilbeck, M. (1976) 'Ideologies and Values', Unit 3 of Course E203, *Curriculum Design and Development*, Milton Keynes: Open University Press.

Skinner, B.F. (1954) 'The science of learning and the art of teaching', *Harvard Educational Review* 24, 86–97.

St John-Brooks, C. (1992) 'Figures in an altered landscape', *Times Educational Supplement Update*, September.

Stenhouse, L. (1975) *An Introduction to Curriculum Research and Development*, London: Heinemann.

Stewart, I. (1990) *Does God Play Dice?: The Mathematics of Chaos*, Harmondsworth: Penguin Books.

Swann Report (1985) *Education for All: The Report of the Committee of Inquiry into the Education of Children from Ethnic Minority Groups*, London: HMSO.

Thomas, K. (1983) *Man and the Natural World: Changing Attitudes in England 1500–1800*, London: Allen Lane.

Tizard, B. and Hughes, M. (1984) *Young Children Learning*, London: Fontana.

Tizard, B., Blatchford, P., Burke, J., Farquhar, C. and Plewis, I. (1988) *Young Children at School in the Inner City*, Hove: Lawrence Erlbaum Associates.

Tyler, R. W. (1949) *Basic Principles of Curriculum and Instruction*, Chicago: University of Chicago Press.

Walden, R. and Walkerdine, V. (1982) *Girls and Mathematics: The Early Years*, Bedford Way Papers 8, University of London Institute of Education.

Warden, J. (1981) 'Making space for doing and talking with groups in a primary classroom', in Floyd, A. (ed.) *Developing Mathematical Thinking*, Wokingham: Addison-Wesley in association with the Open University Press.

Waters, D. (1979) *Management and Headship in the Primary School*, London: Ward Lock Educational.

Whitaker, P. (1983) *The Primary Head*, London: Heinemann Educational Books.

Wragg, E.C. (1987) *Teacher Appraisal: A Practical Guide*, London: Macmillan Education.

Wragg, E.C. (1991) 'Good teaching follows no easy formula', *Observer*, 14 April.

Author index

Subject index